NoSQL and SQL Data Modeling

Bringing Together

Data, Semantics, and Software

first edition

Ted Hills

Published by:

2 Lindsley Road
Basking Ridge, NJ 07920 USA

https://www.TechnicsPub.com

Cover design by John Fiorentino

Technical reviews by Laurel Shifrin, Dave Wells, and Steve Hoberman

ISBN, print ed. 9781634621090
ISBN, Kindle ed. 9781634621106
ISBN, ePub ed. 9781634621113
ISBN, PDF ed. 9781634621120

First Printing 2016

Library of Congress Control Number: 2016930173

To my wife Daphne Woods, who has always believed in me, and gave me the space and support I needed to write this book.

Contents at a Glance

Part I: Real Words in the Real World 17

Chapter 1: It's All about the Words 19

Chapter 2: Things: Entities, Objects, and Concepts 23

Chapter 3: Containment and Composition 29

Chapter 4: Types and Classes in the Real World 35

Part II: The Tyranny of Confusion 43

Chapter 5: Entity-Relationship Modeling 45

Chapter 6: The Unified Modeling Language 59

Chapter 7: Fact-Based Modeling Notations 67

Chapter 8: Semantic Notations 75

Chapter 9: Object-Oriented Programming Languages 83

Part III: Freedom in Meaning 87

Chapter 10: Objects and Classes 89

Chapter 11: Types in Data and Software 105

Chapter 12: Composite Types 117

Chapter 13: Subtypes and Subclasses 137

Chapter 14: Data and Information 155

Chapter 15: Relationships and Roles 167

Chapter 16: The Relational Theory of Data 177

Chapter 17: NoSQL and SQL Physical Design 197

Part IV: Case Study 213

Chapter 18: The Common Coffee Shop 215

APPENDIX: COMN Quick Reference 231

Table of Contents

Acknowledgements xiii

Introduction 1

Taking Care of Data 3

Plant Change Control 2.0 5

Where did the Savings Come From? 5

Why Model? 8

Why COMN? 11

Book Outline 12

Book Audience 13

NoSQL Database Developer 13

SQL Database Developer 14

Data Modeler 14

Software Developer 14

Ontologist 15

Part I: Real Words in the Real World 17

Chapter 1: It's All about the Words 19

References 21

Chapter 2: Things: Entities, Objects, and Concepts 23

Chapter Glossary 28

Chapter 3: Containment and Composition 29

Containment 29

Composition 31

Chapter Glossary 33

Chapter 4: Types and Classes in the Real World 35

Collections of Objects 35

Sets of Concepts 37

Sets of Objects 38

Types and Classes 38
Types Designate Sets 39
Classes Describe Objects 40
Three Aspects of Types and Classes 41
Chapter Glossary 41

Part II: The Tyranny of Confusion 43

Chapter 5: Entity-Relationship Modeling 45
Logical E-R Data Models 45
Multiple Levels of Abstraction 48
Limitations of E-R Modeling Notation 50
NoSQL Arrays and Nested Data Structures 50
Lack of Reusable Composite Types 51
Lack of Place 54
Modeling the Real World 54
Representing Individual Entities 55
Mapping Between Models 55
Data in Software 56
Terminology 56
Entity 56
Conceptual 57
E-R Terms Mapped to COMN Terms 57
References 58

Chapter 6: The Unified Modeling Language 59
Class Diagrams 59
Stereotyping 60
Limitations of the UML 61
Lack of Keys 61
Middling Level of Abstraction 61
Lack of Concept 62
Subclassing versus Subtyping 62
Terminology 63
Relationship, Composition and Aggregation 63
Type and Implementation Class 64
UML Terms Mapped to COMN Terms 64
References 65

Chapter 7: Fact-Based Modeling Notations 67
Facts and Relationships 67
Limitations of Fact-Based Modeling 69
Lack of Instances 70
Incompleteness 70
Difficulty 71
Terminology 71
Fact-Based Modeling Terms Mapped to COMN Terms 72
References 74

Chapter 8: Semantic Notations 75
Predicates and RDF Statements 75
Doubles and Quadruples 78
OWL 79
Graphical Notations for Semantics 80
Terminology 80

Chapter 9: Object-Oriented Programming Languages 83
Classes, Objects, Types, and Variables 83
Terminology 85

Part III: Freedom in Meaning 87

Chapter 10: Objects and Classes 89
Material Objects 90
Objects with States 90
Meaning of States 91
Objects with More States 92
Even More States 93
Methods 94
Material Objects in Computers 94
Summary 96
Computer Object Defined 97
Composing Objects 98
Software Object Composition 98
Authorizing Certain Routines 101
Summary 102
Chapter Glossary 104

Chapter 11: Types in Data and Software 105
Types in Programming and Databases 105
What does a Type tell us? 106
Classes in Object-Oriented Software 107
Separating Type and Class 108
Simple Types 112
References 116
Chapter Glossary 116

Chapter 12: Composite Types 117
Composite Types as Logical Record Types 117
Types Representing Things in the Real World: Identification 119
Stepwise Refinement and Completeness 122
Types Representing Other Types 123
Measures as Composite Types 125
Nested Types 128
Modeling Documents 130
Arrays 132
Chapter Glossary 135
References 135

Chapter 13: Subtypes and Subclasses 137
Subtypes 137
Restriction is Subtyping 143
Subclasses 144
Subtypes and Extensions: Perfect Together 146
Inheritance 151
Using Subtype Variables and Values 151
Using Extending Types and Classes 152
Projection: The Inverse of Extension 153
Chapter Glossary 154

Chapter 14: Data and Information 155
Information 155
Is Information Always True? 157
From Information to Data 157
Data en Masse 159
Variable Names 160
Summary 160

Information and Data as Colloquialisms 161
Information En Masse 161
It's Just Data 161
Putting it all Together 162
"Unstructured Data" and "Semi-Structured Data" 163
Data Object 165
Chapter Glossary 166

Chapter 15: Relationships and Roles 167
Arrivals and Departures 167
Labeling Relationship Lines 170
Cleaning up the Model 171
Roles, Predicates, and Relationships 174
Chapter Glossary 175

Chapter 16: The Relational Theory of Data 177
What is a Relation? 178
The Order of Rows 178
The Uniqueness of Rows 180
The Significance of Columns 181
Summary 182
Technical Relational Terminology 182
Tuple and Relation Schemes 185
Giving Data to the System 185
Data Attribute Versus Attribute 186
Relational Terminology Reprise 187
Composite Data Attributes 187
Relational Operations 190
NoSQL Versus the Relational Model 191
SQL Versus the Relational Model 192
Terminology 193
Chapter Glossary 194

Chapter 17: NoSQL and SQL Physical Design 197
What's Different about NoSQL? 197
Database Performance 198
ACID versus BASE and Scalability 199
ACID 199
Atomicity 200
Consistency 200

Isolation 200
Durability 201
BASE and CAP 201
NoSQL and SQL Data Organization 203
Key/Value DBMS 204
Graph DBMS 205
Document DBMS 206
Columnar DBMS 207
Tabular DBMS 208
Summary 211
References 211

Part IV: Case Study 213

Chapter 18: The Common Coffee Shop 215
Analysis: Documenting Real-World Entities 215
Logical Data Modeling: Designing the Data 220
Physical Data Modeling: Designing the Implementation 226

APPENDIX: COMN Quick Reference 231

Glossary 235

Photo and Illustration Credits 239

Index 241

Acknowledgements

I am very grateful to Tony Shaw of Dataversity for giving me the opportunity to present this new modeling notation to a wider audience, first at the NoSQL Now! conference in San Jose in 2015, and then at the Enterprise Data World conference in San Diego in 2016. Daniel Upton attended my workshop at the NoSQL Now! conference, and introduced me to Steve Hoberman, data modeling enthusiast, leading author, and publisher. I met with Steve to talk about my ideas. Steve accepted my proposal for this book, and that is how it came into being.

The fundamental ideas behind concept and object modeling notation arose from my work on object-oriented programming language design, and from tackling the difficult problem of integrating objects and data. In the latter effort, I was helped tremendously by the many writings of C. J. Date, most especially *Foundations for Future Database Systems: The Third Manifesto, Second Edition* (by C. J. Date and Hugh Darwen). I had the opportunity to correspond with and speak to Mr. Date about this topic, and this finally enabled me to perceive the difference between data and objects. Mr. Date is not aware of the debt I owe him for the clarity of his thinking on all things relational. One should not read this acknowledgement as his endorsement of my ideas.

I have had the opportunity to discuss the Concept and Object Modeling Notation (COMN), and the ideas behind it, with colleagues at LexisNexis, most notably Roger Cass, Matthew Johnson, Michael Khatib, and Paul Rogers. They gave me the opportunity to test my ideas and my expression of them. Roger has the additional distinctions of having introduced me to Object Role Modeling, and of having put the "N" in COMN so that the acronym became pronounceable as "common". My immediate manager and longtime friend Greg Saxton and our chief architect Ian Koenig encouraged me to pursue this work.

My wife Daphne Woods, a brilliant novelist, long ago trained this technologist in the mysteries of English grammar and composition. She also trained our daughter Heather through ten years of home schooling to near perfection in these fields. Consulting with these two during the writing of this book helped me with clarity and structure.

It was wonderful to have my colleague Laurel Shifrin, respected educator Dave Wells, and Steve Hoberman as technical reviewers. Laurel's knowledge of unstructured data and Dave's knowledge of structured data helped keep some unsupported assumptions out of the work. Dave's early enthusiasm for COMN has been a tremendous boost. What a pleasure to have Steve, a leading author of data modeling books and my publisher, encouraging and promoting this work.

Here's to all who have struggled to tame their data. I hope you find this makes the journey more pleasurable and more successful.

Introduction

Joe came barreling into the plant manager's office, clutching a roll of blueprints in one hand. He was so excited. "Sam, have I got great news!" he called out.

Sam looked up from his desk behind the office counter. He looked weary. Well, keeping track of everything that goes on in a 150-acre refinery that processes 200,000 barrels of oil a day could make anyone weary. He pushed back his chair, got up, and ambled over to the counter.

"What's the news?" Sam asked.

"The boys in engineering have figured out that, by just combining a few material flows earlier in the process, the petrochemical plant could reduce emissions, produce more product from the same input flows, and add $5,000 a day to the plant's bottom line in reduced expenses! So I've come down here to find out what it will take to implement these changes." Joe placed the rolled-up blueprints on the counter and spread them out.

Sam started studying the drawings, running his finger over the many lines and shapes that represented the thousands of pipes visible out the office windows. He licked his finger and pulled the top drawing back to look at the next blueprint, and then the next, all while Joe watched excitedly but silently. Sam had a reputation. He knew his stuff. If Sam said it could be done, it could be done, and if he said it couldn't, well, you'd better do a ton of research before you said Sam was wrong.

Finally Sam looked up from the counter. "I think I get it. This isn't too bad. We'll just have to re-route a few pipes and this could be implemented pretty easily."

Joe was happy and relieved. "So, how long do you think it will take?"

Sam kept his look level when he delivered the blow. "I think about six months."

"Six months!" Joe nearly shouted. "I thought you said this was easy! Why, in six months we will have lost"—Joe figured fast in his head—"nearly a million dollars in savings!"

"I know, but it can't be helped," Sam explained. "You see, although the change is easy, we have to be really careful we don't mess up any downstream product flows that could be inadvertently affected by this change. And that takes time to figure out."

"It takes six months to look at these drawings and figure out what the impact of the change is?" Joe asked, somewhat incredulously.

Sam's poker face began to show a little discomfort. "Well, that's the problem," Sam said. "You see, the drawings engineering used weren't up to date, so we have to check them against the actual piping, and update them, and then look at the change request again."

Joe wasn't just going to accept this as the final verdict. "Why do you have to look at the actual piping? Why not pull out the latest drawings that engineering *should* have used, and compare to them?"

Sam began to turn a little red. "I'm not quite sure how to say this, but engineering did use the latest drawings we have on file. The problem is that they don't match what's actually been implemented in the plant."

Joe felt the tension rising, and realized that now was the time to pull out all his diplomatic skills, to avoid a confrontation that could hide the truth. He paused a moment, looked down at the counter to collect his thoughts, put on his best "professor" demeanor, and then looked up at Sam. "So I guess what you're saying is that changes were made in the field, but the drawings weren't updated to reflect them."

"That's right," Sam said quietly. "The project office doesn't like us spending time on drawings when we should be out in the field fixing things, and no one ever asks us for the drawings, so we just do stuff to make the plant run better and the drawings stay in the filing drawer."

Joe was surprised and a bit distressed, but kept his voice level. "Interesting. What kinds of changes do you do out in the field that don't require engineering's involvement?"

"We've got this great guy—Manny. He's worked here for 30 years, and knows where every pipe goes and how every fitting fits together. When something goes wrong, we call Manny, and he usually fixes the problem *and* finds an improvement that the engineering guys overlooked. So we discuss it and then implement the improvement, and everything runs better."

"But no one updates the drawings," Joe said quietly.

"Well, yeah," Sam muttered embarrassedly, looking away from Joe.

"And no one tells engineering what changed," Joe added. Sam didn't say anything. "Well, Sam, thanks for explaining the situation. I'll go back to the project office and we'll see if we can figure out any way to update the drawings with the current process flows in less than six months." Joe turned to go, but then hesitated and turned back. "Could Manny work with the engineers to document his changes? I presume that would be faster than having someone check every single connection."

Sam turned white. He didn't want to break this news. "Manny doesn't work here anymore."

Joe's shoulders slumped. "What happened to him?"

"He retired last month."

Taking Care of Data

This sad story of plant change control gone awry, changes made in the field without engineering involvement or approval, and a lack of any documentation about the current state of things, will likely be all too familiar to many readers. This is often how we treat our databases and our software. When we roll out a new system, our documentation will be pretty good for a few months, but then, as the changes accumulate, the documentation moves from being an asset to being overhead, and eventually even becoming a liability, as there is a risk that someone might rely on what it says when it's completely wrong.

This plant change control story is, of course, fictitious, and not at all representative of what goes on in chemical plants or in most construction-based industries. Such industries learned long ago that they need a strictly controlled process for making changes in a physical plant. Changes can originate with an engineer, a field operator, or a product manager, but all change requests follow the same strict process:

1. Take a copy of the strictly controlled current drawing and update it with the requested change.
2. Obtain engineering approval for the change.
3. Implement the change according to the drawing.
4. Check when the change is complete that the drawing matches the implementation exactly. Update the drawing if necessary to reflect the "as-built" condition of the plant.
5. File the updated drawing as the latest, fully reliable picture of reality.

There is never any debate about whether the "overhead" of following this process is "worth it". Everyone knows that a mistake could lead to a fire or an explosion in a chemical plant, a building collapse, or other possibilities we don't even want to think about.

Unfortunately, we're not so smart when it comes to our data designs. If someone has a bright idea how to make things better, then we say, sure, let's give it a try. It might really be a bright idea, too, but someone needs to think through the potential unintended consequences of what an "improvement" could do to the rest of the system. But it's really hard to think through the potential unintended consequences when an up-to-date drawing of a database design does not exist. Every change, even a trivial change, becomes slow, tedious, and full of risk.

Let's fast forward a year to how things have worked out in our fictitious petrochemical plant.

PLANT CHANGE CONTROL 2.0

Sam was in his office, happily conversing with one of his field operators. Life was good. Costs were down and profits were up. The Environmental Protection Agency was happy about the recent reduction in emissions. And things didn't seem to be breaking as often as they used to.

Joe walked into the plant manager's office. As soon as he saw Joe, Sam came over to shake his hand. "How are things, Joe? Have any more brilliant money-saving ideas for us?"

"Not today, Sam. Just thought I'd see how implementation is going on the last one."

"Well," Sam said, "Robbie is out there right now making a final check on the actual piping versus the as-built drawings. As soon as he's done that, he'll implement the change. He'll be done checking today, and he'll start the changes tomorrow."

"Done today?" Joe exclaimed. "I thought he only started checking today."

"That's right." Sam smiled. "Robbie is fast."

"Faster than Manny," Joe joked, and winked.

"You got that," Sam retorted.

WHERE DID THE SAVINGS COME FROM?

You see, Robbie is a robot. Robbie is comparing the pipes and fittings he sees to an electronic drawing that shows what they should be. If there are any differences—which could only come about if someone deviated from the change-control process—Robbie will report exactly what those differences are, the drawings will be updated to reflect the changes, and engineering will be notified of a change they didn't authorize.

It's relatively easy to envision drawings of pipes and fittings, and the pipes and fittings themselves. With data, it's not so easy. Data is abstract. You can't walk up to it and touch it, or pick it up and move it around. Nonetheless, our databases are very much like the pipes and fittings of a petrochemical plant. They define what the data is and how it is interconnected. A data model gives us a way to visualize the data and its inter-relationships. A data model is our tool to design and plan for our data before a database is created, and to keep track of changes to the database after it's been implemented.

It sounds a bit far-fetched—or at least a little bit futuristic—to imagine a robot looking at pipes and fittings and comparing them to drawings, but this capability exists for the majority of our databases today. Most database designs to this point have been implemented using something called the Structured Query Language, or SQL. Software tool vendors have done a superb job building so-called "data modeling tools" that enable a person to draw a graphical design for a database at a high level of abstraction, progressively add detail to that design (a process called **stepwise refinement**) until it is detailed enough to implement, then literally "push a button" and have the tool generate the database itself. The same tools enable a person to read the design of a database and generate a graphical model which is an "as-built" drawing. The first process—from drawing to implementation—is called **forward engineering**, and the second process—generating a drawing from an actual implementation—is called **reverse engineering**. The forward-engineered model can be compared to the reverse-engineered model in order to ensure that they stay in sync—that no unauthorized changes have been made to the implementation without first updating the design. This process of forward- and reverse-engineering with comparison is called **round-trip engineering**. When combined with a disciplined change-control process that makes sure every change starts with the design drawings, the process is called **model-driven development**.

There are many stories of disciplined data modeling leading to faster delivery and fewer bugs. Figure 1 below shows what happened after data modeling was introduced to the database implementation of one agile software development project.

There are many other such stories that can and have been told, where disciplined data modeling saved a project, and ongoing data modeling processes kept a system healthy.

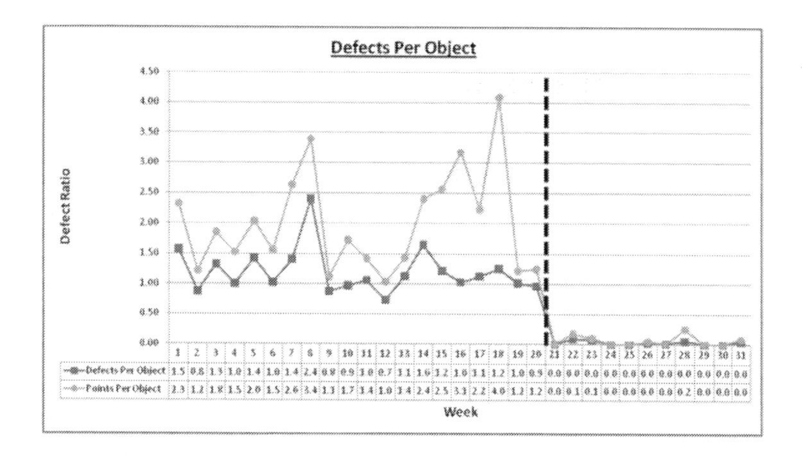

Figure 1. Defects per Object Before and After Data Modeling Adopted. Courtesy of Ron Huizenga.

I have personally had positive experiences in my career with model-driven development. It leads to many happy people:

- Engineers (often referred to as "data modelers", "data architects", and "database administrators" in IT projects) are happy because they know that the database they are responsible for is truly under their control. All changes go through them, and they can look for the far-reaching implications of what may appear to be simple changes.
- Implementers (called "software developers" and "database developers" in IT projects) are happy because they can trust that someone thought about potential unintended consequences before a change was made, and in fact the engineers included them in that process.
- Managers, operational personnel, marketers, sales people, and other business stakeholders are happy because change requests are handled quickly and efficiently, with the utmost automation possible.
- Everyone is happy because the design documentation is a living, breathing thing that is an asset to the corporation.

I have written this book for many reasons, but many of those reasons could be summed up as my desire to see model-driven development become the norm in information technology.

There are two barriers to this happening and this book is aimed at destroying both of them.

First, there aren't enough people who know what data modeling is and how to use it effectively. There needs to be a cadre of well-trained **data modelers** who know how to use data modeling notations, techniques, and tools to do forward and reverse engineering of databases. This book is intended to educate such people.

Second, existing theories of data aren't enough. Although data modeling tools can do forward and reverse engineering of SQL databases, there is a relatively new set of database technologies collectively called NoSQL database management systems (DBMSs) not yet supported by traditional tools. Some of the difficulties the data modeling tool vendors are having adapting to these newer tools originate with defective theories of data. This book refines our current data theories so they work just as well with NoSQL databases as they do with SQL databases. These updated theories of data also mesh with semantics and with software design, so that data designs can make sense as a description of real world objects and concepts, can meet business requirements, and can guide implementation.

Business stakeholders, software developers, and many others need to learn about the pitfalls of poorly managed data and the advantages of model-driven development. For them, there will be white papers, seminars, conference presentations, and more. But for you—whether you are a seasoned data modeler or just getting started—this book will teach you how to be the master of any data design problem that comes your way.

As the title implies, *NoSQL and SQL Data Modeling* teaches techniques for database design that are applicable to both the newer NoSQL (No SQL or Not Only SQL) databases and the traditional SQL databases. It draws connections to representations of the real world, and of meaning (semantics) in the real world and in data. It shows how data is represented in and manipulated by object-oriented software. It introduces the Concept and Object Modeling Notation or COMN (pronounced "common") for documenting data designs.

WHY MODEL?

Creating a model is not an absolutely necessary step before implementing a database. So, why would we want to take the time to draw up a data model at all, rather than just diving in and creating the database and storing data? A data model describes the schema of a database or document, but if our NoSQL DBMS is "schema-less" or "schema-free", meaning that we don't need to dictate the schema to the DBMS before we start writing data, what sense does it make to model at all?

The advantage of a schema-less DBMS is that one can start storing and accessing data without first defining a schema. While this sounds great, and certainly facilitates a speedy start to a data project, experience shows that a lack of forethought is usually followed by a lot of afterthought. As data volumes grow and access times become significant, thought needs to be given to re-organizing data in order to speed access and update, and sometimes to change tradeoffs between the speed, consistency, and atomicity of various styles of access. It is also commonly the case that patterns emerge in the data's structure, and the realization grows that, although the DBMS demands no particular data schema, much of the data being stored has some significant schema in common.

So, some vendors say, just reorganize your data dynamically. That's fine if the volume isn't too large. If a lot of data has been stored, reorganization can be costly in terms of time and even storage space that's temporarily needed, possibly delaying important customers' access to the data. And schema changes don't just affect the data: they can affect application code that must necessarily be written with at least a few assumptions about the data's schema.

A data model gives the opportunity to play with database design options on paper, on a whiteboard, or in a drawing tool such as Microsoft Visio, before one has to worry about the syntax of data definitions, data already stored, or application logic. It's a great way to think through the implications of data organization, and/or to recognize in advance important patterns in the data, before committing to any particular design. It's a lot easier to redraw part of a model than to recreate a database schema, move significant quantities of data around, and change application code.

If one is implementing in a schema-less DBMS without a model, then, after implementation is complete, the only ways to understand the data will be to talk to a developer or look at code. Being dependent on developers to understand the data can severely restrict the bandwidth business people have available to propose changes and expansions to the data, and can be a burden on developers. And although you might have friendly developers, trying to deduce the structure of data from code can be a very unfriendly experience. In such situations, a model might be your best hope.

Beside schema-less DBMSs, some NoSQL DBMSs support schemas. Document DBMSs often support XML Schema, JSON Schema, or other schema languages. And, even when not required, it is often highly desirable to enforce conformance to some schema for some or all of the data being stored, in order to make it more likely that only valid data is stored, and to give guarantees to application code that a certain degree of sanity is present in the data.

And this is not all theory. I have seen first-hand the failure of projects due to a lack of a data model or a lack of data modeling discipline. I have also seen tremendous successes resulting from the intelligent and disciplined application of data modeling to database designs.

Here are some stories of failure and of success:

- A customer data management system was designed and developed using the latest object-oriented software design techniques. Data objects were persisted and reconstituted using an object/relational mapping tool. After the system was implemented, performance was terrible, and simple queries for customer status either couldn't be done or were nearly impossible to implement. Almost everyone on the project, from the manager to the lowliest developer, either left the company or was fired, and the entire system had to be re-implemented, this time successfully using a data model and traditional database design.

- Two customer relationship management (CRM) systems were implemented. One followed the data model closely; the other deviated from the model to "improve" things a bit. The CRM system that deviated from the model had constant data quality problems, because it forced operational personnel to duplicate data manually, and of course the data that was supposed to be duplicated never quite matched. It also required double the work to maintain the data that, in the original model, was defined to be in only one place. In contrast, the CRM system that followed the data model had none of these data quality or operational problems.

- A major financial services firm developed a database of every kind of financial instrument traded in every exchange around the world. The database was multi-currency and multi-language, and kept historical records plus future-dated data for new financial instruments that were going to start trading soon. The system was a success from day one. A model-driven development process was used to create the system, and to maintain it as additional financial instrument types were added, so that all database changes started with a data modeler and a data model change. Database change commands were generated directly from the model. The system remained successful for its entire lifetime.
- A business person requested that the name of a product be changed on a report, to match changes in how the business was marketing its products. Because the database underlying the report had not been designed with proper keys, the change, which should have taken a few minutes, took several weeks.

You see, developing a data model is just like developing a blueprint for a building. If you're building a small building, or one that doesn't have to last, then you can risk skipping the drawings and going right to construction. But those projects are rare. Besides, those simple, "one-off" projects have a tendency to outlive early expectations, to grow beyond their original requirements, and become real problems if implemented without a solid design. For any significant project, to achieve success and lasting value, one needs a full data model developed and maintained as part of a model-driven development process. If you skip the modeling process, you risk the data equivalents of painting yourself into corners, disabling the system from adapting to changing requirements, baking in quality problems that are hard to fix, and even complete project failure.

WHY COMN?

There are many data modeling notations already in the world. In fact, Part II of this book surveys most of them. So why do we need one more?

COMN's goal is to be able to describe all of the following things in a single notation:

- the real world, with its objects and concepts
- *data about* real-world objects and concepts
- objects in a computer's memory whose *states represent data* about real-world objects and concepts

COMN connects concepts, real-world objects, data, and implementation in a single notation. This makes it possible to have a single model that represents everything from the nouns of requirements all the way down to a functional database running in a NoSQL or SQL database management system. This gives a greater ability to trace requirements all the way through to an implementation and make sure nothing was lost in translation along the way. It enables changes to be similarly governed. It enables the expression of reverse-engineered data and the development of logical and conceptual models to give it meaning. It enables the modeling of things in the Internet of Things, in addition to modeling data about them. No other modeling notation can express all this, and that is why COMN is needed.

Book Outline

The book is divided into four parts. Part I lays out foundational concepts that are necessary for truly understanding what data is and how to think about it. It peels back the techno-speak that dominates data modeling today, and recovers the ordinary meanings of the English words we use when speaking of data. *Do not skip part I!* If you do, the rest of the book will be meaningless to you.

Part II reviews existing data modeling, semantic, and software notations, and object-oriented programming languages, and creates the connections between those and the COMN defined in this book. *If you are experienced with any of those notations, you should read the relevant chapter(s) of part II.* COMN uses some familiar terms in significantly different ways, so it is critical that you learn these differences. Those chapters about notations you are not familiar with are optional, but will serve as a handy reference for you when dealing with others who know those notations.

Part III introduces the new way of thinking about data and semantics that is the essence of this book and of the Concept and Object Modeling Notation. Make sure you've read part I carefully before starting on Part III.

Part IV walks through a realistic data modeling example, showing how to apply COMN to represent the real world, data design, and implementation. By the time you finish this part, you should feel comfortable applying your COMN knowledge to problems at hand.

Each chapter ends with a summary of key points and a glossary of new terms introduced. There is a full glossary at the end, along with a comprehensive index. In addition, an Appendix provides a quick reference to COMN. You can download the full reference and a Visio stencil from http://www.tewdur.com/. This will enable you to experiment with drawing models of your own data challenges while you read this book.

Book Audience

Each person who picks up this book comes to it with a unique background, educational level, and set of experiences. No book can precisely match every reader's needs, but this book was written with the following readers in mind in order to come as close as possible.

NoSQL Database Developer

You might be someone excited to use the newest NoSQL database management software, but are aware of pitfalls that can hamper the performance and/or flexibility of NoSQL database designs. You may have found that established data modeling notations, such as E-R, fact-based, or the UML, can't be used directly for NoSQL designs, without at least some non-standard extensions. This book will teach you COMN, which can express your NoSQL designs precisely enough to be used in model-driven development.

You might be surprised to find that the most difficult problems to solve in database design are logical and not physical. Since the differences between NoSQL and SQL databases are mostly physical and not logical, the bulk of this book is focused on enabling you to think through the logical design of data apart from physical considerations, and then to step through the process of physical database design while remaining faithful to the logical design. Make sure you read part I carefully, then dig into part III and learn these techniques. We'll cover the differences between NoSQL and SQL in chapter 17. If you have a software development background, you should also read chapter 9 on object-oriented programming languages.

SQL DATABASE DEVELOPER

You might be an experienced developer of SQL databases who always created designs directly in SQL, or used your own informal or home-grown data modeling notation—perhaps on a whiteboard or the back of a napkin—before you dove into specifying primary keys, indexes, partitions, and constraints. You're intrigued by the idea of data modeling, or you just want to know if there's something you've been missing. This book will teach you how to think about data at a logical level, before those critical physical design decisions come into play. Read part I carefully, then all of part III. We'll get to the physical issues where you're already an expert in chapter 17.

DATA MODELER

You might be an experienced data modeler, already using an E-R or fact-based modeling notation, or the UML, to design your databases. But there are some niggling design problems that you always felt should not be so hard to tackle. Or, you might want to fold semantics into your data models but aren't sure how to do that. You'll find that learning COMN will build on the data modeling knowledge you've already acquired, and expand how far you can use that knowledge to include NoSQL databases, semantics, and some aspects of software development. Make sure you read part I, then the relevant chapters in part II, before you dig into part III and learn how to think differently about data and data models. After you've learned COMN, you'll find that much of the advice on data modeling you've already learned is still valuable, but you'll be able to apply it much more effectively than before.

SOFTWARE DEVELOPER

You might be a software developer who knows that there's more to data than meets the eye, and has decided to set aside some time to think about it. This book will help you do just that. Make sure you read part I, then chapter 9 on object-oriented programming languages. Chapter 9 will be especially relevant for you, as it will draw connections between data and the object-oriented programming that you're already familiar with. If you design software with the Unified Modeling Language (UML), you should also read chapter 6.

ONTOLOGIST

You've begun to apply semantic languages like OWL to describing the real world. However, you find the mapping from semantics to data tedious and also incomplete. It's difficult to maintain a mapping between a model of real-world things and a model of data. COMN is a tool you can use to express that mapping. Make sure you read part I carefully, and chapter 8 on semantic notations, before continuing on to part III.

Key Points

- The Concept and Object Modeling Notation (COMN, pronounced "common") can represent data designs and their connections to the real world, to meaning (semantics), to database implementations, and to software.
- A data model is essential to any successful database design project, and helps to meet requirements, build in flexibility, and avoid quality problems and project failure.
- Everyone should read all of part I of this book.
- Part II contains chapters relevant to those who already know the notations and languages discussed.
- The meat of the book is in part III, but will only make sense to those who read part I and the relevant chapters of part II.
- This book should deliver value to NoSQL and SQL database developers, new and experienced data modelers, software developers, and ontologists.

Part I

Real Words in the Real World

In designing databases and data systems, we seek to accurately represent the real world and data about the real world. But our ability to think about the real world is hampered by the special meanings we have attached to ordinary words, making it difficult or impossible to reason without inadvertently carrying along the intellectual baggage of a particular technical view of reality.

Part I of this book returns us to the ordinary English meanings of words that we have co-opted for special purposes in the field of information technology. By the end of this section, your mind will be refreshed to remember the way we use these words in ordinary speech. This will prepare you to learn new, more precise meanings for these words that will make them powerful tools in analysis and design.

Chapter 1
It's All about the Words

"When *I* use a word," Humpty Dumpty said in rather a scornful tone, "it means just what I choose it to mean—neither more nor less."

"The question is," said Alice, "whether you *can* make words mean so many different things."

"The question is," said Humpty Dumpty, "which is to be master—that's all."

[Carroll 1871]

We are indeed the masters of our words, and we have the responsibility to define them. What I call "the Humpty-Dumpty problem" is the fact that we must define our words in sensible ways, while not contradicting earlier uses of the same words, nor making them mean so many different things.

It is my belief that many of the unsolved problems in the information technology (IT) field remain unsolved simply because our technical vocabulary is impairing our ability to speak and reason about these problems. Our contemporary technical vocabulary often redefines words from everyday use and from mathematics and logic in subtly different, often confusing, and sometimes mistaken ways.

This book sets out to solve these problems by re-examining the definitions of words that we consider to be fundamental to data modeling, semantics, and software development—words like type, class, entity, and relationship—and by tuning them up to make them more precise. We will not redefine these so much as we will *refine* them: we will make them mean *less*, so to speak. When we are done with them, the meanings of these words will overlap less, and this will empower us to think, design, and communicate more clearly than ever before. Certain data model patterns that have always been challenging will become tractable, and there will be less impedance when integrating data with software and semantics.

But since we *can* make words mean so many things, what is to guide this refinement? What safety measures can we appeal to so that we don't just end up with a different version of the soupy mix of words that we already have? My approach is to start with the ordinary words of everyday English—the so called natural language that we all grew up with and knew how to use long before we knew what a computer was. It is this vocabulary, after all, from which the IT industry has borrowed to name its specialized terms. But when we need to specialize a term, we will first judge its specialized definition according to how well it meshes with natural language. Only then will we consider how a term meshes with related terms and with other well-established terminology in the IT field. We will also look for definitions that are more consistent with themselves, and more primitive, depending on fewer external terms—therefore more precise. Finally, we will favor definitions that are useful as building blocks, supporting higher-level definitions based on them.

Once we can get past the assumptions built into today's terminology, we will be able to see clearly the solutions to today's intellectual roadblocks. We will discover why we struggle with certain data modeling challenges, why it is so hard to integrate object-oriented software with databases, and why the expression of meaning is so elusive. Armed with our new terms and understanding, we will look again at design.

Like Humpty Dumpty, folks get very defensive about their ideas of what words mean, and don't take kindly to others changing their meanings. But unless we can open our minds to altering some of our terms' definitions, to make them more precise and more meaningful, we will be stuck without solutions to some of our most important problems. So, although it may at first be difficult to make the shift, please open your mind to accepting new, more precise definitions for old familiar terms. You will be amply rewarded as old problems melt away and analysis and design become easier and more powerful.

To help you remember the new definitions, each chapter that introduces new terms reviews their definitions at the end of the chapter. There is also a full glossary at the end of the book. Most of the natural-language definitions we will use are drawn from Merriam-Webster's Online Dictionary (www.Merriam-Webster.com).

It may be easier to learn the refined definitions than you would anticipate. This book has been carefully edited to ensure that it uses these familiar terms only in ways consistent with their refined definitions. As a result, you should find as you read along that you'll gradually forget about the older, broader, fuzzier definitions of these terms. Being more precise will become easier than returning to the less-precise notions you had before.

Key Points

- Many of our modern technology terms have overlapping and imprecise meanings. This clouds our ability to reason and communicate about design problems.
- We will return to everyday English ("natural language") to judge and refine the meanings of our terms.
- After completing this refinement process, design problems that have stubbornly refused to be solved will yield to our more precise terminology.

References

[Carroll 1871] Carroll, Lewis. *Through the Looking Glass*, 1871, chapter VI. Found at http://en.wikisource.org/wiki/Through_the_Looking-Glass,_and_What_Alice_Found_There/Chapter_VI

Chapter 2

Things: Entities, Objects, and Concepts

The English language has at least four words related to "thing". Consider these definitions from Merriam-Webster:

thing : a separate and distinct individual quality, fact, idea, or usually entity

entity 2 : some*thing* that has separate and distinct existence[1] and objective or conceptual reality

object 1a : some*thing* material that may be perceived by the senses

concept 1 : some*thing* conceived in the mind : thought, notion

I added the italics to the second half of the word "some*thing*" in the definitions above to emphasize that the definitions of entity, object, and concept depend on the definition of thing. You'll also see that there is a partial circularity between the definition of "thing" and the definition of "entity", because each definition uses the other word.

The worlds of software development and database development have heavily overloaded two of these words, namely the words "entity" and "object". (They've avoided the word "thing", I think, because who would boast of being skilled at thing-relationship modeling or thing-oriented programming?) Let's make sure we understand what these words meant before technologists got a hold of them.

In ordinary English, the words "thing" and "entity" are pretty much identical in meaning. "Entity" can be thought of as the technical term for "thing". For those who are familiar with entity-relationship (E-R) modeling, please note how the ordinary English definition of "entity" is completely different from the

---

[1] This is not the best wording, since existence is not a property that things *have*. However, the overall sense of the definition is still quite valuable.

E-R definition. Those familiar with philosophy and semantics will recognize that the word "object" is usually used in those fields to represent the same meaning as the ordinary English meaning of "entity".

The Merriam-Webster definition for "entity" makes a very important distinction between two kinds of things: objective things and conceptual things.

An objective thing is something whose existence can be verified through the senses. Things that stimulate the senses include light and sound, but there's an important kind of objective thing that the dictionary defines as an "object": "something *material* that may be perceived by the senses." Something "material" is something that is made of matter. What is matter?

At the current limits of scientific knowledge of the universe, we believe that all matter consists of so-called elementary particles, which come in a relatively small number of types. (See Figure 2-1.) We call them elementary because, as far as we know, they aren't composed of anything else. All other matter is composed of them. An electron is an elementary particle. Protons and neutrons are composed of the elementary particles called quarks. If a relatively fixed number of electrons, protons, and neutrons remain in a relatively static relationship to each other—protons and neutrons bound together in a nucleus, and electrons orbiting the nucleus—we have what we call an atom. We call atoms that are bound to each other in certain spatial relationships molecules. Molecules can get quite large, and can form, among other things, minerals, proteins and other raw materials of living things, and, very simply, everything that we can see or touch.

In ordinary parlance, when enough matter in relatively static spatial relationships is aggregated together to the point where we can see and touch it, we call the aggregate an object. If, for instance, you looked at your desk and saw a pencil and a pen, you would say that these were two objects on your desk—and you would be right, despite the fact that you will sharpen the pencil and it will get shorter, and the pen will gradually run out of ink. You have an intuitive and approximate but very useful concept of what an object is. In fact, your idea of an object is a concept that is widely shared by many persons.

Based on these observations, we can define the object of ordinary parlance and experience using a technique called induction. Our induction rests on two simple definitions.

1. An elementary particle of matter (that is, an electron or other lepton, or a quark) is an object.
2. Any collection of objects in relatively static spatial arrangements to each other is an object.

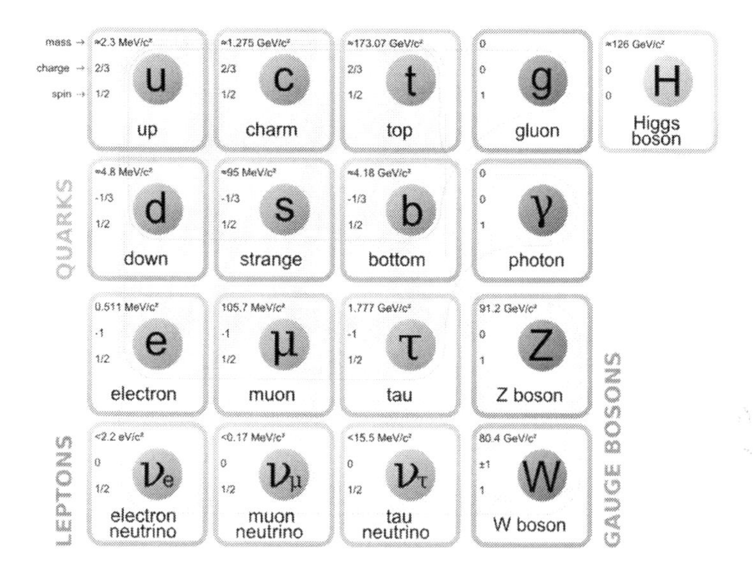

Figure 2-1. The Elementary Particles

The first definition is really just a linguistic definition. It says that we will use the term "object" to refer to, among other things, elementary particles of matter. An electron is an object, a quark is an object, etc.

The second definition is where the trick is. It says that objects are built from other objects. On the surface of it, this sounds like a circular definition: where does the object begin? So let's take this definition apart to see how it works.

If we are going to build objects from objects, what objects can we start with? Well, in definition number one we said that we would call the elementary particles of matter objects, so then we can build our first objects from elementary particles. Let's put together three elementary particles—three quarks—to make a proton. The three quarks stick very closely together—that's a relatively static spatial arrangement. So a proton, built from objects which are elementary particles, qualifies by definition number two as an object. Next, let's grab an electron—which is also an object because it's an elementary particle, too—and put it in orbit around the proton. An orbit is a relatively static spatial arrangement, so the electron/proton combination—which happens to be a hydrogen atom—must be an object, too.

Relax—I won't go on constructing the universe one particle at a time! But hopefully I've gone far enough that you can see how induction works. We start with our starter kit of objects—elementary particles of matter—and from those we can build all objects, eventually up to objects we can see and touch.

This inductive definition reflects the reality that all objects, except the elementary particles, are built from other, simpler objects. We say that they are **composite** objects, *composed* of other objects called **components**.

We've now covered one-half of the definition of entity. We know what objective entities are, and, more particularly, we know what objects are. Let's turn now to conceptual entities: what are they?

A concept is, according to Merriam-Webster's Online Dictionary, a thought or notion; essentially, an idea. We know that persons have ideas, and that they exist in a person's brain as a configuration of neurons, their physical states, and their interconnections. We also know that there are many ideas that are shared by persons—many ideas that are known by the same names, understood in approximately the same way, and enable communication. For instance, if you are reading this book and understanding even a part of it, it is because you and I share some of the same ideas, or concepts, about what the words I am using mean.

The interesting thing about widely shared concepts is that, unlike objects, they have no place or time: they are not confined to a geographic location or a particular point in time, or even to the same set of words. For instance, the concepts of the number "one", of numbers in general, and of counting, are understood by all human cultures, even though people who speak different languages use different names for any given number. In light of this, it would be wrong to say, "The number one is here and not there", or, "The number one began at this point in time and will go out of existence at this other point in time." Perhaps if our knowledge of history were perfect we could identify the point in time at which the first person had the idea of "one" for the first time. But we don't know history to that degree of detail, and it's irrelevant anyway. The only way in which the number one would come to an end would be if all humans ceased to exist. If that happened, there would be no one to record the event, so it would be irrelevant. We therefore treat the number one, and similar shared concepts, as if they have no time or place, and if we are wise we recognize that the names of concepts are just symbols that are quite separate from the concepts they represent.

In summary, then, an **entity** is a thing that exists either objectively or conceptually. An **object** is an objective entity that is either an elementary particle of matter or is composed of other objects in relatively fixed spatial relationships. A conceptual entity is a **concept**; essentially, an idea.

As will be explained in greater detail in subsequent chapters, the word "entity" will be used in exactly the sense of the definition quoted above, un-overloaded, as meaning any thing that exists, whether it is an object (whose existence can be objectively verified) or a concept (whose existence is merely as an idea). The chapter on entity-relationship data modeling will examine the word "entity" as it is used in that context.

The word **object** will also be used in exactly the sense of the definition quoted above, to mean a material entity, in contrast to **concept**, which is a conceptual entity. We will examine the meaning of object in object-oriented programming, but we'll save that for later.

Key Points

- The word "entity" is the technical term for "thing".
- Entities come in two flavors, conceptual and objective.
- Objective entities include material things called objects. All objects, except the elementary particles, are composed of other objects.
- Conceptual entities are concepts or ideas.
- Unlike objects, widely shared concepts have no time or place.
- We will look at overloaded technical definitions of these words in later chapters. For now, we will use their natural-language definitions.

CHAPTER GLOSSARY

entity : something that has separate and distinct existence and objective or conceptual reality (Merriam-Webster)

object : something material that may be perceived by the senses (Merriam-Webster)

concept : something conceived in the mind : thought, notion (Merriam-Webster)

composite : made up of distinct parts (Merriam-Webster)

component : a constituent part (Merriam-Webster)

Chapter 3

Containment and Composition

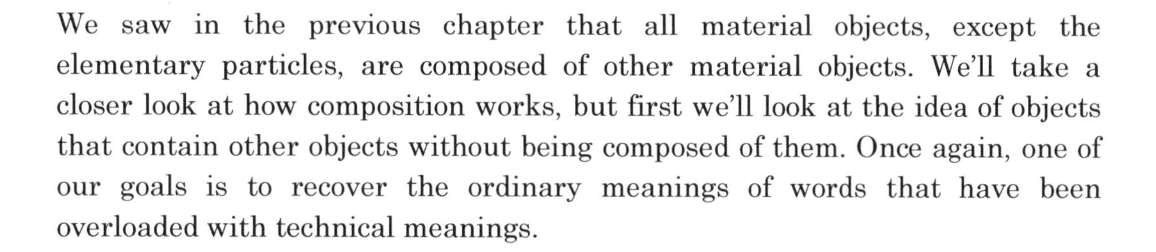

We saw in the previous chapter that all material objects, except the elementary particles, are composed of other material objects. We'll take a closer look at how composition works, but first we'll look at the idea of objects that contain other objects without being composed of them. Once again, one of our goals is to recover the ordinary meanings of words that have been overloaded with technical meanings.

Containment

Suppose I go to a grocery store and buy a dozen eggs. I carry the eggs home in a carton that is made of Styrofoam, fiberboard, or some other material that protects the fragile eggs from breaking. Over the course of a week I eat the eggs, and when the last egg is gone I throw away the carton.

Each egg is an object—a material thing—and the carton is an object, but they are different kinds of objects. The carton was specially designed to hold up to twelve eggs. The carton is a **container** and the eggs are its **contents**. When I brought the carton home it was full. As soon as I took the first egg out of the carton it was no longer full. Once I took the last egg out of the carton it was empty. So the *state* of the container—full, partially full, empty—varied over the course of the week. However, despite its changing state, the *composition* of the carton never changed. I would never at any time say that the carton was composed of eggs. It was composed of Styrofoam or fiberboard.

In general, a container is designed so that contents can easily be added and removed. These operations change the **state** of the container, but do not change its **composition**—that is, what it is made of. If I took a few eggs out of the carton and made a cake from them, it would be correct to say that the eggs were in the cake, but not in the same sense as being in the carton. In the cake the eggs have lost their integrity and can never be removed from it again. Unlike the egg carton, the cake is *composed* of eggs, and flour and milk and sugar and other ingredients, **blended** together.

Observe that *containment is exclusive*, in two senses. First, an egg is either in a carton or not in a carton. It cannot be partially contained. Second, if I had another egg carton, it would be impossible for me to have a particular egg in both cartons simultaneously.

Some containers can nest, like Russian matryoshka dolls. Each container can contain, not only whatever fits, but also another, smaller container, which can contain another smaller container, and so on. With nesting containers, it is possible to say that something in a smaller container is also in the larger container that contains the smaller container, but the contents of the smaller container are not in the large container *directly*. An object can only be *directly* in one container at a time. If the carton of eggs is in a grocery bag, we can say that the eggs are in the bag, but it is more complete to say that the eggs are in the carton in the bag.

Suppose I bring home the dozen eggs from the grocery store, in their protective container, but my refrigerator is so full that I cannot fit the carton of eggs inside. To solve the problem, I remove the eggs from the carton, tuck each of the twelve eggs into little spaces that can accommodate an egg-sized object, and throw the carton away. Even though I have destroyed the container, the twelve eggs continue to exist in the refrigerator. This shows that, in ordinary parlance, a container and its contents can exist independently.

Composition

We saw in the previous section that containment is not composition; that is, a container is not composed of its contents. We also saw one kind of composition, where a cake is composed of its ingredients *blended* together in such a way that they can't be separated again. There are a few more modes of composition—ways in which objects can be composed of smaller objects—that are relevant to our ultimate purpose of representing data, software, and semantics.

Remember that an object is composed of other objects in some kind of relatively static spatial relationship. Certainly a cake is an object, because it is composed of eggs, milk, flour, sugar, and other objects in a relatively static spatial relationship: they are all blended together and will remain that way until the cake is consumed.

Now let's think about a frosted cake. Frosting is applied to the top of the cake and between the layers. This isn't quite blending, because the integrity of the cake and the frosting is still preserved. You can still see the difference between them, though it would be difficult to separate them once again. This kind of object composition is called **aggregation**. An object is formed from other objects in a way that the components keep their integrity, but it would be difficult to extract the components after they've been joined together.

For those who know the UML, please note that, in ordinary English and in COMN, composition is the over-arching term, and aggregation is one particular kind of composition. Likewise, a component is that which is part of any kind of a composite.

For those who are familiar with dimensional modeling, please note that what is called **aggregation** in that discipline is **blending** in ordinary English and in COMN.

In contrast to aggregation, we can have **assembly**. This is a mode of composition where components retain their integrity and can even be removed from the object which they compose, if so desired. A real-world example of an assembly is an engine. Its parts are connected with screws and other connectors that can be disconnected and reconnected at will.

Another important mode of composition is **juxtaposition**, where objects are arranged in a fixed spatial relationship to each other without being blended and without being connected to each other. For instance, dinner plates and silverware are juxtaposed on a dining table to form a place setting.

Regardless of the mode of composition, we call the objects of which another object is composed its **components**. So, the components of a (blended) cake are its ingredients, the components of a layer cake are alternating layers of cake and frosting, the components of an engine include pistons, spark plugs, valves, the block, etc., and the components of a place setting include dishes, silverware, and glasses.

Components are not contents. For instance, the engine assembly, which is composed of many components, will eventually *contain* gasoline, but we would never say that the engine is *composed* of gasoline. The soup bowl will eventually contain soup, but we would never say that the place setting is composed of soup.

In any given real-world object, it is likely that many modes of composition are present at once. For example, one of the components of an engine assembly is a spark plug. A spark plug is an aggregation of ceramic and metal parts joined together such that one can see the different parts but one cannot separate them (without destroying the spark plug and its parts).

Key Points

- A container is an object that can hold other objects in such a way that they can be easily added to and removed from the container.
- Adding objects to and removing objects from a container changes the container's *state* but not its *composition*. We never say that a container is composed of its contents.
- Containment is exclusive. An object can only be in one container at a time, and is either entirely in or entirely out of the container.
- Containers can **nest**: A container may contain another container.
- All objects, except the elementary particles, are composed of other objects.
- Four modes of composition important to us are:
  - juxtaposition
  - blending
  - aggregation
  - assembly
- In any given real-world object, it is likely that many modes of composition are present at once.

Chapter Glossary

container : an object that can contain other objects (like an egg carton)

contents : the objects inside a container (like the eggs in an egg carton)

juxtaposition : arranging objects in a fixed spatial relationship without connecting them (like a place setting)

blending : combining two or more objects in such a way that they lose their integrity (like eggs, flour, milk, and sugar in a cake)

aggregation : combining two or more objects in such a way that they retain their integrity, but it is difficult or impossible to separate them again (like a layer cake)

assembly : combining two or more objects in such a way that they retain their integrity, and it is relatively easy to separate them again (like an engine)

Chapter 4
Types and Classes in the Real World

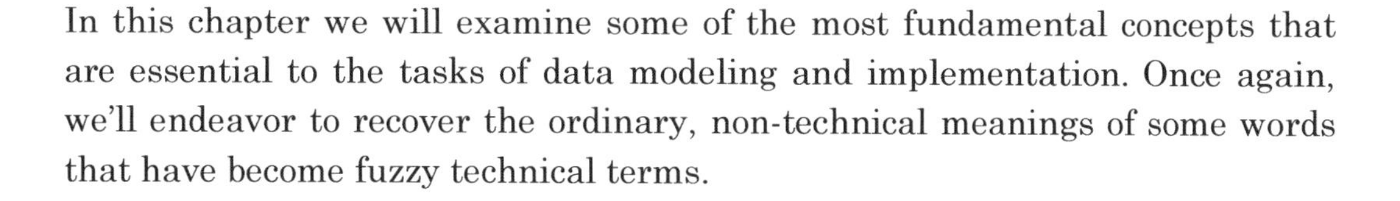

In this chapter we will examine some of the most fundamental concepts that are essential to the tasks of data modeling and implementation. Once again, we'll endeavor to recover the ordinary, non-technical meanings of some words that have become fuzzy technical terms.

Collections of Objects

Art museums usually contain paintings. Based on the previous chapter, we can recognize that a museum is a container, and the paintings are its contents.

Art museum curators often speak of their **collections** of paintings. For example, an art museum may say that it has a collection of Monet paintings, a collection of Morisot paintings, and a collection of Renoir paintings. Unlike containers and their contents, collections are not so strictly tied to physical relationships. Let's see how this works.

It is common in the art world for museums to share their collections with each other, as a benefit to the art world and the public at large. For example, suppose there is an art museum on the East Coast of the United States that has a wonderful collection of oil paintings by the French impressionist Monet. This East Coast museum will package up part of its collection of Monet paintings and send them to a museum on the West Coast, for display there for some months, before they are shipped back to the museum that owns the collection.

Now, while those paintings are on the West Coast, they are still considered part of the collection belonging to the East Coast museum, even though they are not physically contained in that museum. So we can see that a collection can exist inside or outside any particular container.

The paintings on loan to the West Coast museum might be displayed side-by-side with paintings belonging to the West Coast museum, but they would never be considered to be part of any collection of the West Coast museum. The East Coast museum always owns its collection, no matter where the members of that collection might be. This is evidence that our concept of collection, like our concept of containment, involves exclusivity. We often describe this exclusivity in terms of ownership. Something owned by one person or group is not owned by any other person or group. Something that is a member of one collection may not also be a member of another collection—except transitively: a collection may belong to another collection.

We can see from this example that the objects belonging to a collection may or may not be in the same container at any one time. Although a container, being an object, always has but one location at any one time, a collection of objects is not necessarily localized. This gives us a clue that, while a container is an object, a collection is not an object; a collection is merely a concept.

Our hypothetical East Coast art museum has paintings and other drawings of many types, including oil paintings, watercolors, charcoal and pencil sketches, pastels, and engravings. The paintings can have many subjects, including landscapes, still-lifes, and portraits. The museum curators often speak of the paintings in their collection according to any of these characteristics, and will call these collections, too. A painting by Monet might be a landscape and an oil painting, so that, when a curator speaks of "our Monet collection," "our collection of landscapes," and "our collection of oil paintings," the oil landscape by Monet is included every time. Thus, we can see that, in ordinary English, an object can be in multiple collections at the same time, provided that all of the collections have the same owner.

Sets of Concepts

We have seen that a collection is conceptual, even when the members of the collection are objects. It is also possible to have a collection of concepts. In such a case, both the collection and its members are conceptual. However, we don't usually use the word "collection" in connection with concepts. We will usually say that we have a **set** of concepts.

We know that numbers are concepts. Mathematicians have a special notation that they've developed just so that they can talk about sets of numbers (and other things). It is called **set notation**. Very simply, a list of numbers is enclosed in curly braces, as in

$$\{1, 2, 3\}$$

The whole expression is called a **set**. The set just given consists of the numbers one, two, and three.

One of the interesting things about sets of conceptual entities, such as sets of numbers, is that you can destroy the set notation that describes the set, but that doesn't destroy the set itself, nor its members. A set of numbers, and the numbers themselves, don't exist just because they are written down. This is in contrast to collections of objects. A collection of objects can be destroyed in a number of ways:

- The objects themselves can be destroyed.
- The collection can be destroyed by ceasing to consider it as existing. For instance, the East Coast art museum might give away all of its Monet paintings to other museums. The paintings continue to exist, but the collection is destroyed.

Membership of concepts in sets is not exclusive. A single concept can be in multiple sets at the same time. Consider as an example the number 2. It is in all these sets simultaneously:

- the set of natural numbers
- the set of integers
- the set of even numbers
- the set of prime numbers

In fact, we could go on inventing sets *ad infinitum* for 2 to be part of.

Although membership in a set is not exclusive, two sets can be exclusive *of each other*. For example, the set of even numbers is exclusive of the set of odd numbers. Any given integer is a member of only one of those two sets. But, as we have seen, an integer can be a member of many non-exclusive sets at the same time.

Sets of Objects

We have covered collections of objects and sets of concepts. We don't generally speak of collections of concepts. But we can speak of sets of objects. A set of objects is very similar to a collection of objects, except without the concept of ownership. For instance, we could speak of the set of cars in a parking lot at a given moment, and the set would be understood, even though the cars had no one owner. A set, like a collection, is a concept, even though members of the set may be objects.

And, as with sets of concepts, some sets may be exclusive of each other. A given painting may not simultaneously be a pastel and watercolor, and it may not simultaneously be a portrait and a landscape. But a painting may simultaneously be in the pastel set and the landscape set.

Types and Classes

Long before computers were invented, we humans recognized similarities between things, categorized those things by their similar characteristics, and named those categories. For example, humans observing a herd of elephants roaming the African plains would recognize that all the individual animals in the herd shared common characteristics, including that they were gray in color, had long snouts, and grew to enormous size. These humans developed a shared concept of the common characteristics, and in order to be able to communicate about that shared concept would give that shared concept a name; in English, the name of the shared concept is "elephant". Once the category of animals was named, every time such an animal was seen, instead of describing the animal's characteristics, a reference to the category ("an elephant") was sufficient to communicate about it. Other animals were similarly categorized based on common characteristics, and the categories were given names; for example, lion, tiger, zebra, etc.

There is a rich set of words in English related to this innate human activity of classification, and these words are synonyms of each other. Some of these words are:

category	class	classification	division	family
genus	kind	order	species	type

The worlds of database and software development have heavily overloaded two particular words related to classification, namely the words "type" and "class", giving them specialized meanings that are actually at the core of one set of problems plaguing computer science. In our refined terminology we will use these two words with great caution and specificity. Since "type" and "class" are synonyms in ordinary English, this choice of specialized meanings is arbitrary from an English point of view. We will see in part III how these choices are influenced by object-oriented programming languages, but how quite different definitions for these terms clarify our thinking.

We will use the word **type** to mean *something that designates a set,* usually a set of concepts but also possibly a set of objects. We will use the word **class** to mean *a description of the structural and/or behavioral characteristics of potential or actual objects.* In cases where we don't have enough context to choose between "type" and "class", the word "kind" will be used, meaning "some kind of category, but we're not sure whether it's a type, a class, or something else".

TYPES DESIGNATE SETS

What does it mean for a type to "designate" a set? We mean that there is some means by which we can identify the members of the set, and distinguish those from things that are not in the set. It turns out that there are many ways to designate sets. Here are some examples of types that designate sets of concepts:

- by **naming**; for example, "natural numbers" is the name of a well-known set and therefore that phrase designates the set and is a type.
- by **selection** using some condition; for example, all those natural numbers which are divisible by two.
- by **enumeration**—in other words, by listing the names of the members of the set; for example, {1, 2, 3}.

There are additional ways to designate sets which we'll see later in the book.

It's important to keep in mind that a type—a designation of a set—is not the set itself. For example, the phrase "natural numbers" consists of words, but the set it designates is quite different, consisting only of numbers.

Here are some examples of types that designate sets of objects:

- by **selection** using some condition; for example, "all red cars".
- by **enumeration**; for example, I could designate a set of objects by listing their names; let's say, "scissors, ruler, matches, twist tie".
- by **location**: This is a special case of selection. For example, I could designate a set of objects as "those objects found in the junk drawer in my kitchen." In fact, this set could be the same set as I just designated by enumeration. It is significant that objects can be designated by their location in space and time. Concepts cannot be so designated.

Again, there are additional ways to designate sets of objects, and again, the designation of the set is not the set itself.

CLASSES DESCRIBE OBJECTS

Above we said that a **class** is *a description of the structural and/or behavioral characteristics of potential or actual objects*. In our refined terminology, we would say that the word "elephant" is a class, because it references a structural description of the animals in question. Another example of a class is a set of drawings and blueprints describing a house or houses that are built or to be built.

The term "elephant" indirectly designates a set of animals; specifically, all those animals matching the description associated with the shared concept of an elephant. This would include elephants that currently exist, elephants that have existed, and even elephants that might yet come into existence. We don't know exactly how many elephants are or will be in this set, but the word "elephant" nonetheless identifies the set. A class, therefore, is a kind of type. It differs from other types in that a class can only designate sets of objects. One cannot have a class of concepts, in this restricted sense of the term.

When we get into the specialized terminology of Concept and Object Modeling Notation (COMN) in part III, we will see that these definitions of type and class line up to some extent, though not exactly, with their definitions in object-oriented programming. (The differences are significant.) When discussing software and data, the term **class** will be used solely to refer to a designation of a set of objects that exist or might exist in a computer's memory or storage, by describing the structural and/or behavioral characteristics of objects belonging to the class. The term **type** will be used to refer to the designation of sets of concepts or objects which may exist in the computer or in the real world, and which are not designated solely by descriptions of structure or behavior.

THREE ASPECTS OF TYPES AND CLASSES

With regard to types and classes, we have three things separately:

- the type or class, which designates, through some means (condition, description, enumeration, etc.), the things that are members of the set
- the actual members of the set designated by the type or class
- the name of the type or class; for example, "natural number", "elephant".

CHAPTER GLOSSARY

type : something that designates a set

class : a description of the structural and/or behavioral characteristics of potential or actual objects

collection : a set of objects having a single owner

Key Points

- Objects may belong to collections. An object may belong to several collections, but only if all the collections have the same owner.
- The objects belonging to a collection need not be in the same container or even in the same vicinity.
- A collection is a concept, even though it consists of objects.
- We generally don't speak of collections of concepts. We speak of sets of concepts. A concept may be a member of more than one set at a time.
- We may also have sets of objects.
- Some sets, of objects or concepts, may be exclusive of each other.
- Sets and collections of objects may be destroyed by destroying the objects themselves, or by simply ceasing to consider the set or collection to exist.
- Sets of concepts are not destroyed merely by destroying some representation of them.
- The terms "type" and "class" are synonyms in English, but are not synonyms in information technology, nor in COMN.
- We will use the term "kind" when we don't care to distinguish between type and class.
- Types designate sets; classes describe objects.
- A type may designate a set through many means, including naming, selection, enumeration, and (for sets of objects only) location.
- A class indirectly designates the set of all potential or actual objects which match its description.
- A type or class is not the same as the set it designates.

Part II

The Tyranny of Confusion

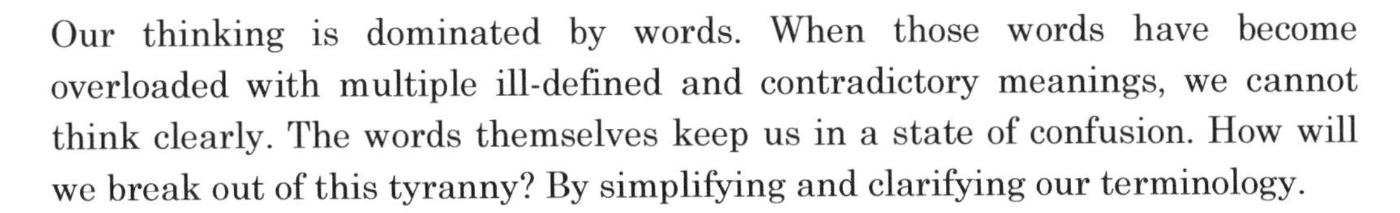

Our thinking is dominated by words. When those words have become overloaded with multiple ill-defined and contradictory meanings, we cannot think clearly. The words themselves keep us in a state of confusion. How will we break out of this tyranny? By simplifying and clarifying our terminology.

Part I of this book returned us to the ordinary English meanings of words that we have co-opted for special purposes in the field of information technology. For those with knowledge of established modeling notations and/or programming languages, it will be important to re-interpret those notations using the clarified vocabulary of everyday English. This next section contains a chapter on each of five major modeling notations. Each chapter provides a brief overview of the notation, and focuses on what those notations really mean in ordinary English. This will bring out a number of intellectual short circuits inherent in each notation that limit our ability to analyze requirements and design solutions.

If you know one of these notations, it is very important that you read the relevant chapter, so that you can make the translations necessary from the terminology you are familiar with to the terminology of COMN. By learning the refined terminology, new vistas of analysis and design will open up to you. You may be surprised at all the ideas you took for granted that turn out to have more to them than the notation teaches. But *you will only be able to gain these insights* if you can rise above the terminology and related concepts that are integral to the notation you already know. The chapters in this section are intended to help you do that.

You may read just the chapters that apply to the notations with which you are familiar. You may read all the chapters if that suits your interest. And, if you don't have a background in any of these notations, feel free to skip this entire section.

The same example data modeling problem is used in each of these chapters so that if you are reading more than one chapter it will be easy to compare the notations to each other.

If you are an enthusiastic user or supporter of one of the notations discussed in the following chapters, please keep in mind that each chapter is not intended to be a complete presentation of the notation. Rather, it is intended to orient the reader who is already familiar with the notation to how the same concepts are represented in COMN, and to highlight the areas where COMN can represent things that the subject notation cannot.

Chapter 5

Entity-Relationship Modeling

Entity-relationship (E-R) modeling was formally proposed by Peter Chen in 1975 [Chen 1976], and is almost certainly the dominant form of data modeling in use today. The notation of E-R modeling has evolved significantly since Chen's paper, and has forked into several variants, including Integration DEFinition for Information Modeling (IDEF1X), Barker-Ellis, Information Engineering (IE), and other variants. IE notation is common but not standardized, and exists in several variants. For the purposes of this chapter, we will use the variant of IE notation implemented in a Microsoft Visio drawing tool stencil.

E-R modeling defines three stages of data modeling: conceptual, logical, and physical. We will start our review of E-R modeling with logical data models, where the focus is on the design of data structures to hold data relevant to the problem to be solved.

Logical E-R Data Models

A logical E-R data model starts with simple rectangles representing data that is to be stored about various things, and lines between rectangles representing relationships expressed in data. See Figure 5-1 below. (For the UML equivalent, see Figure 6-1 in chapter 6.) Most E-R data modelers refer to the rectangle as an **entity**. This is not incorrect, because it's never wrong to call anything a thing. But this terminology covers up the fact that the rectangle represents up to three things simultaneously:

1. The rectangle represents a **logical record type**. This is not a type in the sense of a generalization/specialization hierarchy. It is a type in the sense that it designates a set. A logical record type is a list of data attributes aggregated together, and it implicitly designates the set of all possible values of those data attributes taken together—the Cartesian product of the data attributes' types. Sometimes the display of these

data attributes is suppressed, and only the name of the entity is visible, but the rectangle represents the data attributes nonetheless.

2. The rectangle represents a table of data conforming to the logical record type, which presumably is or will be created in keeping with the model.

3. By labeling a rectangle with the name of a real-world entity type—for example, "Person"—an implicit connection is made from the rectangle to the real-world entity type that records of this type are about. Not every entity rectangle relates directly to a real-world entity type. Some entities are needed just to relate some data to some other data.

For those readers familiar with E-R modeling, the most important idea to take away from this chapter is that the entity of E-R modeling in fact denotes a logical record type, a table of data, and possibly also a real-world entity *type*. In ordinary English, the word entity means an individual thing—what an E-R modeler would call an instance or an entity instance—not a type of thing nor a table of data. COMN uses the term entity to mean an instance, and entity type to mean a type of thing (generally, though not always, a type of real-world thing).

An entity rectangle is divided into three sections. The top section gives the name by which the "entity" (logical record type/table/real-world entity type) is known in the model. The middle and bottom sections list data attributes. The middle section lists the logical record type's identifying data attributes, which make up its **primary key**. These are the data attributes whose values are unique on each record of the type in a single table, and thus serve to identify individual records. The "PK" designation indicates exactly which data attribute (or data attributes) form the primary key for records of the type in a single table. The bottom section lists the ordinary data attributes of the logical record type.

Some of the data attributes are so-called **foreign keys**: data attributes which are keys to other logical record types. It is a foreign key that represents a relationship between two entities. In fact, the relationship is between the data in the two tables. Foreign key data attributes are indicated by an "FK" designation. In the data model of Figure 5-1, the Person ID data attribute of both the Person Phone Number and Person Address tables are foreign keys that reference the Person ID primary key of the Person table.

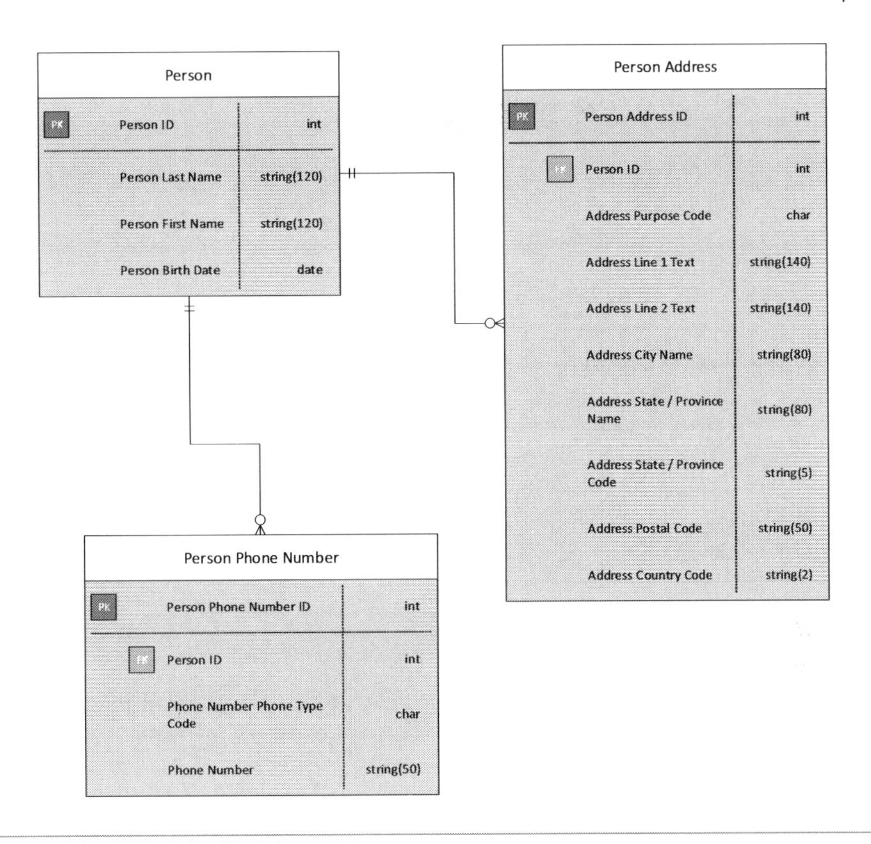

Figure 5-1. A Logical E-R Data Model

The relationship lines connecting the rectangles use what is called "crow's feet" notation, and indicate how many records matching a foreign key are found in the table at each end of a relationship. Two lines crossing a relationship line mean "one and only one" record at that end. In Figure 5-1, the Person ID of each Person Address record references only one Person record. This makes sense, since Person ID is the primary key of the Person table. A primary key value is always unique and will always reference exactly one record. Reading the same relationship line in the other direction, we see a circle and then what look line three lines fanning out to the Person Address record. The circle indicates optionality, and the three lines indicate "many". This indicates that one Person record may be referenced by any number of Person Address records, including none.

It should be pointed out that the model of Figure 5-1 is not ideal, because it creates the possibility that the same data might be stored repeatedly in a database. For instance, two people who live at the same address will have Person Address records that are identical except for the Person ID foreign key values. But this design has been chosen to illustrate issues relevant to COMN, so, for now, please ignore these otherwise important design issues.

Multiple Levels of Abstraction

It is customary to use E-R data models at three levels of abstraction:

- conceptual (the highest level)
- logical
- physical (the lowest level)

Each rectangle in a conceptual data model may relate to one or more rectangles in a logical data model, and each rectangle in a logical data model may relate to one or more rectangles in a physical data model.

A conceptual data model is similar to a logical data model, in that each rectangle represents a logical record type and eventually a table whose records conform to that type. But a conceptual data model simplifies a logical data model in two important ways:

1. It is customary to hide the display of data attributes within the rectangles of a conceptual data model, in order to allow the modeler to focus more on the relationships between entities.

2. A conceptual data model will depict many-to-many relationships between entities with a simple relationship line. In a logical data model, such many-to-many relationships are "resolved" by inserting an **associative entity** between the pair.

A conceptual data model is usually developed as a first-order approximation of a logical data model. Data-related details are omitted in order to support the early stages of model development, where too much attention to data-related details could distract from the task of documenting the data requirements that are present in a given set of business requirements. The conceptual data model is then used to derive a logical data model, where details such as data attributes and associative entities are added.

With just a little training, non-technical personnel can interpret and interact with conceptual data models. When interviewing business stakeholders, a conceptual E-R data model is a useful tool for capturing data requirements, validating terminology, and scoping application efforts.

Lower in the layers of abstraction, a physical data model enables the expression of the details of how a data design will be implemented in a particular database management system (DBMS). A rectangle in a physical data model no longer represents a logical record type, but rather a physical record type as the layout of a row in a table. A list of names and data types inside the rectangle expresses the names and types of the table's columns. The names of tables and columns are spelled in a way that is dictated by the technical requirements of the chosen DBMS; the most noticeable difference from names in the logical data model is that physical data names do not usually contain spaces.

Just as a logical data model can contain associative entities that are not depicted in a conceptual data model, a physical data model can contain tables that are not represented in a logical data model; for example, a physical data model might include tables that combine data from multiple logical data model entities for faster read access. In a disciplined data modeling process, such tables are limited solely to those needed for some implementation purpose, and do not represent a short circuiting of the logical data modeling process.

This approach to modeling at three levels of abstraction can be thought of as a stack of five planes. The uppermost plane is where most of the things mentioned in business requirements are to be found. This plane is called the **real world**. The next plane down is inhabited by the conceptual data model. Many entities in the conceptual data model correspond to real-world entities, and are named so as to reflect that fact. The middle plane is inhabited by the logical data model. Most of the entities and their relationships on this plane correspond one-for-one to those on the conceptual data model plane. As mentioned above, some logical data model entities correspond to many-to-many relationships from the conceptual data model. The next plane down is inhabited by the physical data model. Again, most things correspond one-for-one to the things on the next higher plane. Finally, the bottom-most plane is the database implementation. In a fully model-driven database implementation, everything in the database has a one-for-one correspondence to something in the physical data model. In fact, there are data modeling software tools available that support the generation and maintenance of SQL databases directly from physical data models. These tools make possible the ideal of model-driven development, where a connection can be maintained between the business requirements captured in the conceptual data model, through the several planes of modeling, all the way to the tables of the database.

Limitations of E-R Modeling Notation

The disciplined use of E-R modeling notation has enabled many database design processes to progress efficiently and correctly from requirements analysis through data design and all the way into implementation, following a model-driven development process all along the way. E-R notation has been a workhorse of the information technology (IT) industry in this regard. But E-R notation does have limits that prevent it from fully expressing some valuable aspects of database design, as we shall now see.

NoSQL Arrays and Nested Data Structures

Logical and physical E-R notation assumes that database implementation will be in a DBMS, such as a SQL DBMS, that stores data in tables. It does not, therefore, have any way of expressing two modes of data storage that NoSQL databases make possible:

- arrays
- nested data structures (often called "nested documents" by NoSQL DBMSs)

Arrays can be useful ways for storing some small and simple data structures. For example, it might be preferable to store a person's list of telephone numbers directly as an array attribute on the Person entity of Figure 5-1. This avoids the overhead of a separate table and foreign key just to store phone numbers. (If one is to do this, one must consider whether the telephone numbers need an index to support fast searching, and, if so, whether the NoSQL DBMS chosen for implementation can index array-type data attributes. We'll look at that question in greater depth in chapter 17.) E-R notation has no way to express an array.

We'll look at nested data structures in the next section.

Both arrays and nested data structures are modeled in E-R notation in a way that corresponds to their necessary implementation in a SQL database. This is what is shown earlier in Figure 5-1. The array or nested data structure is split out into its own table. That table has a foreign key back to the table from which it was split. Additionally, that table must have its own primary key.

NoSQL DBMSs support the direct aggregation of arrays and nested data structures in enclosing data structures, without the use of keys. E-R notation has no way to show data structures that are related to each other without keys. As a result, E-R notation cannot be used for NoSQL database design.

Some organizations have nonetheless used E-R notation for NoSQL designs, and use notes or other means to communicate to humans that a relationship line between two entities / logical record types does not represent a foreign key relationship. Such models can be useful, but cannot be used in a model-driven development of a NoSQL database, because the modeling tool can't tell the difference between foreign-key relationships and aggregation of arrays or nested data structures in a single "entity". Such models also require extra discipline on behalf of the data modeler, to make sure that the meaning of the non-foreign-key relationships is preserved as the model is updated, since the modeling tool used can't know the difference.

LACK OF REUSABLE COMPOSITE TYPES

Consider the Person Address logical record type of Figure 5-1. Most of the data attributes of this logical record type are not specific to persons, but are related only to postal addresses. The only person-specific data attributes are the keys, and these would not be present in a NoSQL database design that nested this information. If one removed these person-specific data attributes, one would have a generic postal address type, which could be used to store the addresses of persons, organizations, factories, ports, government entities—in other words, any postal address. This would clearly be quite useful.

However, in the current state of things, individual E-R data models must specify the structure of postal address data over and over. A modeler could define a **domain** to capture the types of individual data attributes. For instance, it might make sense to define a domain called Address Line Text as string(140), and then reuse this domain to specify the types of Address Line 1 Text and Address Line 2 Text. But this works only at the level of an individual data attribute. The type of an individual data attribute in an E-R model is always what we call a **simple type**, because it has no components. There is no way to create what is called a **composite type** that has multiple components—such as the entire postal address structure—and then include it by name in many designs. Programmers for decades have had the concept of a subroutine, which enables a routine written just once to be incorporated without alteration in hundreds of programs, saving development and debugging time, and making implementations more consistent with each other. But in the world of E-R modeling, the work of designing common data structures and integrating them into multiple models is done repeatedly, wasting time and making results less consistent.

Remember that a rectangle in a logical E-R data model represents a logical record type *and* a particular set of records that conform to that type. There is sometimes a debate as to whether the rectangle should be named after the type (for example, the singular Postal Address) or the set of records (for example, the plural Postal Addresses). The established convention is to name the rectangle in the singular, after the type. If the modeler wants to refer to the set of records and not the type, he must say so, and this isn't a problem in conversation. But there's no way to distinguish between the two in a logical model. There is therefore no way for an E-R modeler to say, "This rectangle represents just a type and not any particular set of records," which would define a reusable composite type.

The relational database mentality behind E-R notation explains why this limitation has been so persistent. One of the main goals of relational database design is to eliminate **redundancy** in data, which is where the same data is stored in several places in the database. Redundancy leads to the possibility of inconsistent data, where an update of certain data in the database changes the logically identical data items in one physical place but leaves them out of date in another. Inconsistent data is devilishly hard to deal with, reduces the quality of data, and can lead to costly operational mistakes as fundamental as shipping a package to the wrong address.

On the surface, it appears that supporting composite types in E-R notation would enable redundant data in spades. A simplistic use of composite types would certainly do that. But there are many cases where legitimate uses of composite types would make designs simpler and more robust. As we have seen, being able to specify the structure of a postal address just once, and then incorporate that structure in many places, perhaps in models for multiple databases, could be quite useful.

Composite types are especially useful when the data to be represented has a structural pattern but there is no benefit to organizing that data around a key. Consider the logical data model of Figure 5-2, which depicts a foreign exchange transaction. A foreign exchange transaction is a financial transaction in which one exchanges the currency of one nation for the currency of another. For instance, one might exchanges euros for British pounds, or American dollars for Canadian dollars.

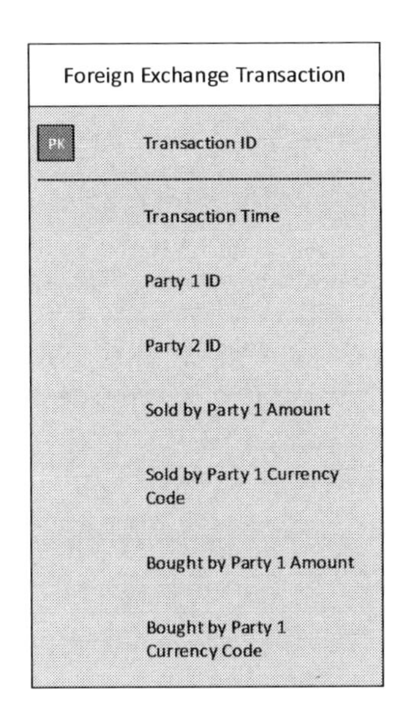

Figure 5-2. A Foreign Exchange Transaction E-R Entity

As the model shows, a record of a foreign exchange transaction needs to show:

- the amount and currency that was "bought" or taken in
- the amount and currency that was "sold" or given out
- the identity of the "counterparty" who provided the currency that was bought and accepted the currency that was sold
- the date and time, or "timestamp", of the transaction

There is a clear pattern in the data attributes. Two pairs of data attributes are highly similar in their structure and naming, specifically the two pairs of currency amount and currency code. Each pair is in effect a use of an unnamed composite type, which perhaps we could call "Currency and Amount". Since E-R notation has no way to identify, name, and reuse composite types, we must content ourselves with naming the individual data attributes in a way that reflects that the amounts and currency codes are in pairs.

We know intuitively that an amount and a currency are related in a special way, but we have no way of depicting this directly in an E-R model. This is a deep subject, especially so for those database designers who have known only E-R notation and SQL DBMSs. Chapter 12 is devoted to an in-depth exploration of composite types and their representation in COMN data models.

LACK OF PLACE

An E-R model is meant to illustrate the design of a single database, which is implemented in a single place. But the reality in almost all cases is that, at any one time, data belonging to a single logical record type can be found in multiple physical records, in multiple databases. A major task of enterprise data management is to get one's arms around this reality, to identify the one physical place which is to be used as the authoritative source for a given type of data, and then to ensure that all other records of the same type of data take their data from the authoritative source. An E-R model, with its one-for-one mapping from logical record type to physical table, cannot represent the complexities of this reality. It is not possible in an E-R model to show that a single logical record type has multiple instantiations in multiple databases. E-R notation is limited to depicting one database at a time.

MODELING THE REAL WORLD

As we have seen, the so-called entities of conceptual and logical E-R data models are typically given names that imply the real-world entity types that they are about. Consider our logical data model above which has a logical record type named "Person". The name of the logical record type clearly implies that records of this type hold data about the real-world entity type known as "person".

Sometimes data modelers will add so-called entities to a conceptual model to depict things in the problem space about which no data will be stored. These are in fact not logical record types at all, but are actually real-world entity types. Data modeling tools enable a data modeler to tell the tool not to carry such "entities" forward to the logical data model, but no visual indication is given that the symbol does not represent a logical record type. This shows that it would be very useful if E-R notation could graphically distinguish real-world entity types from logical record types.

REPRESENTING INDIVIDUAL ENTITIES

If one wishes to connect one's data model to the real world, it can be very important to represent, not only real-world entity types, but also particular instances of those types—particular entities—and relationships to data about those instances. For instance, a model of the legal system of the United States would need to include an entity type called "Court", but may need to represent the Supreme Court, which is an entity and not an entity type, since it is a very special one-of-a-kind court. The model would need to show relationships between the Court logical record type and a particular record representing the Supreme Court—but it can't. An E-R model can represent "Court" but not "the Supreme Court". Such individual entity instances are left implicit in a model, and there is an unsatisfied need to show that records of a certain type always connect to data about those implicit entity instances.

MAPPING BETWEEN MODELS

As we have seen, the five planes of modeling—from the real world, through E-R data models at three levels of abstraction, to the physical database implementation—have mappings between them which are one-to-one or very close to one-to-one. The mappings are controlled by simple rules and are relatively straightforward.

E-R notation does not have a notation for expressing these mappings. This is not a problem except when the mappings between layers are not simple. For example, it may be decided that a single physical table will be used to represent data from three logical record types, representing a decision to denormalize data for faster read access. The logical data model can represent the three logical record types, the physical model can represent the one combined table, but there is no way to express the mapping from the one table back to the three logical record types. You can think of that mapping as lost between the planes. When denormalization is required, or when novel NoSQL data organization methods result in the physical layer not being mapped one-to-one to logical record types, the need to show the mapping increases.

DATA IN SOFTWARE

E-R notation was developed in order to support the design of databases. As such, it did not take into account any of the needs of software development. Software developers cannot use E-R notation to represent their software designs. This leaves quite a gap between the modeling notation used by database developers and the modeling notations or languages of software developers.

TERMINOLOGY

Let's review the terms that E-R modeling has specialized, and compare them to their ordinary English meanings and their use in COMN.

ENTITY

As we have seen above, the E-R term "entity" can mean any of the following things:

- a logical record type
- a set of records that conform to the logical record type
- (in a conceptual model) a real-world entity type

Calling a logical record type an entity is convenient shorthand, and can't be called incorrect, since the term "entity" just means "thing", and everything is a thing. But it only works because E-R notation cannot express the idea of individual things, but only *types* of things—specifically, types of logical records. Taking the ordinary term for thing—entity—and using it to mean a *type* of logical record or a *set* of records makes it difficult or impossible to talk about *individual* records.

In a conceptual model, an E-R entity may represent a *type* of real-world thing. Again, this makes it difficult to model or discuss an *individual* thing.

As will be seen in Part III of this book, it can be very valuable to be able to talk about individual things, not just types of things.

As mentioned above, the presence of a so-called "entity" in an E-R data model implies that there is or soon will be a table of records in a database corresponding to the entity of the model. Thus, the rectangle of an E-R model has a number of explicit and implicit meanings, depending on the kind of model in which it is found and the context in which it is discussed. E-R notation does not make it possible to indicate the exact meaning using a graphical symbol.

CONCEPTUAL

As mentioned, the meaning of the term "conceptual" in "conceptual data model" is used to mean "first approximation" of a logical data model. This is analogous to the use of "concept" in an "artist's concept drawing" of a building: it's just supposed to give the viewer a preliminary idea or "concept" of the final result.

Using "conceptual" this way makes it more difficult to talk of "concepts" in distinction to "objects". Both are important when discussing data, as data exists both as concepts (at the logical level of abstraction) and as objects (at the physical level of abstraction). When using the word "conceptual", we must pay close attention to the context. A concept can be a very precise thing, and treating "conceptual" as a synonym for "approximate" can prevent us from seeing the intended precision.

E-R TERMS MAPPED TO COMN TERMS

A mapping from E-R terms to the corresponding COMN terms is given in the table below. Where more than one COMN term is given for a single E-R term, it indicates that the E-R term is ambiguous.

E-R Term	COMN Term
entity	**logical record type**, which is a kind of **composite type**
	table of logical records
	(possibly) real-world **entity type**
instance	**entity**
data type	**simple type**
domain	**simple type**
data attribute	**data attribute**; more generally, **component** of a **composite type**
(no equivalent)	**composite type**
conceptual	approximate
(no equivalent)	**conceptual**: relating to a concept or concepts

Key Points

- Entity-relationship (E-R) data modeling is probably the most widely used notation for database design and development, and supports these processes well for SQL databases. However, the notation has its limits.
- E-R data models cannot represent arrays or nested data structures, both of which are supported by many NoSQL DBMSs.
- E-R notation cannot express composite types, which would be very useful to increase design reuse, reduce labor and reduce inconsistencies.
- E-R data models cannot represent the reality that data conforming to a single logical record type might be in multiple physical places in an enterprise.
- E-R notation cannot represent individual data records.
- E-R notation cannot represent types of real-world things or individual things in the real world.
- E-R notation cannot represent the mappings between the real world, the three planes of data models, and a database implementation.
- E-R's overload of the word "entity" to mean "logical record type" makes it difficult to talk about individual records, real-world types, and real-world things.
- E-R's use of "conceptual" to mean "approximate" can make it difficult for us to grasp that many concepts are precise.
- The language of E-R modeling is completely disconnected from the language of software design and from programming languages.

REFERENCES

[Chen 1976] Chen, Peter Pin-Shan. "The entity-relationship model—toward a unified view of data." *ACM Transactions on Database Systems (TODS)*, 1, 1. New York: Association for Computing Machinery, 1976.

Chapter 6
The Unified Modeling Language

"The Unified Modeling Language (UML) is a general-purpose visual modeling language that is used to specify, visualize, construct, and document the artifacts of a software system." [Rumbaugh 1999, p. 3] Although the UML's first purpose was for the modeling of software, the UML's class diagrams (just one of about nine kinds of diagrams in the UML) have been used to model data and databases. The *UML Database Modeling Workbook*[Blaha 2013] describes how to use UML along with E-R modeling to design databases.

Class Diagrams

A UML class diagram uses simple rectangles, divided into three sections, to represent **classes** of **objects**. See Figure 6-1 below. (For an E-R equivalent, see Figure 5-1 in chapter 5.) The top section of the rectangle gives the name of the class. The middle section lists the **attributes** of the class. The bottom section, which in Figure 6-1 is empty in all three classes, lists the **operations** and/or **methods** of the class. Methods are the software routines that implement a class's operations.

In an object-oriented software system, the methods of a class are ordinarily the only routines that have direct access to the attributes of objects of that class. This kind of restriction is called **encapsulation**, and represents one of the most valuable contributions that object-oriented software design has made to the reliability of software. By limiting the routines that can operate on attributes, it is much easier to ensure that the totality of the routines in any software is operating correctly.

However, data in a database is not (or should not be) encapsulated, at least not while it resides in a database management system. The reasons for this are covered in chapter 12. The UML provides a notation to indicate whether a class attribute is encapsulated. If an attribute's name is preceded by a minus sign, then the attribute is encapsulated and can only be accessed by the class's methods. If the name is preceded by a plus sign, then any routine can access the attribute. All of the attribute names of the classes in Figure 6-1 are shown with + signs preceding them, indicating that these attributes are not encapsulated.

Each object of a class has a "slot" to hold the value of each attribute of its class. The term "slot" is used by the UML but never defined. Reading between the lines, we conclude that a "slot" is a part of a computer's memory that is allocated to an object.

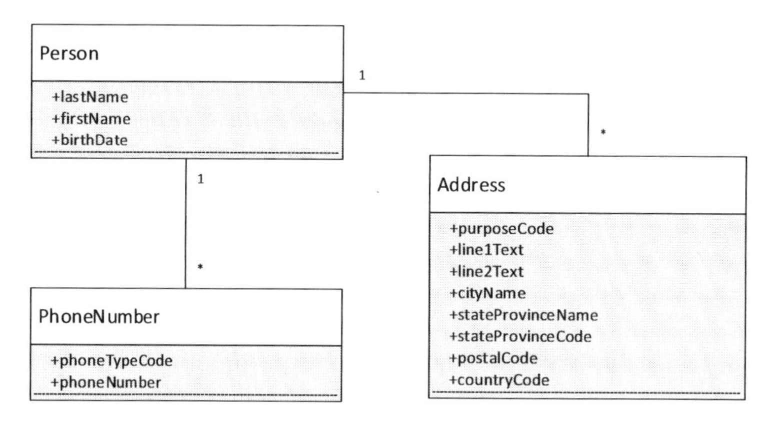

Figure 6-1. A UML Model of Data

The lines between the class rectangles in Figure 6-1 express what the UML calls **associations**. They indicate that objects of the classes will have "connections" to each other. Just as objects are instances of classes, links are instances of associations. Just as an object has a slot to hold the value of each class attribute, a link has a slot to hold a reference to each object at the ends of the association. For example, a link that is an instance of the association between a Person object and one or more Address objects would have exactly one reference to the Person object and one or more references to Address objects.

STEREOTYPING

A stereotype is "a new kind of model element defined within the model based on an existing kind of model element." A stereotype appears on a model as a name enclosed in guillemets (« »). Stereotyping is the UML's main mechanism for extending the language beyond what is already built in.

LIMITATIONS OF THE UML

LACK OF KEYS

In the original conception of the UML as a language for specifying software, associations were conceived to be implemented as references between objects in a computer's memory. Those references are generally implemented as pointers. However, pointers do not translate well to databases. Early database management systems used pointers to represent data relationships, but they were difficult to maintain and did not perform well, and were eventually retired in favor of the now-dominant SQL database management systems, which use foreign keys to represent data relationships.

The UML does not have a notation for identifying key attributes, and therefore cannot represent foreign keys. This means that the UML cannot fully specify a database design. There are workarounds for this deficiency. Michael Blaha in the *UML Database Modeling Workbook*[Blaha 2013] lays out an approach where diagrams in the UML are used for higher-level database design, and then database-specific details, including keys, are specified using the Information Engineering (IE) variant of entity-relationship (E-R) data model notation.

Thus, as a graphical notation for database design, the UML cannot stand on its own.

MIDDLING LEVEL OF ABSTRACTION

The UML is aimed at just about the same level of abstraction as an object-oriented program. The classes of the UML and of a program are both analogous to similarly named real-world entity types (concepts and real-world objects).

One can use the UML to denote real-world classes and real-world objects, provided that one makes it clear in notes on a diagram as to which classes and objects should be interpreted as existing in the real-world and not in a computer's memory.

The UML depends on the notion of a "slot" which it does not define. The UML also does not enable the depiction of a "slot" in any of its graphical symbols. This is a pretty clear indication that the UML considers lower-level physical implementation details to be taken care of by things that should not be diagrammed. This approach makes it difficult to use the UML to express implementation details with the rigor and completeness necessary for model-driven development. It also requires the assistance of other notations, such as E-R, for complete specification of a database design.

LACK OF CONCEPT

The UML defines an object as "a discrete entity with a well-defined boundary and identity that encapsulates state and behavior; an instance of a class" [Rumbaugh 1999, p. 360]. It defines a class as "the descriptor for a set of objects." [*ibid.*, p. 185]

This is all well and good, but the UML lacks any ability to describe entities that do not have state or behavior; that is, concepts. Concepts are expressible in the UML, but only implicitly and only in connection with classes, objects, or other things that the UML can express.

Concepts appear frequently in requirements, and an inability to model them directly means that a model can only represent things related to a concept. For example, an order is a concept. A model often focuses on the record of an order, which can be represented in the UML, but the order itself is just the idea that a customer has made a request of a supplier, and the order might not even be recorded—it might merely be spoken. Another important concept to represent is that of a role played by an actor. In the examples given in writings about the UML, a role is a structural piece of some object, rather than a concept independent of any object. Actors, such as humans, can take on and shed many roles, and the inability to model this apart from an object seems rather limiting.

If one needs to represent a concept and how it, and not a record of it, relates to other concepts in the problem space, one will need to use stereotyping. It seems that something as basic as "concept" ought to have a direct representation in a modeling notation.

SUBCLASSING VERSUS SUBTYPING

In *The Unified Modeling Language Reference Manual* [Rumbaugh 1999], the term "supertype" is explicitly called out as a synonym for "superclass". Strangely, the term "subtype" is not similarly called out as a synonym for "subclass". Perhaps this is merely an omission in the documentation.

As we will see in chapter 13, subtypes and subclasses are very different, and therefore so too are supertypes and superclasses.

TERMINOLOGY

One of the chief challenges I find when trying to apply the UML is that several key UML terms have repurposed ordinary English words in ways that seem strange, given their ordinary meanings.

RELATIONSHIP, COMPOSITION AND AGGREGATION

The UML defines a relationship as "a reified semantic connection among model elements. Kinds of relationships include association, generalization, metarelationship, flow, and several kinds grouped under dependency" [Rumbaugh 1999, p. 411]. Thus, the UML term "relationship" is an over-arching category of various types of connections between model elements.

In contrast, a relationship in COMN is simply an assertion that is true or false (that is, a proposition) about two or more entities. The entities involved in the relationship are "semantically connected" by virtue of being referenced by the same proposition. Chapter 15 examines relationships in depth. Relationships are foundational to semantics.

Although the UML has a concept called "aggregation", it is explicitly ill-defined, and called a "modeling placebo" [Rumbaugh 1999, p. 148], intended to pacify those who claim that it is important. Apparently there is no consensus among those who think it is important as to what it means.

In contrast, in ordinary English the term "aggregate" refers to a composite material, such as concrete, where the components of the aggregate retain their integrity, but there is little chance that they can be separated again. This is exactly how COMN uses the term.

Despite aggregation being ill-defined, composition is defined in terms of aggregation as "a form of aggregation association with strong ownership and coincident lifetime of parts by the whole" [Rumbaugh 1999, p. 226]. Once again reading between the lines, one gets the impression that several objects related by composition are joined in the sense of an assembly, where the objects may be joined or removed, with the additional proviso that, if one of the assembled objects is destroyed, all of the objects in the assembly are destroyed.

TYPE AND IMPLEMENTATION CLASS

In the UML, a type is a stereotype of a class, meaning that it is a class used in a restricted way, merely to specify a subset of objects. An implementation class is another stereotype of a class, and effectively restricts the class to correspond to a programming language class.

COMN has type, which is a fundamental classifier and specifies a set of anything, be it a set of concepts or a set of objects. It corresponds approximately to a UML type stereotype, but can specify more than just sets of objects. COMN has class, which is effectively an implementation class.

UML TERMS MAPPED TO COMN TERMS

A mapping from UML terms to the corresponding COMN terms is given in the table below. Where two COMN terms are given for a single UML term, it indicates that the UML term is ambiguous.

UML Term	COMN Term
class	**class** or **type**
implementation class	**class**
attribute	**component** of a type or class; possibly a **data attribute**
type stereotype of class	**type**
data type	**type** where the members of the type are simple concepts
"slot"	object component of a class
relationship	no direct equivalent; see the various kinds of UML relationships listed below
association	**relationship**
no UML equivalent	**composition**, which is the over-arching term for the formation of composite things from component things
composition	**assembly** with the additional constraint that destruction of one component leads directly to destruction of all components
aggregation	ill-defined in the UML, so no COMN equivalent

UML Term	COMN Term
no UML equivalent	**aggregation**, which is the form of composition of the components (UML attributes) of a type or class

Key Points

- The UML was designed to support the specification of software systems, and it does this well. However, it lacks a few features needed for data modeling.
- The UML lacks the concept of a key, which is essential to data modeling. It can only express the identification of objects by their physically distinct existence.
- The UML aims at a middling level of abstraction. It can represent types and classes, and objects in the real world. It cannot represent many things at a lower, physical implementation level, making it difficult to use for fully specifying a database design.
- The UML lacks direct support for modeling concepts as distinct from objects.
- The UML does not distinguish between subclassing and subtyping.

References

[Rumbaugh 1999] Rumbaugh, James, Ivar Jacobson, and Grady Booch. *The Unified Modeling Language Reference Manual.* Reading, Massachusetts: Addison-Wesley, 1999.

[Blaha 2013] Blaha, Michael. *UML Database Modeling Workbook.* Westfield, New Jersey: Technics Publications, LLC, 2013.

Chapter 7
Fact-Based Modeling Notations

While working at Control Data Corporation in the Netherlands in the early 1970s, Dutch computer scientist Sjir Nijssen developed what came to be known as the Natural-language Information Analysis Methodology, or NIAM, which incorporates **fact-based modeling**. The unique central aspect of fact-based modeling is an approach where modeling starts with statements of facts about a problem domain, provided by domain experts in their own language. The data analyst deduces patterns from these fact statements called fact types. A **fact type** is a statement in natural language that has one or more blanks or "roles" to be filled in. The roles are played either by object types or by label types.

Several very similar graphical notations, and associated methodologies, have been developed to support fact-based modeling, including Object Role Modeling (ORM) and Fully Communication-Oriented Information Modeling (FCO-IM). The examples in this section were drawn in ORM notation using the NORMA tool [NORMA] and Microsoft Visual Studio.

Facts and Relationships

Fact-based modeling starts with statements of fact in the problem domain. Here are some such statements.

> Sam Houston works at 123 East Main Street, Dallas, Texas 75208.
>
> Dolly Doolittle works at 123 East Main Street, Dallas, Texas 75208.
>
> Sam Houston lives at 456 Pine Street, Fort Worth, Texas 76104.
>
> Dolly Doolittle lives at 789 Elm Street, Fort Worth, Texas 76104.
>
> Sam Houston's mobile phone number is 214-555-1212.
>
> Sam Houston's FAX phone number is 214-555-9999.
>
> Dolly Doolittle's home phone number is 214-555-1234.

A fact-based modeler would recognize the patterns in these statements and reduce them to the following fact types:

. . . works at . . .
. . . lives at . . .
. . . has mobile phone number . . .
. . . has FAX phone number . . .
. . . has home phone number . . .

This would lead to the model shown in Figure 7-1 below.

Each rounded rectangle represents what is called either an object type or a value type. An object type typically represents a type of real-world object or concept in the problem domain. A value type represents something that is expressed entirely through a symbol or string of symbols—in other words, numbers and/or text.

Fact-based modeling notations are somewhat unique in the universe of data modeling notations in that they do not support the direct expression of data attributes within the symbol for an object type. Attributes of an object type are shown via relationships to object types or value types. This approach can be seen with the definition of the Postal Address type and its relationships to its component parts. This approach also leads to relational database designs that are already fully normalized (in fact, are in fifth-normal form), making the normalization process that is normally part of logical database design nothing more than a bad memory.

The rounded rectangle representing a Person type is shaded because no "reference mode" has been established for it. A reference mode is a manner in which some value refers to an object. If we were further along in our design, we would have chosen some symbolic identifier type for Person, and shown that as a value type in a dashed rounded rectangle.

Similarly, the Postal Address type is shaded. In truth, the aggregate of the postal address's parts provide the postal address itself, but given the way this model is drawn, an additional value type will be needed to enable reference to an individual postal address. This is desirable in any case, from a database design point of view, for efficient access to postal addresses.

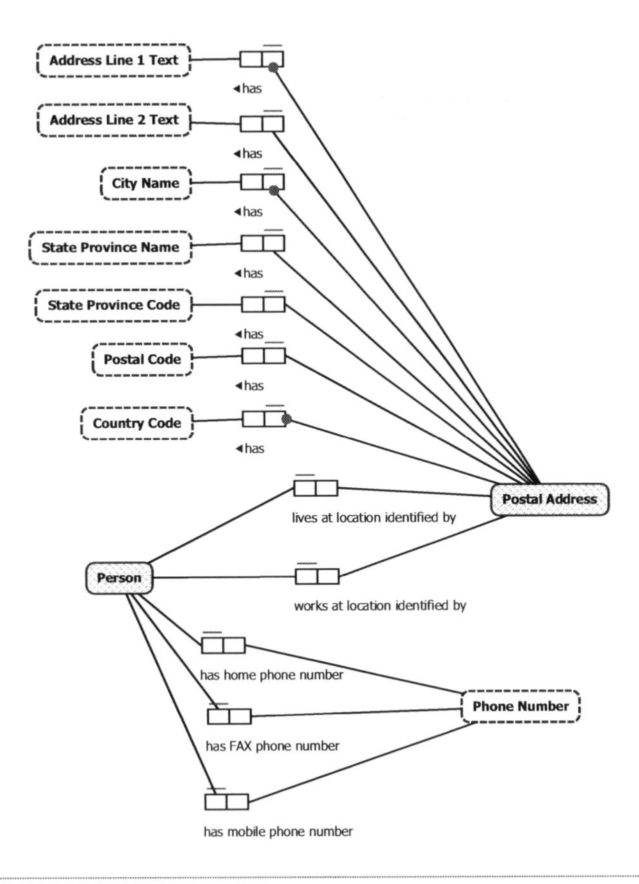

Figure 7-1. An ORM Model

A distinct advantage of fact-based modeling is that it is relatively straightforward to verbalize relationships in natural language; so straightforward, in fact, that modeling tools can do it. This is a wonderful tool for confirming that the model expresses the intended semantics. For example, the relationship from Person to Postal Address via "works at location identified by" is verbalized by the NORMA tool as follows:

Person works at location identified by Postal Address.
Each Person works at location identified by **at most one** Postal Address.
It is possible that more than one Person works at location identified by **the same** Postal Address.

Not shown in Figure 7-1 are additional constraints that can be imposed on any of the relationships in a model. Fact-based modeling has a full set of constraint symbols that allow the constraints of reality and of business requirements to be expressed. This captures more meaning in the model and increases the likelihood that the implementation will meet requirements.

LIMITATIONS OF FACT-BASED MODELING

LACK OF INSTANCES

If one wishes to connect one's data model to the real world, it can be very important to represent, not only real-world entity types, but also particular instances of those types—particular entities—and relationships to data about those instances.

For instance, a model of the legal system of the United States would need to include an entity type called "Court", but may need to represent the Supreme Court, which is an entity and not an entity type, since it is a very special one-of-a-kind court. The model would need to show relationships between the Court object type and the Supreme Court—but it can't. A fact-based model can represent "Court" but not "the Supreme Court". Such individual entity instances are left implicit in a model, and there is an unsatisfied need to show that objects of a certain type always connect to data about those implicit entity instances.

INCOMPLETENESS

The latest edition of Halpin and Morgan's book [Halpin 2008] positions ORM as a tool that should be used to ensure that a conceptual model is valid before proceeding to use E-R modeling or UML modeling to express physical database design details. In this approach, the details of the mappings from ORM to the final database design can be lost between the models.

The FCO-IM book [Bakema 2002] does not recommend the use of other established modeling notations to express physical database schemas. Instead, the book illustrates relational schemas with sample tables and words. In both cases, the fact-based notations exclude the possibility of illustrating physical design details. This is deliberate, as a way to reduce the chance that physical database design considerations will enter into the data analysis phase of a project. It is certainly a problem if such a thing happens, but to prevent the possibility by making those very important physical design decisions inexpressible limits the value of the notation.

Fact-based modeling follows the observation from NIAM that we do not actually represent the real-world in our data, but rather representations of the real-world. COMN accepts this reality, but enables us to model exactly how those representations work. COMN also recognizes that our representations are ultimately realized in a computer as otherwise meaningless physical states of material objects. It is important to grasp this reality, and to be able to express the mapping of the meaningless physical states of material objects to things that have meaning. Thus, COMN supports the expression of physical design alongside conceptual and logical design. If a designer has allowed physical details to drift into conceptual and logical models, that will be apparent from COMN's very different graphical notation for implementation details.

Tools such as NORMA (for ORM) and CaseTalk (for FCO-IM) enable the automatic generation of relational database schemas from conceptual models. This minimizes the need to graphically display the generated schema, but does not handle NoSQL databases. It also provides no means for a database designer to express physical design decisions graphically, nor to map them to the object types to which they relate in order to ensure a complete and correct implementation.

DIFFICULTY

Fact-based modeling is a powerful technique for analysis, and its associated notations can capture requirements in about as complete a manner as possible. However, it has been found to be difficult to learn for data modelers, and difficult to read for business users. In my experience, business users find it much easier to relate to the record-oriented graphics of E-R notations and of the UML. Somewhat counter-balancing this difficulty is the availability of relationship verbalizations generated from the fact-based modeling tools, which are quite easy for business users to grasp.

TERMINOLOGY

The terminology of fact-based modeling uses the terms object, object type, entity, entity type, value, and value type in important ways that cannot necessarily be deduced from the ordinary meanings of the words.

The most basic term in fact-based modeling is **object**, which means thing (the generic "entity" of English and of COMN). Objects come in two flavors: entities and values. An **entity** is either a "real object" (presumably meaning a material object and not to be confused with the "object" we started with above), or an "abstract object" (presumably meaning a concept, and again not to be confused with the "object" we started with above). A value is fully defined by the string of symbols that express it. So, for example, "123" is a value, and "abc" is a value. This terminology is expressed as a type hierarchy in COMN in Figure 7-2.

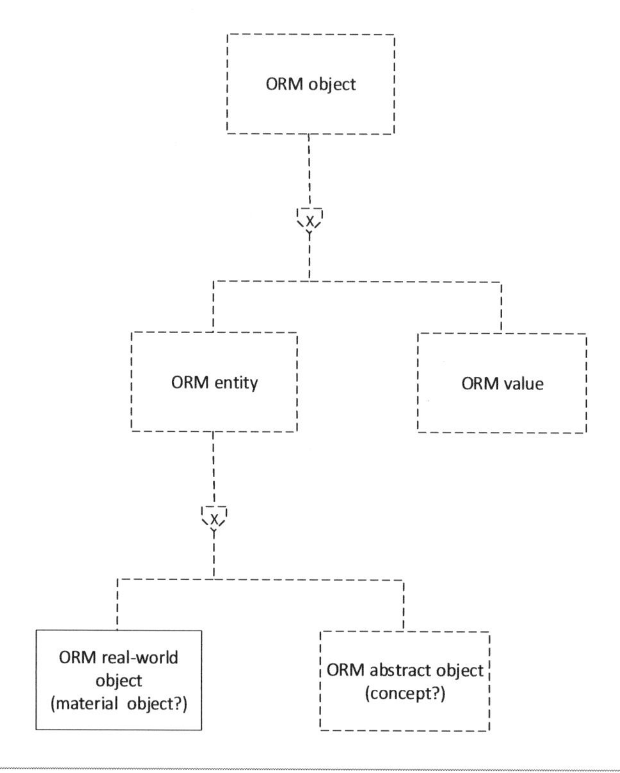

Figure 7-2. The Ontology of ORM in COMN Notation

There can be types of entities, types of values, and types of objects. As in COMN, a type designates a set. It is unclear whether an object type is a type of real or abstract object, or a type of generic object.

ORM has a special place for **measures**, which are quantities of some units; for example, centimeters or kilograms. Measures in COMN are discussed as special kinds of composite types in chapter 12.

The view of relationships and roles in fact-based modeling is very similar to the view in COMN. This should become evident as you read chapter 15 on relationships and roles.

FACT-BASED MODELING TERMS MAPPED TO COMN TERMS

A mapping from fact-based modeling terms to the corresponding COMN terms is given in the table below. Where two COMN terms are given for a single fact-based modeling term, it indicates that the fact-based modeling term is ambiguous.

Fact-Based Modeling Term	COMN Term
object	**entity**
entity	**real-world object** or **concept**
value	that which is fully represented by a **symbol**, or the symbol itself
label	**identifier**
reference mode	**identifier type**
fact type	**relationship type**
role	**role**
predicate	**predicate**

Key Points

- Fact-based modeling is aimed at the conceptual level of abstraction, in order to capture business requirements as completely as possible.
- Fact-based models have a rich constraint language that can capture more of the meaning of business requirements and help ensure a correct implementation.
- Fact-based models have no symbols to represent instances.
- Fact-based models cannot represent logical or physical database designs. The expression of these levels of abstraction must be left out, left to text, or expressed in other notations such as E-R or the UML.
- Fact-based modeling seems to be difficult to learn. Its graphical notations seem to be difficult for business users to read, although its automatically generated verbalizations are more easily understood.

REFERENCES

[NORMA] NORMA for Visual Studio. Available for download at https://www.ormfoundation.org/.

[Halpin 2008] Halpin, Terry and Tony Morgan. *Information Modeling and Relational Databases*, second edition. Burlington, MA: Morgan Kaufmann Publishers, 2008.

[Bakema 2002] Bakema, Guido, Jan Pietr Zwart, and Harm van der Lek. *Fully Communication Oriented Information Modeling (FCO-IM)*. Netherlands: BCP Software, 2002.

Chapter 8
Semantic Notations

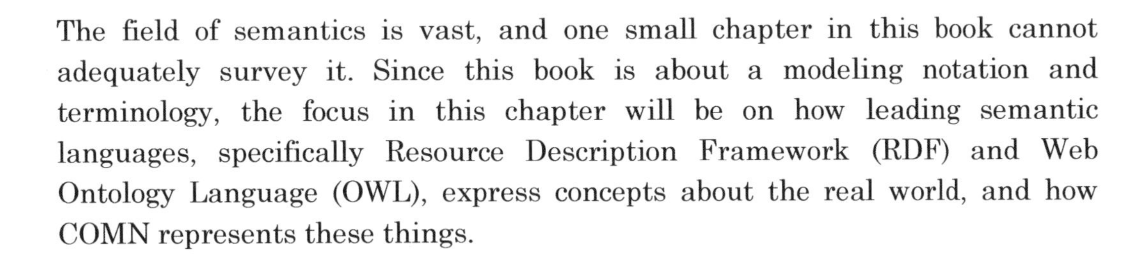
The field of semantics is vast, and one small chapter in this book cannot adequately survey it. Since this book is about a modeling notation and terminology, the focus in this chapter will be on how leading semantic languages, specifically Resource Description Framework (RDF) and Web Ontology Language (OWL), express concepts about the real world, and how COMN represents these things.

PREDICATES AND RDF STATEMENTS

There has been a great interest for some time in enabling computers to understand natural language: to be able to interpret the meaning of sentences, and then to be able to respond to the meaning of full-sentence queries and commands. Think of the robots and computers of science fiction, which have artificial brains and can carry on conversations with humans. There is a serious effort that believes that we can achieve this in the next few decades, but it requires that computers be able to process meaning. The field of semantics has as its goal the reduction of meaning to something that can be processed by a computer.

The effort to reduce meaning to something computable has been hampered by the heavy overloading of the term "predicate". It is used in at least three senses that are relevant to semantics. The three meanings are as follows.

In English grammar, the predicate of a complete sentence is "the part of a sentence or clause that expresses what is said of the subject and that usually consists of a verb with or without objects, complements, or adverbial modifiers" (Merriam-Webster). For example, the predicate is underlined in the following sentence.

Employee #952 works in department 4567.

The English grammar meaning of "predicate" is relevant when one is analyzing natural language text.

In the Resource Description Framework (RDF), the "predicate" is the middle part of an RDF statement, which also has a "subject" and an "object". These terms, borrowed from English grammar, don't quite line up with their English grammar definitions. We can ignore that fact as long as we can keep English grammar definitions out of our minds.

RDF would break down the above sentence as follows:

- the subject: Employee #952
- the predicate: works in
- the object: department 4567

These three parts taken together are called a "triple". (A triple is any group of three things). A triple of this sort forms what is called an **RDF statement**.

The RDF statement above could be expressed in XML as follows:

```
<rdf:Description
rdf:about="http://www.company.fake/employee#952">
  <ns:worksInDept>4567</ns:worksInDept>
</rdf:Description>
```

In this XML example, the subject is expressed as a resource referenced by a URL, the predicate is given by an XML element named `<ns:worksInDept>`, and the object is the value 4567.

You will see in chapter 14, Data and Information Defined, how logicians use the term "predicate", which is entirely different from how the word is used in RDF (and in English). We will preview that chapter here, and map RDF predicates to logical predicates.

In logic, a proposition is "an expression in language or signs of something that can be believed, doubted, or denied or is either true or false" (Merriam-Webster). The statement, Employee #952 works in department 4567, is a proposition.

We would expect the Human Resources department of a corporation to record many similar propositions about many employees; for example:

> Employee #952 works in Department 4567.
>
> Employee #956 works in Department 4567.
>
> Employee #891 works in Department 4566.

As shown above, each of these propositions could be expressed as an RDF statement.

These propositions clearly follow the same pattern. We can express that pattern by creating an English sentence where the variable parts of the propositions are represented by symbols—called, appropriately enough, variables. Here is such a sentence, with the variables underlined.

> Employee #EmpId works in Department DeptNr.

This English sentence is now in the form of a logic **predicate**. In logic, a predicate is a formula with variables that will yield an answer, true or false, when all of its variables are bound to appropriate values. By "appropriate", we mean values that are consistent with the type expected by the corresponding variable.

In our example above, we expect that the variable EmpId will be bound only to EmpId values found in the table of employees, and that the variable DeptNr will only be bound to DeptNr values found in the table of departments. Such restrictions on the possible values of variables are expressed by **types**, which are very similar to what OWL calls classes. We will dig deeply into types in chapter 11.

To this point, then, we've seen that an RDF statement is a proposition, and that the pattern of a proposition can be expressed as a logical predicate with two parameters. The RDF predicate identifies the logical predicate, and the subject and object are the values for the logical predicate's two variables.

DOUBLES AND QUADRUPLES

Not every statement that we would like to make about things come in triplicate form. Sometimes we need to be able to say something that has four parts and can't be sensibly subdivided.

For instance, consider this statement:

> John threw the ball to Mary.

There is no good way to reduce this statement to three parts. There really are four parts, and dropping any part leaves out some important meaning.

Here are two possible approaches to reducing this four-part statement to triples. In the first approach, we place the direct object (the ball) and the indirect object (Mary) in their own triple, and then make that triple the object of another triple that includes the subject and verb (predicate). This can be expressed in pseudo-code using functional syntax as:

```
// triple #1
thrownToSomeone(ball, Mary)

// triple #2
threw(John, thrownToSomeone(ball, Mary))
```

You can see that the second triple incorporates the first triple as its third part.

The second approach places the subject, predicate, and direct object in a triple, and then makes that triple the subject of another triple.

```
// triple #1
someoneThrewSomething(John, ball)


// triple #2
thrownTo(someoneThrewSomething(John, ball), Mary))
```

Logical predicates don't care how many arguments they take: any number greater than zero will do. A logical predicate corresponding to the above statement in functional notation might look like this:

```
threw(< Person_t who, Object_t what, Person_t toWhom >)
```

The above statement would appear in the same functional notation as:

```
threw(John, ball, Mary)
```

Forcing an extra level of factoring of such statements into triples could be disabling to some Big Data applications.

There is a lesser problem in the other direction, when we have only a subject and a verb/predicate; for example,

> Horses exist.
>
> Unicorns do not exist.

These statements could be represented as triples as long as there is a placeholder for the missing object. Such statements do not occur as frequently as those in the form of triples and quadruples, and the extra overhead of the missing object placeholder is probably not a performance problem.

OWL

The Web Ontology Language, or OWL, is a language for expressing ontologies. It has its own implicit ontology, described in the abstract syntax of the language.

COMN can be used to represent ontologies, because its symbology enables the depiction of real-world things, their relationships, and their properties. However, COMN has at its foundation a strong distinction between things that are concepts and things that are material objects. This distinction is present in order to ensure that COMN can represent not only real-world things, but also the real-world material objects of which computers are made, and can show how the meaningless states of those objects can be used to represent meaning.

This strong distinction in COMN leads to very different uses of words like type, class, and object than in OWL. Despite these differences, there is nothing in COMN that is incompatible with the abstract syntax of OWL. Consult the terminology mapping table in the Terminology section below for guidance.

Graphical Notations for Semantics

There is no single graphical notation that is dominant for the expression of semantic information. The semantic community seems to embrace a rich diversity of graphical notations in order to express different aspects of meaning. Notations in use include:

- simple graphs with nodes represented by circles, ellipses, or rectangles, and edges connecting them represented by lines or arcs: Nodes represent the subjects and objects of triples, and edges represent RDF predicates.
- UML-like drawings showing objects/entities with attributes.

Diagrams using these notations are sometimes organized into a particular style, such as state transition diagrams, cluster maps, and trees.

COMN offers the field of semantics a notation that is suitable for many of these purposes. A COMN model can be drawn more like a simple graph or more UML-like. Some of the possibilities will be explored in chapter 17. But the most important aspect of COMN is that the same notation used for ontologies can be used for expressing data and the static structure of software. This enables the modeler to ensure that the translation from a model of reality to a running system is complete and correct, and to express and therefore control the physical realization of the model.

Terminology

RDF Term	COMN Term
statement	an ordered list of three values. The second value (the RDF predicate) identifies a **logical predicate** with two variables. The first and third values (the RDF subject and RDF object, respectively) supply the values for the predicate's two variables. The statement forms a **logical proposition**.

RDF Term	COMN Term
predicate	the name of a **logical predicate** with two variables
no RDF equivalent	**logical predicate**: a logical formula having one or more variables which, when the variables are bound, forms a proposition

OWL Term	COMN Term
individual	**entity**, whether conceptual or objective
class	**type**
no OWL equivalent	**class:** a description of the structure and/or behavior of material objects
datatype	**type** of something lexical
property	**attribute**
ObjectProperty	**attribute** whose value is a reference to some entity
DatatypeProperty	**attribute** whose value is lexical
restriction	**restriction** (a means of subtyping)

Key Points

- The field of semantics today is dominated by the Resource Description Framework (RDF) and the Web Ontology Language (OWL).
- RDF statements and triples are inefficient for representing information that are not in the form of a logical predicate with two variables.
- COMN uses words like type, class, and object differently than OWL, but their abstract syntaxes are compatible.
- COMN offers the field of semantics a single modeling notation that can represent the real world, representations of the real world in data, and the static structure of software. This can help ensure a complete and correct translation of an ontology into a running system.

Chapter 9
Object-Oriented Programming Languages

Programming languages have undergone almost continuous evolution since they were first introduced as a way to express through symbols what instructions should be given to computers. A major change in programming occurred when the Simula programming language introduced the idea of objects in the late 1960s. The concepts of objects and classes were further developed in SmallTalk, C++, and other programming languages.

Today, most programming languages in wide use (other than C) are object-oriented and don't make much of a fuss about it. This chapter will focus on two of the currently most popular object-oriented programming languages, namely Java and C#.

Classes, Objects, Types, and Variables

Chapter 4 in part I explained the type/class split, where types designate sets and classes describe objects. Chapters 10 and 11 will explore in depth the implications of this split for data modeling. For those readers who have a background in object-oriented programming, we'll preview those chapters here, and relate them specifically to Java and C#.

As chapter 11 explains, the idea of a "type" in object-oriented programming languages was inherited directly from high-level languages that pre-dated the object-oriented revolution. The definition of a traditional programming-language type is built in to the language definition, and specifies two things:

- the set of values that can be represented by variables of the type
- the amount of storage to be allocated to variables of the type

These two aspects of a traditional programming-language type cannot be separated.

When object orientation came along, the programming language construct called "class" gave the programmer the ability to extend the set of types that a compiler knew about and could enforce. A class enabled a programmer to specify two things:

- the structure of an object in memory composed of variables and/or other objects
- a set of routines exclusively authorized to operate on the components of objects of the class, called **methods**

Since the built-in types of programming languages had very simple structures, this led to the belief that types are always simple or primitive, and classes always describe structures.

COMN's goal is to be able to describe all of the following things in a single notation:

- material objects in the real world
- concepts
- data about real-world objects and concepts
- objects in memory whose otherwise meaningless states represent data about real-world objects and concepts

To achieve this, COMN separates the two aspects of type that were inherited from early programming languages. The term **type** is reserved for designating a set of values or objects that a variable might represent *completely apart from any specification of memory allocation or structure*. Thus, a type is completely abstract. A type can also be as complex as any class except that it doesn't dictate memory allocation. Types are not necessarily primitive or simple. The term **class** is reserved for describing the structure and/or behavior (that is, the methods) of computer objects in a computer's memory or storage. The physical states of the objects of a class, in COMN terms, have no meaning unless the class declares itself to represent a type. If a class represents a type, then each state of each object of the class represents a member of the set designated by that type.

One of the main advantages of this approach is that it takes those "built-in types" that have been inherent in programming languages ever since there were programming languages and makes them quite a bit less special. There is still the necessary set of "predefined" types, but now these types are not tied to any particular programming language's assumptions about how they are represented in memory, including such things as endian-ness. An integer type simply gives a range of integers that the type designates. Whether that type is represented in memory by a little-endian binary two's complement integer, a string of Unicode decimal digits, or something else is not specified by the type. That kind of information is given (eventually) by a class representing the type that has all the details of the implementation— and the class encapsulates those details so that programs can't become coupled to them.

This is tremendously powerful for data modeling (and for software design, but this book is not about software design!). A data modeler can first capture descriptions of requirements and data as types, variables, and values, without even thinking about how they will be represented in a computer's memory or a database. Then, in a separate stage of design, a data modeler can specify exactly how those things should be represented in physical classes and objects that are available for use on the implementation platform.

So, as you read further in the book, keep in mind that, in COMN, a type tells you the range of values a variable can take on or the set of things the variable can represent, but doesn't give you any clue as to how those things will be represented. And a class can tell you all about a structure in memory and how it can be manipulated through its methods, but is meaningless unless it indicates the type it represents. The next two chapters go into these facts in depth.

TERMINOLOGY

Java Term	COMN Term
class	**class**
primitive type	a **class** representing a simple type
reference type	the class of a pointer or reference to a computer object
variable	a **computer object** whose class is either a class representing a primitive type or the class of a pointer or reference to a computer object
no Java equivalent	**variable**: a symbol which may or may not be represented by a computer object in a compiled program
object	**computer object**

Java Term	COMN Term
value	value
no Java equivalent	**state**: the meaningless physical state of a computer object

C# Term	COMN Term
class	**class**
interface	**class interface**
simple type	a **class** representing a **simple type**
enum type	a **class** representing a **simple type** whose values are named
struct type	a **class** without encapsulation
nullable type	a **class** that includes a representation that a value is unknown
array type	an array class
variable of value type	a **computer object** whose class represents a simple type, enum type, struct type, or nullable type
variable of class type or of interface type	a **computer object** whose class is a pointer or reference to a computer object
variable of array type	a **computer object** whose class is a pointer or reference to a computer object representing an array
no C# equivalent	**variable**: a symbol which may or may not be represented by a computer object in a compiled program
object	**computer object**
value	value
no C# equivalent	**state**: the meaningless physical state of a computer object

Key Points

- Object-oriented programming languages inherited types from early programming languages that specified both value sets and memory structure.
- COMN separates the designation of a set of values from the description of computer object structure and behavior. *Types designate sets* without specifying memory structure. *Classes describe computer objects* in terms of their structure in memory and the routines (methods) exclusively authorized to operate on them. The otherwise meaningless physical states of objects only have meaning if their classes represent types.

Part III
Freedom in Meaning

Part I of this book returned us to the ordinary English meanings of words that we have co-opted for special purposes in the field of information technology. Each chapter in part II reviewed a modeling notation or language, in order to prepare you to see the issues in those notations that may not be evident, that COMN addresses.

Part III introduces COMN in earnest. It is the knowledge in part III, built on the foundation of the clear and simple meanings of words introduced in part I, that will enable you to use COMN to develop models of the real world, of data, and of software that are complete and precise, and that can become, with proper tool support, the basis of a highly efficient and accurate model-driven development process of data and software systems.

Chapter 10

Objects and Classes

Recall from chapter 2 that we have restored the words entity, object, and concept to their ordinary English meanings—meanings that these words possessed for centuries before computing machines were even imagined, let alone constructed. For your reference, here are the definitions again that give those meanings, all of which are quoted from Merriam-Webster's Online Dictionary.

entity 2 : something that has separate and distinct existence and objective or conceptual reality

object 1a : something material that may be perceived by the senses

concept 1 : something conceived in the mind : thought, notion

In this chapter we will take steps toward using these ordinary English words to describe software and data, but without distorting their ordinary meanings. It is the distortions that have made it so difficult for us to think clearly about real-world problems and their solutions in computer systems.

We will go down to a very low level of abstraction, specifically the level of computer hardware. We don't want to stay there, because designing data one storage location at a time or developing software one computer instruction at a time is a laborious and inefficient way to work. But we do have to glance at this basement level, because that's where the foundation is. Understanding that everything rests on very physical objects and their very physical states gives the more abstract things we do a solid foundation.

If you are familiar with any of the notations or languages discussed in part II of this book, make sure you refer frequently to the relevant terminology maps at the end of each chapter in part II, to keep your mind clearly focused on the simpler, more natural terminology of COMN.

Material Objects

Figure 10-1 below shows a fundamental example of an object in the ordinary English sense of the word "object". The object pictured is a rock. It is certainly material, and it can certainly be perceived by the senses.

Figure 10-1. A Rock; a Material Object

Admittedly, a rock is not a very interesting object. A more instructive example of a material object is a flashlight, or electric torch. See Figure 10-2 below.

Figure 10-2. A Flashlight; a Material Object

From this point onwards, unless it is already clear from the context, I will qualify the word "object" with the adjective "material" to mean an object in the natural language sense.

Objects with States

Let us consider the flashlight's characteristics. It is an object in the same sense that a rock is an object, because it can be perceived by the senses: you can see it—even when it's off—and touch it.

However, a flashlight is interesting for more than its capability to be seen and touched. A flashlight can be turned on and off. We describe this capability by saying that the flashlight can hold a **state**. A flashlight has a built-in mechanism for changing its state from off to on and back to off: it's a switch. (In the commonly accepted terminology of computer science, mechanisms built into an object to change its state are called **methods**—but then we're getting ahead of ourselves.)

In contrast to the flashlight, the rock has no states—at least not in the sense that the flashlight has states. More precisely, the rock is in a single state (solid), and offers no mechanisms of its own for changing that state. We call objects like the flashlight **stateful**, while we call objects like the rock **stateless**.

In summary, then:

- A **material object** is an object in the natural-language sense of the word; in other words, something you can see and touch.
- Some objects have states and methods to change those states (for example, a flashlight), and some do not (for example, a rock).
- Objects capable of having more than one state are called **stateful**. Objects having only one state are called **stateless**.

MEANING OF STATES

Some material objects have states with intrinsic meaning. Consider the lighted sign in Figure 10-3.

Figure 10-3. Lighted Sign

This stateful material object does have intrinsic meaning. If this sign is over a doorway to a studio, and it is lit, then it indicates that there are live microphones inside the studio transmitting all sounds to a recording device. This object has two states and two meanings, and the meanings are fixed to the states.

In contrast, consider the flashlight again. I have conducted a fun little experiment with several groups of people. I hold a flashlight in front of the group, and, without any other preamble, ask everyone in the group to call out the state of the flashlight as it changes. I then begin to operate the flashlight's switch, and everyone dutifully calls out, in unison, "on ... off ... on ... off".

I then stop the experiment and tell everyone that this time I want them to call out, not the flashlight's state, but rather its *value*. As I begin to operate the switch, unanimity is gone. I still hear a few calling out "on ... off", but then I hear some calling out "one ... zero" (those are the programmers), some calling out "useful ... useless", some calling out "light ... dark", and some saying nothing except by the confused looks on their faces.

The point is this: There is widely accepted nomenclature for the states of a flashlight (on and off), and no explanation is needed in order for a person familiar with natural language to name each state. But there is not such a widely accepted nomenclature for the *values* of these states. That is because *state and value are very different things*. At least in the case of a flashlight, meanings must be assigned to the states—or not: if one wishes to use the flashlight simply to see in the dark, no assignment of meaning is required.

In summary, we have learned the following about objects and their states:

- The states of some objects have intrinsic meaning, while the states of other objects have no intrinsic meaning.
- It is not always necessary to assign meanings to the states of an object in order for the object to be useful.

OBJECTS WITH MORE STATES

Next let us consider a slightly more complex object than a flashlight or a lighted sign. Consider an important stateful object from the history of the American Revolution: the Old North Church in Boston, Massachusetts.

Figure 10-4. The Old North Church in Boston, Massachusetts, US

On the night of April 18, 1776, the American revolutionaries in Massachusetts learned that British soldiers were going to leave Boston the next day and march to the towns of Lexington and Concord, in order to confiscate the guns and ammunition cached there. The revolutionaries wanted to alert the towns along the route to be ready for the incursion. However, they were not absolutely sure of the route, because they did not know whether the soldiers would leave the Boston peninsula by boat, or march up the peninsula to the mainland. The plan was that when Robert Newman, the sexton of the Old North Church, learned of the route, he would signal it by carrying lighted lanterns up to the church tower: one lantern would signify the land route, and two lanterns would signify the route across water. Robert Newman placed two lanterns in the tower, indicating that the soldiers were coming "by sea".

Thus, on the evening of April 18, 1776, the tower of the Old North Church was used as a stateful object, with the following states and meanings:

- no lanterns: information unavailable
- one lantern: the soldiers were coming by land
- two lanterns: the soldiers were coming by sea

The advantage of this system of signaling was that, although anyone could observe the state of the church tower (no lanterns, one lantern, two lanterns), only those who *knew the values assigned to each state* could interpret and act upon the signal. The revolutionaries could communicate secretly to each other even though the soldiers could see the signals, because only the revolutionaries knew the meanings of the signals.

Even More States

Let us consider a hypothetical modification of the Old North Church tower. Suppose that two lanterns were permanently affixed in the tower, and Robert Newman were to signal by lighting one or two lanterns. Then the states of the church tower would have meanings as follows:

- neither lantern lit: information unavailable
- the first lantern lit, the second lantern unlit: the soldiers were coming by land
- the first lantern unlit, the second lantern lit: the soldiers were coming by land
- both lanterns lit: the soldiers were coming by sea

Now we have four states, but only three meanings! From this we learn that

- We sometimes have stateful objects with more states than meanings.

METHODS

Object-oriented technologists talk much about **methods**, which, in terms of material objects, are mechanisms that are part of those objects that enable one to change their states. Let us consider the methods that are part of the material objects we have considered so far.

- rock: no methods (which makes sense, since it has but one state)
- flashlight: one method, the on-off switch
- lighted sign: a method to turn the sign on or off
- Old North Church: a method to light either lantern

Just to keep you nimble, here is one more material object to consider: a tricycle.

Figure 10-5: A Tricycle

This is a material object that definitely incorporates a mechanism, namely pedals attached to the front wheel. Yet one can see that operation of this mechanism does not change the state of the tricycle: no particular position of the pedals has any significance over any other positions. We thus learn that

- Some material objects have methods but not states.

MATERIAL OBJECTS IN COMPUTERS

Digital computers are composed of vast arrays of a single kind of material object called a **flip-flop**. A flip-flop is a small electronic device built to hold one of two states at any time (either *flip* or *flop*, so to speak), and having methods to change the flip-flop from one state to the other. See Figure 10-6 for a symbol representing a flip-flop. The state of a flip-flop can be observed by checking the voltage on a wire labeled Q. This voltage might be high (not very high; typically about 3 volts or the same as two AA batteries tied together) or low (that is, about 0 volts). The input labeled S is used to *set* the flip-flop to a high-voltage state, and the input labeled R is used to *reset* the flip-flop-to a low-voltage state. This kind of flip-flop is called an R-S flip-flop, after its two inputs.

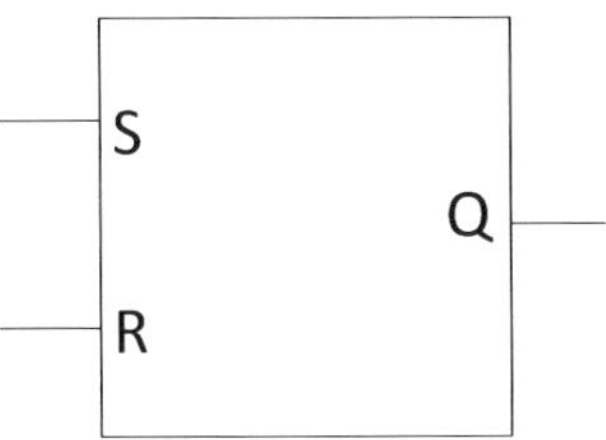

Figure 10-6. A Symbol Representing an R-S Flip-Flop. A Computer's Memory Is Made of Billions of These.

The vast majority of the flip-flops in a computer—those composing the so-called **main memory** of a computer—have no predefined significance, and are specifically designed so that their states can be assigned different meanings at different times. It is this ability to assign and re-assign meaning to states that gives rise to the great utility of digital computers to process a wide variety of information.

When electronic circuit designers are dealing with flip-flops, they avoid even the appearance of assigning meaning to the two states. They simply name the two states **H** and **L**, for high-voltage and low-voltage, respectively. It is irrelevant to the designer of a memory circuit whether the H state is called one and the L state is called zero, or vice-versa. After all, the user of the memory may eventually call the H state "green" and the L state "red", or the H state "stop" and the L state "go": the possibilities are endless.

Despite all this care that electrical engineers take to avoid the appearance of meaning, once the memory chip has left their care, it is very common for users of the chips to assign the number zero to one state (perhaps the H state; perhaps the L state) and to assign the number one to the other state. These two numbers, zero and one, become the standard names for the state of a flip-flop in a computer's memory, and we don't need to know or care about voltages. But it is important to remember that those abstract values zero and one *are represented by the meaningless physical states of material objects*; specifically, the high- and low-voltage states of R-S flip-flops.

Flip-flops in a digital computer are more often used in combination with each other than singly. In fact, computers usually make memory available only in groups of eight flip-flops called **bytes**. Each of the eight flip-flops has two states, so a byte has 2 x 2 x 2 x 2 x 2 x 2 x 2 x 2, or 2^8, or 256, states.

If we look at each of the eight flip-flops in a byte as representing a **bi**nary digi**t** or **bit**, then we can think of a byte as representing an 8-digit binary number. Eight binary digits can represent numbers in the range from zero to 255. Now we can refer to each of the 256 states of a byte with a number.

With regard to the material objects found in computers called flip-flops, we have learned that:

- For practical purposes, the meaningless physical states of material objects are often numbered. The states of objects with two states are often numbered 0 and 1.
- For different purposes, at different times we may assign different meanings to the same states of an object.
- Objects are often combined into a composite object. In general, the composite object has a number of states which is the product of the number of states of its component objects.

SUMMARY

In summary then,

1. A **material object** is an object in the natural-language sense of the word; in other words, something you can see and touch.
2. Some objects have states and methods to change those states (for example, a flashlight), and some do not (for example, a rock).
3. Objects capable of having more than one state are called **stateful**. Objects having only one state are called **stateless**.
4. The states of some objects have intrinsic meaning, while the states of other objects have no intrinsic meaning.

5. It is not always necessary to assign meanings to the states of an object in order for the object to be useful.

6. We sometimes have stateful objects with more states than meanings.

7. Some material objects have methods but not states.

8. For practical purposes, the meaningless physical states of material objects are often numbered. The states of objects with two states are often numbered 0 and 1.

9. For different purposes, at different times we may assign different meanings to the same states of an object.

10. Objects are often combined into a composite object. In general, the composite object has a number of states which is the product of the number of states of its component objects.

Computer Object Defined

When using the term “object” *in any context within computer science or technology*, we will use the following definition.

> **computer object:** a stateful material object whose state can be read and/or modified by the execution of computer instructions

If context makes it clear that a computer object is meant, the modifier “computer” will often be dropped.

A computer object is a material object that has two distinct qualities beyond those possessed by most material objects:

1. A computer object is a **stateful mechanism**. This means that it has two or more possible states, and means for changing those states.

2. A computer object’s state may be read by a computer, or modified by a computer, or both.

This latter distinction will, for the most part, restrict an object to be something internal to a computer. However, to the extent that material objects are hard-wired to a computer, they fall under this same definition. For example, the internal mechanisms of a laser printer that are directly controlled by a processor inside the printer are computer objects in the sense of this definition. In contrast, material objects might be *observable* by a computer, for example via a digital camera, without their states being directly read by the execution of computer instructions, and so would not qualify as computer objects in this sense.

This generic definition of "object" is meant to be a building block. (Remember, a good definition is a building block.) Let us see how this definition is used in the definitions of two more specialized kinds of objects that make the composition of complex objects possible.

COMPOSING OBJECTS

We have two kinds of computer objects: hardware objects and software objects.

- **hardware object:** a computer object which is part of the physical composition of a computer
- **software object:** an object composed of hardware objects and/or other software objects by exclusively authorizing only certain routines to access the component objects

If all we had to work with were hardware objects, we could only write assembly-language programs at a very low level of abstraction. We need a way to compose hardware objects into more complex objects, so that we can have mechanisms that are more complex than computer hardware. The definition of "software object" is crafted to serve this purpose.

We'll defer looking at what it means to exclusively authorize only certain routines, and focus first on how software objects are composed.

Software Object Composition

If we drew a graph of the composition of any software object, it would form a *strict tree*, where

- all of the leaves of the graph would be hardware objects; and

- no software object would be composed of itself, either directly or indirectly through other software objects.

Figure 10-7 shows some example graphs of possible software object compositions using COMN. Each hexagon is an object. A hexagon with an X through it is a **simple hardware object**; that is, a hardware object that is not divided into component parts. Recall from chapter 2 that all material objects, except for the fundamental particles, are composed of other objects. However, when we are illustrating the component parts of computer objects in COMN, we are not concerned with the physical composition of R-S flip-flops. Rather, we are concerned with whether or not the computer is able to address any smaller part of a hardware object. For example, an 8-bit byte in memory, even though it clearly consists of eight R-S flip-flops, would be considered a simple hardware object if the computer can't address its individual bits separately.

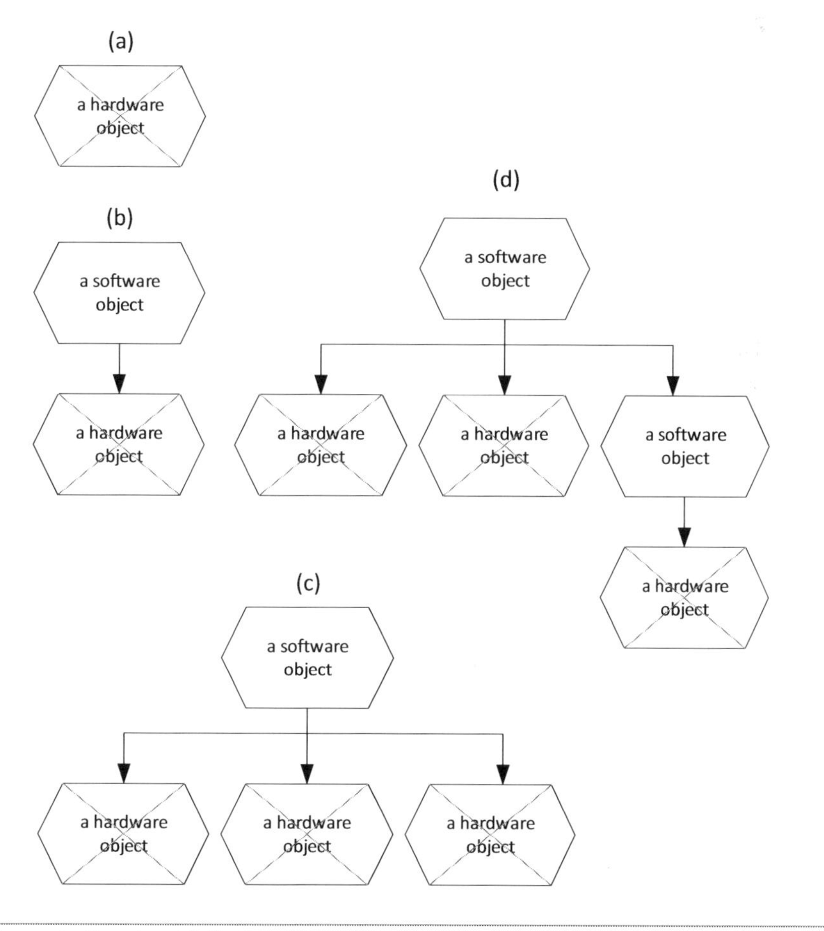

Figure 10-7. Example Graphs of Software Object Compositions

A hexagon with no X through it is a software object. Software objects always have components, which are either hardware objects or other software objects. An arrow with a solid arrowhead from one object to another indicates *composition by aggregation*; that is, the referencing object has the referenced (pointed-to) object as a component.

For the programmers among you, here is an extremely precise description of the composition of a software object. The underlying hardware objects—the R-S flip-flops—are *aggregated* on a silicon chip. They retain their identity, but there's no breaking them apart. In object-oriented programming languages, a software object is (directly or eventually) formed from a group of adjacent hardware objects in memory. The adjacent objects are *juxtaposed* to each other. Memory allocation manages a single software object as if it were an aggregation of the juxtaposed hardware objects. Therefore, we consider that software object composition is by aggregation.

We are concerned here with software objects that are composed by aggregation. If one of the components of a software object references another object by address (pointer), that could be composition by assembly, or it could be merely reference.

The graphs in this figure show the following:

a) a hardware object

b) a software object composed of a single hardware object, where access to the hardware object is restricted to only certain routines

c) a software object composed of three hardware objects, where access to those hardware objects is restricted

d) a software object composed of two hardware objects and one other software object, which in turn is composed of a hardware object

Thankfully, the composition of software objects from hardware objects is, in most cases, taken care of for us by compilers and database management systems. We are usually focused on composing software objects from other software objects. But it's really important to understand that at the bottom of every software object are hardware objects—material things having meaningless physical states to which we assign meaning. It is also critical to the completeness goal of COMN that it be able to illustrate this ultimate outcome of any software or data development effort, even if it is just to enable a modeling tool to generate the low-level picture. If we can rely on the fact that a valid COMN design, no matter how high level, can concretely map to a COMN illustration of how that design can be realized in computer hardware and memory, then we know that COMN is both complete and precise.

Authorizing Certain Routines

The second part of the definition of a software object says that access is restricted to a software object's components "by *exclusively authorizing* only certain routines to access the component objects".

How does this exclusive authorization work? The widespread practice in so-called object-oriented software development is that an object-oriented programming language (e.g., Java, C++, or C#) is used to express both the composition of software objects and the routines that may access the component objects. In this context, it is the software written by a programmer that authorizes only certain routines to operate on certain objects, and it is a compiler for the programming language used that enforces this exclusive access. If a programmer writes code that references a software object's components, and that code is part of a routine not authorized by the program to access those components, the compiler will not allow that code to be translated into computer instructions.

An object-oriented programming language has a construct called a **class**, which is a specification having two parts:

- some number of components which are objects of other classes, giving the *structure* of objects of the class
- some number of routines exclusively authorized to access those components, called the **methods** of the class, collectively establishing the *behavior* of objects of the class

A class can describe the composition of any software object of any degree of complexity.

This object-oriented programming-language idea of "class" is in line with the definition introduced in chapter 4:

class : a description of the structural and/or behavioral characteristics of potential and/or actual objects

We say that a class **encapsulates** the components of a software object by exclusively authorizing only the class's methods to access the components. Encapsulation contributes significantly to the reliability of software systems, by making it easier to confirm that a software object's states will be manipulated only in legitimate ways. Only the object's class's methods need to be validated in order to ensure that the object will "behave" correctly. Objects become the building blocks of larger systems, and those larger systems are more reliable when they are built from objects whose correct operation has been verified.

It is interesting to observe that a software object shares some characteristics with hardware objects.

- A hardware object has a fixed built-in set of mechanisms, accessible by computer instructions, for accessing and/or changing its state. Similarly, a software object has a fixed set of routines for accessing and/or changing its state.
- A hardware object may be composed of other hardware objects not directly accessible by computer instructions. Similarly, a software object may be composed of other (hardware or software) objects not directly accessible by its routines, if those objects are encapsulated within higher-level software objects that are part of the software object.

SUMMARY

Computer objects are entirely physical. Hardware objects have physical states that, for the most part, have no meaning. We refer to the states of these hardware objects using numbers, but that doesn't necessarily mean that the states represent numbers. They may; they may not.

Software objects can be constructed from hardware objects and other software objects in a tree-like fashion, but—at least as far as we know at this point—the composite states of software objects have no more intrinsic meaning than the states of the hardware objects of which they are composed.

Objects as seen in this light may have states that are useful even though they have no meaning. Think of the flashlight whose "on" state is useful for seeing in the dark, but which has no meaning. When one assigns meaning to an object's state for some signaling purpose, the state itself still does not express the meaning. A British soldier could stare all night at the two lanterns in the Old North Church tower and never discover the meaning assigned to them. In general, the meanings of an object's states must be supplied from some source outside the object itself. In the next chapter we'll see how meaning is supplied.

In addition to the states of objects having no intrinsic meaning, so far the concepts of "value" and "data" are also not associated with objects. This will be shocking to many in the industry. This is a major departure from established thought and terminology. This will be justified in the next chapter.

Key Points

- A material object—that is, an object in the natural-language sense of the word—is something you can see and touch.
- A stateful material object is an object that has more than one state. A stateful material object may have mechanisms to change its state.
- The states of material objects may or may not have any meaning. Their states may be assigned meaning. Their states might be useful apart from any meaning.
- Computers are composed of stateful material objects which we call hardware objects.
- Software objects are composed of hardware objects and/or other software objects, in a tree.
- In general, the states of software objects have no more meaning than the states of the hardware objects of which they are composed. In general, meaning must be assigned to states by something other than the objects having those states.

Chapter Glossary

computer object : a stateful material object whose state can be read and/or modified by the execution of computer instructions

hardware object : a computer object which is part of the physical composition of a computer

software object : an object composed of hardware objects and/or other software objects by exclusively authorizing only certain routines to access the component objects

method : a routine authorized to operate on the components of software objects of the class of which it is a part

encapsulate : to authorize only a certain set of routines (called **methods** of the class) to operate on the components of objects of a class

state : the physical condition of an object

stateful : having more than one state

stateless : having only one state

value : a concept that is fully specified by a symbol for the concept; also, a symbol for such a concept

Chapter 11

Types in Data and Software

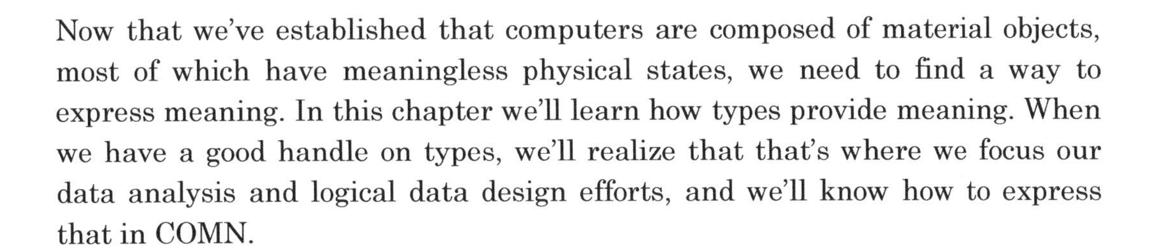

Now that we've established that computers are composed of material objects, most of which have meaningless physical states, we need to find a way to express meaning. In this chapter we'll learn how types provide meaning. When we have a good handle on types, we'll realize that that's where we focus our data analysis and logical data design efforts, and we'll know how to express that in COMN.

TYPES IN PROGRAMMING AND DATABASES

The term "type" began to be used in the earliest of so-called "high-level programming languages" in the 1950s in a way that was very different than its English meaning, which is related mostly to classification. "Type" was used as a way for a programmer to inform a compiler that a variable could take on any value in the set designated by the type, and simultaneously that a variable needed a certain amount of memory so that it could represent all the values of that set. So, for instance, in the days when 16 bits of memory were commonly used for storing numbers, a variable whose type was `INTEGER` required 16 bits of memory and could take on any value that could be represented using 16 bits—that is, any integer in the range from -32,768 to +32,767. A variable whose type was `REAL` required 32 bits of memory and could take on a much larger range of numbers that also included fractional digits; that is to say, digits to the right of the decimal point. (`REAL` was a misnomer, since such variables could not take on irrational real numbers such as pi or the square root of two; `FLOATINGPOINT`, meaning floating decimal point, would have been a better name for the type.) Thus, the name of the type *designated the set of values* the associated variable could take on, and additionally *communicated a memory allocation requirement*.

This notion of type naturally extended to database management systems (DBMSs), which came along about a decade after high-level programming languages were created. Each DBMS defines a fixed, relatively small set of "types" that describe what values can be represented in individual fields in a database. Since a DBMS usually uses a mass storage medium such as hard disk or flash memory, its types can be quite different than those supported in main memory by programming languages. Designers took advantage of the greater flexibility they had with mass storage than with main memory to define types differently than programming languages types, and incompatibilities between programming language types and DBMS data types were born.

Nowadays, the programming language type called `int` and the DBMS type called `INTEGER` are most likely to occupy 32 bits of memory or storage and are able to represent numbers in the range of negative two billion to positive two billion, while the programming language type called `double` and the DBMS type called `DOUBLE PRECISION` are most likely to occupy 64 bits of storage and are able to represent a large range of floating-point rational numbers. Other types exist to handle the expression and storage of such things as character strings and dates.

WHAT DOES A TYPE TELL US?

Let's look closely at what a traditional database or programming language type communicates. A DBMS uses a data type and a high-level language compiler uses a variable's type for the same two purposes:

- a logical purpose: A traditional type specifies the possible values a variable or field can take on. This is extremely valuable in helping to ensure the correctness of programs and data through a process called **type checking**. A compiler or DBMS either checks when compiling a program, or generates executable code to check when the program is running, to ensure that only values in a variable's type's range are assigned to the variable. For example, a DBMS will refuse to allow a program to store the character "X" in a field whose type is `DOUBLE PRECISION`. Similarly, when compiling code to assign the value of a variable of type `DOUBLE PRECISION` to a variable of type `INTEGER`, a compiler will generate code to report an error if the value of the variable of type `DOUBLE PRECISION` exceeds the range of values that can be represented by a variable of type `INTEGER`.

- a physical purpose: A traditional type specifies the memory or storage required for a variable or data item. A compiler or DBMS ensures that the proper amount of computer memory is allocated so that it can represent all of the values in the type's range. In the examples above, 32 bits (four bytes) of storage is typically allocated to a variable whose type is `INTEGER`, while 64 bits (eight bytes) of storage is typically allocated to a variable whose type is `DOUBLE PRECISION`.

Thus, while the English word "type" can mean a classification, in DBMS and high-level programming language terminology the word "type" means a constraint on values and a specification of the storage required for any variable declared to be using that type. But the two meanings still have something important in common: both designate a set, either implicitly or explicitly. Type as classification *designates the set* of things that belong to the classification. Likewise, the DBMS or programming language type *designates the set* of values that may be represented in memory or storage. This is consistent with what we said in chapter 4, that *types designate sets*.

Classes in Object-Oriented Software

As mentioned above, in ordinary English the words "type" and "class" are synonyms. However, with the advent of object-oriented languages in the late 1960s [Holmevik 1994], the world of IT gradually adopted the term "class" to mean something different than "type". "Type" for the most part retained its early meaning of set of values plus storage specification. Additionally, because the term "type" was adopted early in the history of programming language development, types were generally quite simple or "primitive", specifying little more than sets of letters and/or numbers. In fact, in some contexts the terms "primitive type" and "data type" are considered synonyms, and the adjective "primitive" considered unnecessary. In contrast, the "class" of object-oriented programming is associated with the enablement of programmers to define structures of arbitrary complexity, leading to a terminology that considers "classes" to be more powerful in their descriptive capabilities than mere "[primitive/data] types". Both class and type retained their use as specifying storage in addition to designating a set. In programming and database development (though not in data modeling), both terms lost their meaning related to classification.

Unfortunately, this vocabulary leaves the programmer or database developer with several problems. One problem is that it becomes difficult for the analyst or designer to talk of types and classes of things in the real world without confusing those terms with the very different meanings of "type" and "class" in data and software. Modeling the real world, and translating those models into their representations in software and data, can get quite confusing. Making this worse is the fact that the fields of semantics and philosophy use the terms "type" and "class" differently than their ordinary English meanings and differently than their programming-language and DBMS meanings.

Another problem is that there is no substantial difference between the programming / DBMS meanings of "type" and "class" other than degree of complexity. We are left with two words for things that appear, at least on the surface, to be very similar.

SEPARATING TYPE AND CLASS

It turns out that it can be very helpful to separate the two functions of a programming language or DBMS type, namely the specification of a constraint on values and the specification of memory or storage requirements. This separation preserves both terms as very useful, but by clearly focusing each term on only one meaning, thought and communication about data, semantics, and software becomes much clearer and more powerful.

As we have seen in chapter 10, the term "class", when properly understood, can be used to describe the composition and "behavior" of computer objects—that is, software objects and hardware objects—all the way down to the level of the hardware objects of which computers are composed. We will preserve this use of "class".

Classes therefore can be used to specify storage allocation requirements. We will remove this aspect of types, and limit types to designating sets of things—that is, sets of concepts or objects. Types become our means to specify the values that are to be represented in storage, without any presuppositions about how much storage will be needed or how those representations will be constructed.

A class indicates the meaning of the physical states of its objects by declaring that it represents a type. A class represents a type if its objects are designed so that each state of an object represents a member of the set designated by the type.

That's a mouthful, and a lot to remember, so let's draw that in COMN. See Figure 11-1. Starting at the top of the drawing, we see two rectangles with a line connecting them. The solid rectangle on the right represents a class, and the dashed rectangle on the left represents a type. In COMN, classes are drawn as rectangles using solid lines, in an allusion to the solidity of matter, while types are drawn as rectangles using dashed lines, to indicate that they are conceptual, not physical.

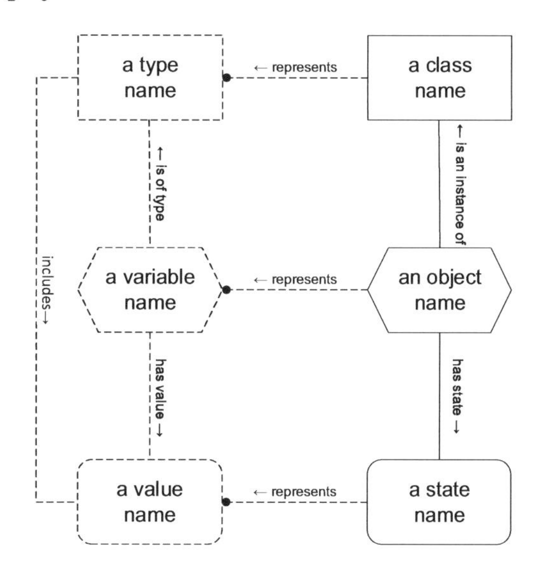

Figure 11-1. Representation Relationships (The relationship labels are unnecessary.)

The line from class to type with the solid ball on one end expresses the assertion that this class **represents** this type. The small arrow to the left of the word "represents" indicates the reading direction. Since a line with a ball on the end always indicates a representation relationship in COMN, the word "represents" isn't actually necessary. It's just included in this diagram to help you remember what that kind of line means. Because the representation relationship is conceptual and not physical, it is drawn with a dashed line.

In the middle of the diagram we have two hexagons also connected with a representation relationship. We saw the solid hexagon in chapter 10. It represents a software object. The dashed hexagon represents a variable in a program or a field declaration (perhaps a table column, perhaps a document component) in a database. This diagram says that the object represents the variable. In other words, something solid and material, capable of having multiple physical states, represents something symbolic that is declared to be able to take on any of the values of its type. It is usually a compiler or DBMS that allocates an object to represent the variable or field specified symbolically by a programmer or database designer.

At the bottom of this diagram we have two rounded rectangles. The solid-outline rounded rectangle on the right represents a physical state of the object above it. The dashed-outline rounded rectangle on the left represents a value of the type, to which the variable above it is bound. This, finally, shows the mapping of an otherwise meaningless physical state to a value of a type. The declaration that the class at the top represents the type at the top is only valid if in fact every possible state of any of the class's objects represents a value of the type.

By this means, the representation mapping expresses the meaning of the states of otherwise meaningless objects.

The unadorned lines in this figure (all of which happen to be vertical) have meanings based on the symbols they connect:

- The line from object to class indicates that the object is an instance of the class.
- The line from object to state indicates that the object may have the state.
- The line from variable to type indicates that the variable has the type.
- The line from variable to value indicates that the variable is bound to the value.
- The line on the far left, from type to value, indicates that the type includes the value.

Again, in the case of the unadorned lines, the words are not needed, as there is only one possible interpretation for these lines. Lines in COMN drawings either have a meaning given by arrowheads and tails, such as the ball at the head of the "represents" line, have a meaning given by what they connect, such as the unadorned lines connecting dissimilar symbols, or have a meaning given explicitly in words and other symbols. We will see examples of these later.

Connecting lines are dashed or solid based on whether the relationships they represent are conceptual (dashed) or physical (solid). Any relationship involving something conceptual must itself be conceptual. Relationships between physical things may be physical, but may also be merely conceptual.

Computer objects are physical, and their states are physical phenomena, but *descriptions* of computer objects—that is, software and DBMS classes—are conceptual. Nonetheless, we draw classes in solid outline to indicate that they are descriptions of physical things.

What is gained by the separation of type and class? Exactly what the world of computer science has been striving for decades, through modeling notations, high-level programming languages, data languages, virtual machines, and other means that have never quite achieved these goals:

1. Specification of the "what" independent of the "how": Existing modeling notations, programming languages, and data languages have tried to enable the expression of software and data requirements independent of particular computer architectures, but the fact that the most basic types assumed some particular representation meant they always failed. A virtual machine is not devoid of such assumptions: it simply specifies a particular set of representation assumptions independent of any real computer (even including the arbitrary choice of endian-ness). In contrast, COMN can truly describe the "what" in terms of types independently of any assumed virtual or real representations.

2. Description of the "how" independent of the "what": Classes can be used to describe the mechanisms and states of raw computer hardware before any meaning has been attached to those states. Most modeling notations and high-level programming languages cannot express ideas at this low level.

3. Specification of the representation of requirements separately from specification of the requirements: Once a pure description of the "what" has been drawn in COMN, the design of the "how" can be completed by

building up classes and objects from those available on the implementation platform, and those classes and objects can be mapped to the types in the requirements using representation mappings. Most existing notations and languages cannot express this mapping, either because they've tangled the concept of types with assumed representations and implementations, or they've prohibited the expression of implementation concerns, or (strangely but commonly) both.

Simple Types

We have seen how hardware objects are simple objects, having no components (from the point of view of software), and how we will rarely deal with hardware objects directly. We leave that difficult and tedious work to compilers and DBMSs.

Not so with simple types. Database designers must deal with simple types, and composite types, throughout the analysis, design, and implementation phases of any project.

The implementers of DBMSs and programming languages have done us a great favor by creating large collections of so-called "types"—which we now think of as classes representing types—that name and describe particular implementations of representations of values. We can use these implementations to build our systems. But if, at analysis time, we ignore these implementations and focus only on specifying the sets of values to be represented—types in the COMN sense—we can specify our systems' requirements—the "what"—without even a glance at what particular implementation systems provide for us. For example, if we need some variable to range between -1 and 100,000, we can specify that as a type, and defer until later the exact choice of an implementation of some class whose objects can represent just those values. We can also specify that type without recourse to the arbitrarily distinct idea of a so-called "domain" supported by some E-R modeling tools. These modeling tools need the concept of "domain" in addition to the concept of "type" because they've hard-wired "type" to the fixed set of mostly simple types provided by DBMS implementations. If, instead, types have nothing to do with implementations, then a type is a type is a type, whether it is directly supported by an implementation out of the box or will require some programming. The E-R modeling concept of "domain" is just redundant.

In addition to the simple type starter kits provided to us by DBMSs and programming languages, we often need to make up our own simple types. One of the most common of these is an enumeration. An enumeration is a type that is specified by listing the names of the members of the set it designates. Here are some example enumerations:

- account status: open, closed, suspended, abandoned
- organization type: corporation, government entity, non-profit
- order status: ordered, shipped, back-ordered, canceled

In general, enumerations have no components. Now, their *representations* do: the example enumerations listed above represent enumeration values with words and phrases which are composed of letters and punctuation. But what these representations *represent* have no components. For instance, an account status of "open" can't be broken down into any constituent parts. Likewise, an order status of "shipped" has no components. Don't confuse the value, which is simple, with information about what these values represent. For instance, we can learn of the date on which an account was opened, or the reason an order was canceled. But the enumerated values that these data are about, "open" and "canceled", are simple values.

Figure 11-2 below shows a COMN diagram for account status. Such a drawing is most useful for enumerated types that designate relatively small and stable sets of values. Stable enumerated types of those sorts can be extremely important in a data design, as it enables distinct parts of a system to communicate with each other. For larger and/or more fluid enumerated types, the type names are often kept in a database table. (There are well documented standard techniques for managing such lists of reference values in databases.) For the more fluid enumerated types, a model will typically just show the type rectangle and omit the enumerated values.

The rectangles and rounded rectangles in Figure 11-2 are dashed because they represent concepts, and are in bold outline because they represent the concepts in the real world, not as expressed in data. The lines crossing through the shapes indicate that these are a simple type and simple values, having no components.

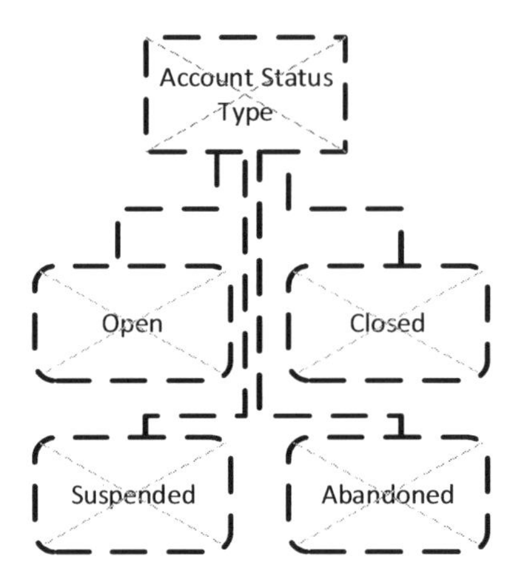

Figure 11-2. An Enumerated Type in COMN

How will these enumerated values be represented in a running system? That is a physical design decision that is expressed through classes. It is possible that a program would represent the values using integers in the range 0-3, and a database would store each status as a single letter code. A user interface would wish to display the values using their full character string form. All three modes of representation can be expressed in COMN, separately from the type diagram but mapped to it. Figure 11-3 shows just one possible representation of the enumerated type, as letter codes. Other representations could be shown on the same or different diagrams.

This figure gives more detail than would ordinarily be shown, for the purposes of teaching the notation. It's easy to see that each possible state of an object of the Account Status Char Class represents a value of the Account Status Type, and it is therefore valid to say that the Account Status Char Class represents the Account Status Type. In the upper right-hand corner we've shown that the Account Status Char Class is composed of something called CHAR{1}, which is a DBMS type. The solid arrowhead indicates that the composition is by aggregation, meaning that the DBMS type is an integral part of the class, though it can still be seen as a separate component of the class. (Recall the definition of aggregation back in chapter 3.) The CHAR{1} class is composed of a simple hardware class, a byte, again through aggregation. We'll look more closely at composition in chapter 12.

A conceptual modeler will focus solely on the abstract definition of Account Status Type and its enumerated values without giving a thought to its eventual representation and implementation. Database designers and programmers will focus on the middle section, giving thought to how to represent the abstract values in symbols such as characters and numbers. A data modeler will not normally show the details of representation at the lowest levels on a COMN model, but if he wanted to, he could. Furthermore, a data modeling tool could generate the low-level details from information in the model, in order to assist in analyzing physical design details, and as the final and heavily automated step in model-driven development.

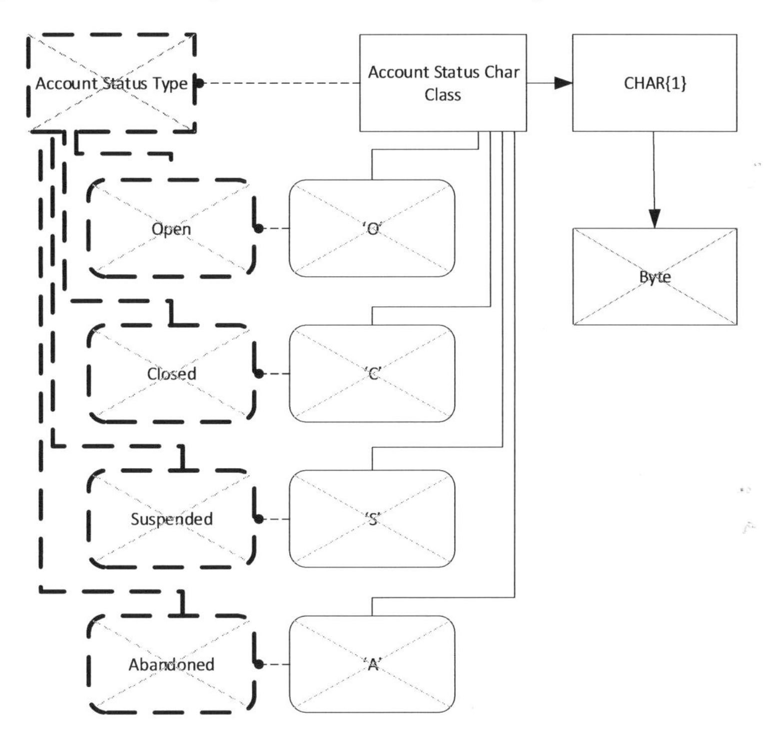

Figure 11-3. Physical Representation of an Enumerated Type

Figure 11-3 is just a small representative sample of how COMN supports high-level analysis, decisions about representations for information, and physical design decisions. We will look at representation more closely as part of chapter 12, when we look at composite types.

As we will see in chapter 13, the type/class split makes it easier to work with subtypes, which are a powerful tool for analysis and design.

References

[Holmevik 1994] Holmevik, Jan Rune (1994). "Compiling Simula: A historical study of technological genesis". *IEEE Annals of the History of Computing* 16 (4): 25–37. doi:10.1109/85.329756.

Key Points

- Classification is an innate human activity. When stripped of their technical meanings, the English words "type" and "class" are synonyms, and are used to designate sets of things with similar characteristics. We say that *types designate sets*.
- The word "type" was co-opted by the information technology industry to express both a potential set of values and memory storage requirements for representations of those values.
- The word "class" grew up later to describe more complex structures than those that could be described directly by the types of the previous earlier decade. "Type" alone took on the connotation of being simple or "primitive"; data types were also considered primitive.
- In COMN, we keep the programming-language concept of a class, which is very physical. We strip any notion of physicality from the concept of a type, and use types solely to designate sets.
- Classes may optionally declare that they represent types.
- Our type/class split enables us to specify systems in terms of types without reference to any default or implicit representations or implementations. This enables us to specify systems in highly portable and machine-independent ways, and defer all implementation considerations to a later stage of design.

Chapter Glossary

simple type : a type that designates a set whose members have no components

composite type : a type that designates a set whose members have components

Chapter 12
Composite Types

In the previous chapter we have seen how very basic types, such as integer types, are simple—having no components—but classes describing software objects are always composite. In this chapter we will dig into types that have components—so-called composite types—which actually dominate the work of data modeling.

Composite Types as Logical Record Types

A COMN model may show a composite type as a simple dashed rectangle without crossing lines through it, or it may show the details of the composition of the type using a dashed rectangle with three sections, in a manner very similar to the UML's three-section rectangle showing the name, components, and methods of a class.

Figure 12-1 uses a rectangle with three sections to illustrate a hypothetical design for a record for the United Kingdom Department for Work and Pensions to keep track of National Insurance Numbers (NINOs) and the people to whom they are assigned. The top section of the rectangle contains the name of the type. The middle section contains the components of the type, often called its **data attributes**.

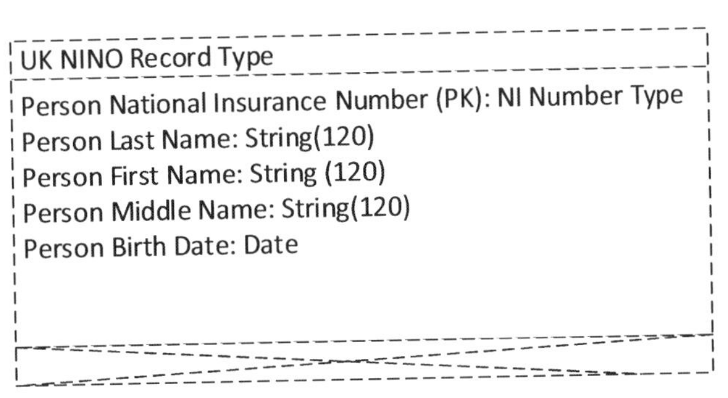

Figure 12-1. UK NINO Logical Record Type

The name of the first component of the UK NINO Record type, the Person National Insurance Number, is followed by the letters "PK" in parentheses. This means that it is a component (in this case, the only component) of the primary key of the record type. A key is a component or set of components whose values are always unique in any set of records of the type. Without a key, records in a set of records can be difficult or impossible to distinguish from each other.

The bottom section of the rectangle has lines crossing through it. This notation asserts that this type has no methods. When a composite type has no methods, it does not encapsulate its components. They are visible and directly manipulatable by all. Now, encapsulation is incredibly valuable. By controlling what routines can access or modify the component objects of a software object, encapsulation makes software much simpler, therefore easier to write and easier to avoid generating bugs in the writing. Encapsulation has led to a significant increase in the reliability of software, and a concomitant decrease in the cost of software development. But upon reflection, one realizes that the value of encapsulation is related to the encapsulation of *mechanisms*. We want to limit the routines which can operate the internal mechanisms of an object. But in the case of data, we actually *want* data to be visible to others—we don't want to hide it as we want to hide internal mechanisms. "Information hiding" *a là* David Parnas [Parnas 1972] should be about hiding information about mechanisms, not about hiding information *per se*.

So, when we define a logical record type, we typically don't define any particular methods. We might do so at a higher level than an individual logical record type. For example, we might have a higher-level type that references several different record types, and that provides mechanisms to manipulate groups of records of those various types in ways that ensure that their values remain consistent with each other. By encapsulating access to groups of related records of different types, and allowing only the methods of the encapsulating type to access them, we achieve all the benefits of encapsulation, without forcing the overhead of encapsulation on the very methods designed to manipulate instances of those record types. We also enable powerful relational operations (see chapter 16) which are not possible on encapsulated data. This form of composition of records and objects through reference is composition by assembly.

TYPES REPRESENTING THINGS IN THE REAL WORLD: IDENTIFICATION

It is very common, and fundamental to data modeling, to use types of values to represent types of things in the real world. Consider an identifier: a number or alphanumeric string assigned within a computer system to identify a real-world object. The example in the previous section mentions the UK National Insurance Number (two letters, six digits, one letter), which is used to identify people. Other countries have their own national identifiers, such as the US Social Security Number (a 9-digit decimal number). Drivers' license numbers also represent people, though a slightly different set of people than national identifiers do; namely, those licensed by some state or nation to drive vehicles. Lottery tickets are identified by numbers. Houses on streets are usually identified by numbers assigned by a postal authority. Individual automobiles are identified by Vehicle Identification Numbers (VINs) assigned at the time of manufacture. And so on.

We can diagram in COMN exactly how identification works. Figure 12-2 shows that same logical record type for UK national insurance numbers, but now it's shown connected to a collection of records, through that collection to the real-world persons that the records are about, and to the NI Number type.

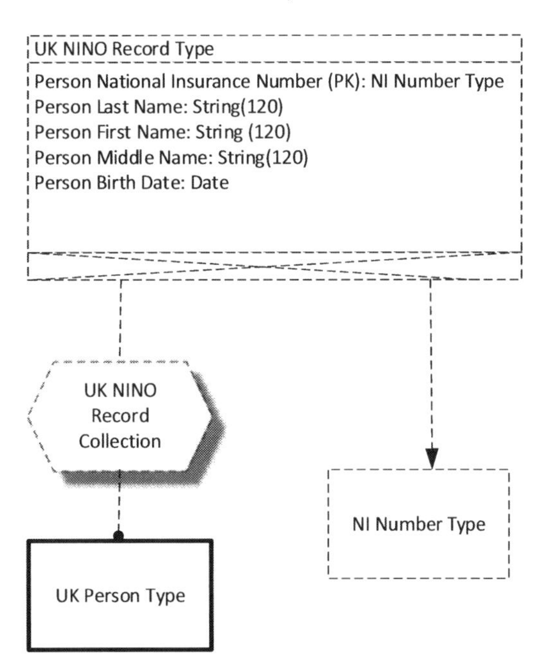

Figure 12-2. UK NINO Logical Record Type with Related Types

We've seen rectangles in COMN before, but the UK Person Type rectangle is drawn differently: it has a solid bold outline. A solid outline indicates that the type represented designates objects, not concepts, and people are material objects, because they can be perceived by the senses. The bold outline indicates that these objects exist in the real world and not in the computer. A person is a material object but not a computer object. We named this type UK Person Type because it's not the type of all persons, but only the type of persons known to the UK Department for Work and Pensions.

In between the UK NINO Record Type and the UK Person Type we have a dashed hexagon with a shadow labeled the UK NINO Record Collection. A dashed hexagon is the COMN symbol for a variable, and the unadorned line connecting it to the UK NINO Record Type tells us that that is the type of the variable. The shadow indicates a collection, so the shadowed hexagon represents a collection of variables. Since we're focused on logical data design and not implementation, we haven't decided yet whether the collection will be represented by a table in a SQL database, a collection of documents in a NoSQL document database, or something else. In any case, we think of this collection of records as a collection of variables, where each variable has the UK NINO Record Type. Each variable will eventually be a table row, a document, or something similar.

The representation line from the UK NINO Record Collection to UK Person Type indicates that the record collection represents the UK Person type. This means that each value of a record in the UK NINO Record Collection represents a UK Person. Since we know that the key of a UK NINO Record—the Person National Insurance Number—is always unique, we know that in fact it is the Person National Insurance Number that represents, or **identifies**, a UK Person.

It is not true that *every* NINO identifies a UK Person. It is only a NINO that has been assigned to a person, as recorded in a UK NINO Record, that identifies a UK Person. This is where the NI Number Type on the right of Figure 12-2 comes in. The NI Number Type designates the full set of NINO numbers, whether assigned or not. The full set is defined as all those strings of characters starting with two letters, then six decimal digits, and finally one suffix letter, minus certain prohibited combinations as defined by the UK

Department for Work and Pensions. NINOs to be assigned to people must be drawn from this set.

Let's look more closely at the relationship from the UK NINO Record Type to the NI Number Type. The definition of the UK NINO Record Type includes a component, the Person National Insurance Number, whose type is NI Number Type. The UK NINO Record Type incorporates the NI Number Type by aggregation; in other words, the NI Number Type is part of the UK NINO Record Type and can't be separated from it, although it remains a recognizably separate part. The line with the solid arrowhead pointing from the UK NINO Record Type to the NI Number Type indicates this. As is standard in COMN notation, arrowheads always point in the direction of reference. The UK NINO Record Type mentions the NI Number Type, and not the other way around.

We can now see that we have two subtly different sets of values that have two different functions. The NI Number Type designates a set of strings of characters in a certain format. The UK NINO Record Collection includes a subset of all possible NI Number Type strings, specifically only those NI Number Type values actually assigned to identify persons. This subset of NI Number Type values is what represents or identifies the UK Person Type.

In striving toward our goal of efficient development of reliable systems, both the UK NINO Record Type and the NI Number Type are valuable. The NI Number Type can be used at points of data entry to ensure that character strings entered as purported NINOs are at least in the right format, whether or not they are assigned to anybody. This level of type checking is a valuable first line of defense in ensuring high data quality, and might be all that's possible if access to the UK government's authoritative NINO database isn't readily available. To be really sure that a NINO identifies a UK Person, one must look in the authoritative UK NINO Record Collection to find a matching value there.

In place of the logical record type rectangle, the record collection shadowed hexagon, and the UK Person type rectangle, an E-R data model would show a single rectangle. In an E-R data model the rectangle would be called an "entity", but it would in fact represent three things simultaneously: the record type, the actual collection of records, and the real-world objects represented by the identifiers on the records. An equivalent model could be drawn in COMN using a single shadowed hexagon with components recorded directly in it, as long as the details of the representation relationships were not important—and we will do exactly this in chapter 13. But for the representation of reusable composite types such as measures, this separation is essential. We will also see in chapter 15 how separating the three things can give us important insights to our data.

STEPWISE REFINEMENT AND COMPLETENESS

Perhaps you've seen a pattern as to how COMN can be used to depict varying degrees of detail in a model. A type or class may be depicted as a simple rectangle containing nothing more than its name, or it may be expanded and divided into three sections so that its components and methods may be shown. When components are shown, their types or classes may also be shown. A type or class that is referenced by another type or class may optionally be added to a diagram, whether or not the referencing types or classes are drawn with three sections, calling out their components and their types by name, or just one section.

However, if a type or class is added to a diagram, then every relationship it has to other types or classes on the same diagram must be drawn. This principle, which is called the **completeness principle**, is essential, because if drawing relationship lines were optional, one could never know from a COMN drawing whether what it depicted was complete. The fact that two types were on the same drawing but without relationship lines between them could *not* be taken as indicating that they were not directly related. The completeness principle lets the reader know without any doubt whether any two types on a drawing are related or not. It also leads to a strategy for laying out large models such that limits on clutter require subdividing diagrams into clusters of closely related types. This makes for more readable and more logically organized models.

This flexibility in showing varying levels of detail enables an analyst or designer to approach a modeling problem a little bit at a time. One can start by drawing the simple rectangles for composite types that aren't split into three sections. One can gradually add additional rectangles to show relationships to other types and classes, and perhaps hexagons to show instances of data and objects relating to those types and classes. Finally, one can begin to expand some of the type and class rectangles to show details of their components and methods. This approach to modeling is called **stepwise refinement**, where the high-level details of a design are first captured, and then additional details are gradually added, until the model is complete. Unlike with E-R modeling, a COMN model supports stepwise refinement at every level of abstraction—conceptual, logical, and physical—without changing models or model types. A suitable modeling tool would enable one to alter the level of detail displayed dynamically, after the details had been added, and to separate a model into diagrams showing just the parts relevant to a particular subject or audience.

TYPES REPRESENTING OTHER TYPES

It is very common—and fundamental—that we use values to represent other values. As an example, let's look at good ole' ASCII, that character set and encoding that is foundational to all computer-to-computer and computer-to-human communication.

The American Standard Code for Information Interchange, or ASCII, has two parts, as shown in Table 12-1:

1. a set of 95 graphical characters that can be printed on paper and used to express human-readable text, plus a set of 33 so-called "control characters" that are useful for computer-to-computer communication

2. integers in the range 0 to 127, each of which is used to represent one of the 128 characters described by ASCII

Figure 12-3 shows the ASCII encoding expressed in COMN. The type being represented is named ASCII Character, and designates the set of characters given in Table 12-1. The ASCII Character rectangle has lines crossing through it because an ASCII character has no components, even though its representations have components. The type doing the representing is called ASCII Type, and is a composite type with one component. The component is called Ordinal. It is an integer in the range of 0 to 127 that corresponds to one of the 128 ASCII characters.

ASCII Type encapsulates its component. Only its methods can access the integer variable in order to manipulate it. In this way ASCII Type can make sure that the integer is manipulated only in ways that make sense given that it represents a character and not an integer. For instance, although one can multiply two integers together, it makes no sense to multiply two ASCII characters together, so ASCII Type does not offer a multiplication method. It is possible, however, to flip alphabetic letters between upper case and lower case. ASCII Type has methods toUpper and toLower that can manipulate the integer component Ordinal in ways to make this happen. These methods and others are shown in the bottom section of the ASCII Type rectangle.

<table>
<tr><td>0</td><td>NUL</td><td>16</td><td>DLE</td><td>32</td><td>SP</td><td>48</td><td>0</td><td>64</td><td>@</td><td>80</td><td>P</td><td>96</td><td>`</td><td>112</td><td>p</td></tr>
<tr><td>1</td><td>SOH</td><td>17</td><td>DC1</td><td>33</td><td>!</td><td>49</td><td>1</td><td>65</td><td>A</td><td>81</td><td>Q</td><td>97</td><td>a</td><td>113</td><td>q</td></tr>
<tr><td>2</td><td>STX</td><td>18</td><td>DC2</td><td>34</td><td>“</td><td>50</td><td>2</td><td>66</td><td>B</td><td>82</td><td>R</td><td>98</td><td>b</td><td>114</td><td>r</td></tr>
<tr><td>3</td><td>ETX</td><td>19</td><td>DC3</td><td>35</td><td>#</td><td>51</td><td>3</td><td>67</td><td>C</td><td>83</td><td>S</td><td>99</td><td>c</td><td>115</td><td>s</td></tr>
<tr><td>4</td><td>EOT</td><td>20</td><td>DC4</td><td>36</td><td>$</td><td>52</td><td>4</td><td>68</td><td>D</td><td>84</td><td>T</td><td>100</td><td>d</td><td>116</td><td>t</td></tr>
<tr><td>5</td><td>ENQ</td><td>21</td><td>NAK</td><td>37</td><td>%</td><td>53</td><td>5</td><td>69</td><td>E</td><td>85</td><td>U</td><td>101</td><td>e</td><td>117</td><td>u</td></tr>
<tr><td>6</td><td>ACK</td><td>22</td><td>SYN</td><td>38</td><td>&</td><td>54</td><td>6</td><td>70</td><td>F</td><td>86</td><td>V</td><td>102</td><td>f</td><td>118</td><td>v</td></tr>
<tr><td>7</td><td>BEL</td><td>23</td><td>ETB</td><td>39</td><td>‘</td><td>55</td><td>7</td><td>71</td><td>G</td><td>87</td><td>W</td><td>103</td><td>g</td><td>119</td><td>w</td></tr>
<tr><td>8</td><td>BS</td><td>24</td><td>CAN</td><td>40</td><td>(</td><td>56</td><td>8</td><td>72</td><td>H</td><td>88</td><td>X</td><td>104</td><td>h</td><td>120</td><td>x</td></tr>
<tr><td>9</td><td>TAB</td><td>25</td><td>EM</td><td>41</td><td>)</td><td>57</td><td>9</td><td>73</td><td>I</td><td>89</td><td>Y</td><td>105</td><td>i</td><td>121</td><td>y</td></tr>
<tr><td>10</td><td>LF</td><td>26</td><td>EOF</td><td>42</td><td>*</td><td>58</td><td>:</td><td>74</td><td>J</td><td>90</td><td>Z</td><td>106</td><td>j</td><td>122</td><td>z</td></tr>
<tr><td>11</td><td>VT</td><td>27</td><td>ESC</td><td>43</td><td>+</td><td>59</td><td>;</td><td>75</td><td>K</td><td>91</td><td>[</td><td>107</td><td>k</td><td>123</td><td>{</td></tr>
<tr><td>12</td><td>FF</td><td>28</td><td>FS</td><td>44</td><td>,</td><td>60</td><td><</td><td>76</td><td>L</td><td>92</td><td>\</td><td>108</td><td>l</td><td>124</td><td>|</td></tr>
<tr><td>13</td><td>CR</td><td>29</td><td>GS</td><td>45</td><td>-</td><td>61</td><td>=</td><td>77</td><td>M</td><td>93</td><td>]</td><td>109</td><td>m</td><td>125</td><td>}</td></tr>
<tr><td>14</td><td>SO</td><td>30</td><td>RS</td><td>46</td><td>.</td><td>62</td><td>></td><td>78</td><td>N</td><td>94</td><td>^</td><td>110</td><td>n</td><td>126</td><td>~</td></tr>
<tr><td>15</td><td>SI</td><td>31</td><td>US</td><td>47</td><td>/</td><td>63</td><td>?</td><td>79</td><td>O</td><td>95</td><td>_</td><td>111</td><td>o</td><td>127</td><td>DEL</td></tr>
</table>

Table 12-1. ASCII Chart

On the far right we show the integer type of the Ordinal component of ASCII Type, but this is for illustration purposes only. The model is complete without this rectangle.

Since ASCII Type is a type and not a class, no storage allocation has been specified. We need a class before there's anything to implement in a computer. A class implementing ASCII Type would quite reasonably store each character code in a byte, but the methods of the class would limit the byte to entering only 128 of its 256 possible states. The other 128 states would have no meaning in this usage. If we wished to show this level of detail, we would draw a class that represents the ASCII Type, and show that its only component is an integer class having a byte component.

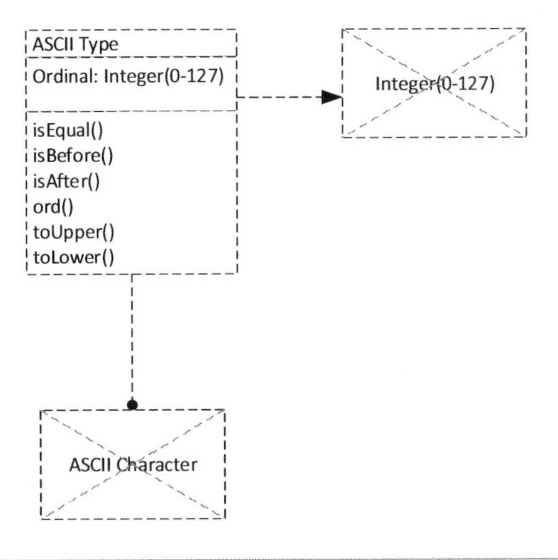

Figure 12-3. ASCII

Measures as Composite Types

We've seen how composite types can be used to represent other types. Now we'll look at how composite types can be used to express measures. A **measure** is a combination of a number giving a count, quantity, or amount, and a type of thing that is being measured. Here are some example measures:

- 5 kilograms
- 2 cups
- $39, or USD 39
- 20 million people (perhaps the population of a metropolitan area)
- 1.9 children (perhaps the average number of children in a family)

We are used to units of measurement being related to space (for example, distance or volume) and time (for example, seconds or days), but in fact measures apply to anything that can be counted or measured.

A measure can be modeled as a composite type with two components. For the sake of illustration, let us consider a measure of currency, where the number component is a decimal number to five decimal places, and the currency is identified by a 3-character ISO 4217 currency code. See Figure 12-4.

Currency Amount Type
Currency Amount: Number(18,4) Currency: ISO 4217 Currency Code Type
sum() difference() amount() currency()

Figure 12-4. A Measure of Currency

A measure is a very special thing, because it encapsulates a multiplicative relationship between a numeric measure (in this case, the Currency Amount) and a type of things that's being measured or counted (in this case, Currency). In other words, "5 kilograms" really means "5 x kilogram", and "$39" really means "39 x USD". Because of this, not all of the operations valid on plain numbers are valid on measures. For instance, it is only valid to add or subtract two currency measures together if they are measures of the same currency. Multiplying two currency measures together probably makes no sense, although multiplying measures of physical units is quite sensible and yields measures of different types; for example, multiplying distance by weight yields energy. Because of this, encapsulating the two components of a measure and providing methods that only allow correct operations on the measure provides a higher level of correct operation than if the two components remained unencapsulated.

Composite types, including measures, are wonderful as units of reuse. The structure of a composite type can be specified just once and reused in hundreds of places without modification, enabling the original design to be carried through to many unrelated designs— just as standardized parts in manufacturing enabled the industrial revolution. A composite type can also be used to express an organizational decision to use that structure as a standard. Let's look at a foreign exchange transaction. In a foreign exchange transaction, one party "sells" or gives up some amount of a certain currency, in exchange for some amount of a different currency. The other party is the mirror image: that party "buys" the currency being given up by the first party, by supplying the requested amount of the different currency. This is exactly what happens if you travel from continental Europe to the United Kingdom and "buy" British pounds with your euros, or if you cross from the United States to Canada and "buy" Canadian dollars with your America dollars.

The design for a logical record type of a foreign exchange transaction is depicted in Figure 12-5. Its first component is a simple integer Transaction ID, enabling us to distinguish transaction records from each other. Next we have a date and time on which the transaction took place, as a variable whose type is "timestamp". We have two identifiers that identify the parties to the transaction. Finally, we have two variables: Amount Sold by Party 1 (which is bought by Party 2) and Amount Bought by Party 1 (which is sold by Party 2). These two variables have the same type, which is the Currency Amount Type introduced earlier. The number "2" near the aggregation arrowhead indicates that the Currency Amount Type has been included in the Foreign Exchange Transaction Record Type twice.

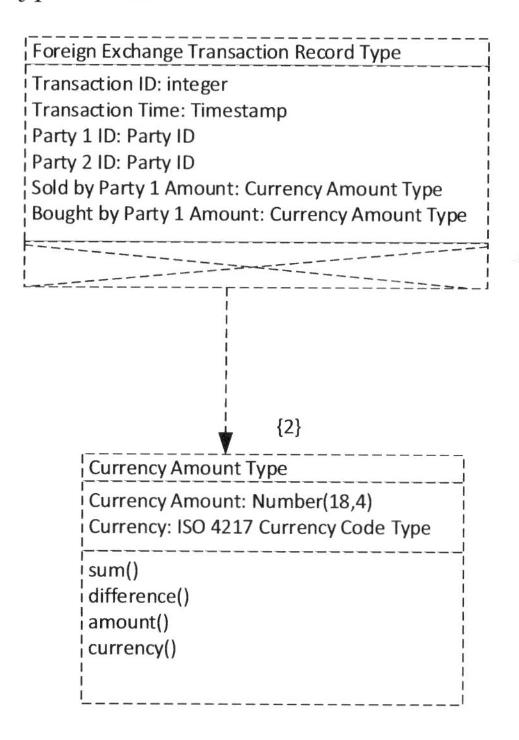

Figure 12-5. A Foreign Exchange Transaction Logical Record Type

By re-using the Currency Amount Type, the designer of the Foreign Exchange Transaction Record Type does not have to define four variables as components of Foreign Exchange Record, but only two. The designer does not have to look up how many decimal digits the organization wishes to use when recording currency amounts. That standard has already been built into the Currency Amount Type, and the designer merely has to reference the composite type in order to incorporate that standard. Finally, the names of the two variables reflect their role in the record type, and aren't lengthened or complicated by the names and types of the individual components of Currency Amount Type. All these benefits are in addition to the additional type safety gained by encapsulating the components of the measure.

In a large or even a medium-sized enterprise, there are typically hundreds of composite types that need standardization and thousands of opportunities to re-use those standard types. Examples of such composite types include postal addresses, personal names, telephone numbers, and various identifiers: the list could go on for quite some time. Most data modeling notations either can't express reusable composite types, or can but insist that their components always be encapsulated. (For the reasons why, review the relevant chapters in part II). In COMN, expressing these things is straightforward.

Incidentally, the world of database design has standardized on names to use with measures, to make it easier to judge from the name of a component what it indicates. Conventional use will make sure that a measure's name ends in one of the three words count, quantity, or amount, as follows:

- count: an integral number of things that are counted; for example, Access Attempt Count
- quantity: a possibly fractional number of things that are measured, not counted, including the result of statistical functions on counts; for example, Order Item Quantity, Average Children Per Family Quantity, Fuel Capacity Gallon Quantity, Distance Kilometer Quantity
- amount: a quantity of some currency; for example, Price Amount

NESTED TYPES

Types that represent other types are only useful if they are incorporated into composite types as the types of some components. Measures are composite types that are most useful when incorporated into other composite types by aggregation, as the Currency Amount Type was incorporated twice into the Foreign Exchange Transaction Record Type.

There is nothing that says that this composition by aggregation must be limited to a single level. It can go on for as many levels as are useful. We call this **nesting** of types. In Figure 12-6 below, we have nesting to four levels, as follows:

- ASCII Type is nested three times inside Char{3}.
- Char{3} is nested inside ISO 4217 Currency Code Type.
- ISO 4217 Currency Code Type is nested inside Currency Amount Type.
- Currency Amount Type is nested (twice) inside Foreign Exchange Transaction Record Type.

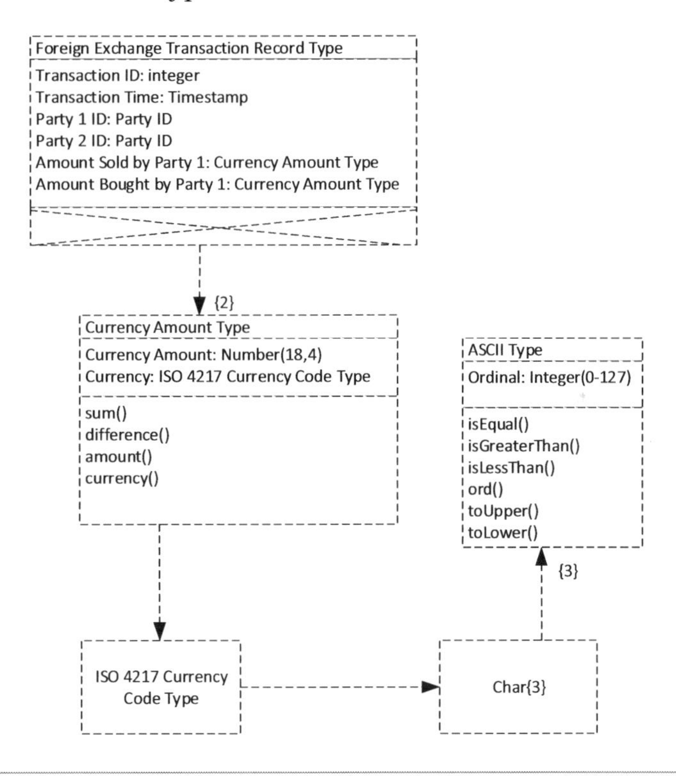

Figure 12-6. Nested Types

The Unified Modeling Language (UML) and object-oriented programming languages can express arbitrary nesting like this. The eXtensible Markup Language (XML) and JavaScript Object Notation (JSON) can express nesting. Entity-relationship models and SQL cannot express nesting. This is often blamed on the relational model, but chapter 16 will show that the limitation is in implementations, not relational theory.

One must be careful to consider that all of the types in question here are not classes. They say nothing about the layout of these types in storage. When one is focused on logical design, the goal is to create a model that most efficiently expresses requirements. It is only at the stage of physical design (discussed in chapter 17) that storage layouts should be considered. To read COMN types as entity-relationship's "entities", as SQL database tables, or as the UML's classes, is to jump prematurely to the physical level and get tangled up in physical design decisions before the requirements are fully articulated.

MODELING DOCUMENTS

Some vendors offer what they call "document databases", which are presumably structured in such a way that they can efficiently store the electronic equivalents of what we would recognize in printed form as documents: contracts, tax forms, papers, even entire books. A document in this parlance is a composite type, and should be modeled in COMN as such. Documents often include nested types, and as we have just seen, these can be modeled in a straightforward manner in COMN.

The eXtensible Markup Language (XML) is a common form for exchanging documents in electronic form. See Figure 12-7 for a snippet of an XML document. The names enclosed in angle brackets are called **tags**, and constitute the markup of what is otherwise plain text. Most tags come in pairs with text between the start tag and end tag, and the whole construction is called an **element**. For example, in Figure 12-7 the plain text "Chapter 1" is surrounded by the start tag `<title>` and the end tag `</title>`. Elements can next. For example, the Chapter 1 title is nested inside a `<chapter>` element. The same `<chapter>` element also contains two <para> elements. The `<chapter>` element is nested inside the `<book>` element.

```
<?xml version="1.0" encoding="UTF-8"?>
 <book xml:id="simple_book" xmlns="http://docbook.org/ns/docbook"
version="5.0">
   <title>Very simple book</title>
   <chapter xml:id="chapter_1">
     <title>Chapter 1</title>
```

```
      <para>Hello world!</para>
      <para>I hope that your day is proceeding
<emphasis>splendidly</emphasis>!</para>
    </chapter>
    <chapter xml:id="chapter_2">
      <title>Chapter 2</title>
      <para>Hello again, world!</para>
    </chapter>
  </book>
```

Figure 12-7. An XML Document Snippet

An XML document is an instance of some document type—whether that type is articulated or not. An XML document's type—the structure of its elements and the way in which they nest—might be expressed in a variety of schema languages, such as Document Type Definition (DTD), XML Schema, and RELAX NG (RNG). COMN notation can directly express exactly what these schema languages can express, with the same precision and without ambiguity, using nested composite types—something that cannot be done in E-R notations or in fact-based modeling.

JavaScript Object Notation (JSON) is a very simple language for expressing values. JSON is built around two kinds of composite structures: array and object. An **array** is a set of values which are distinguished solely by the order in which they appear, while an **object** is a set of values which are distinguished by their names. A unit of JSON text is called simply that: a JSON text. See Figure 12-8 for an example of a JSON text.

```
{
  "firstName": "John",
  "lastName": "Smith",
  "isAlive": true,
  "age": 25,
  "address": {
    "streetAddress": "21 2nd Street",
    "city": "New York",
    "state": "NY",
    "postalCode": "10021-3100"
  },
  "phoneNumbers": [
    {
      "type": "home",
      "number": "212 555-1234"
    },
    {
```

```
      "type": "office",
      "number": "646 555-4567"
    }
  ],
  "children": [],
  "spouse": null
}
```

Figure 12-8. A JSON Text

As with XML, a JSON text may or may not have its type described by some other document using a schema language such as JSON Schema. As with XML, COMN can directly express exactly what a JSON schema language can express, using nested composite types—something that, again, cannot be done in E-R notations or in fact-based modeling.

JSON is often compared to XML as a more efficient language with the same expressive power. This is not quite accurate. The confusion has arisen because XML has been heavily used as a data interchange language, although that was not its original design intent. XML is a **markup language**, which means that it is focused primarily on adding annotations to human-readable text; those annotations are most often used to express the meaning or significance of the text that they mark up. In contrast, JSON is a language for expressing data, which might include human-readable text as data but not marked-up text in the same sense as XML. It is unfortunate that the term “document” is commonly used to describe a piece of JSON text. The JSON spec never uses that term, and simply refers to “a JSON text”.

Notwithstanding the confusion between “a JSON text” and “document”, COMN can be used to model a JSON text’s type as a composite type.

ARRAYS

An array is a special kind of composite type. It consists of some non-negative integral number (possibly zero) of variables all of a single type. Each variable is called an **element** of the array. The entire collection of variables is known by the name of the array, and each element within the array is identified by an integer known as its **element number** or **index**.

An array type is defined by the element type plus the range of possible numbers of elements that may be possessed by a variable of the array type. The possible numbers are called the **multiplicity** of the array. (The actual number of elements in any particular array variable or value is called its **cardinality**.) Here are some example array multiplicities and the COMN notation for expressing them:

- a plus sign ("+"), indicating that one to any integral number of elements may occur

- an asterisk ("*"), indicating that zero to any integral number of elements may occur

- integer expressions enclosed in a pair of curly braces("{" and "}") giving the possible numbers of elements. The expressions can take the following forms:

    - a single positive integer, indicating exactly that many elements will occur; for example, "{3}"
    - a range of integers specified as two non-negative integers separated by a hyphen; for example, "{0-2}"
    - a comma-separated list of non-negative integers giving allowable numbers of elements; for example, "{0, 2, 4, 6}"
    - any combination of number ranges and non-negative integers; for example, "{0, 2-5, 9}"

Arrays can be represented in COMN diagrams in two ways:

- When a type or class is depicted with a rectangle having three sections, the multiplicity of a component can be indicated using one of the above expressions after the element's type.

- When one type or class is composed of another by either aggregation or assembly, the arrowhead pointing to the element type or class may have a multiplicity expression next to it, at the element type end.

One kind of array we can't live without is the character string. We've already seen a three-character array type, Char{3}, as a component of the ISO 4217 Currency Code Type. It is quite common to use variable-length character strings to represent human-readable text in various contexts. For example, you might see character string components defined like this:

- Person Last Name: ASCII Type{1-200}
- Product Name: Unicode Type{1-1000}
- Postal Code: Unicode Type{2-50}

These simple arrays are heavily used in data design. However, an array's element type can be of arbitrary complexity. We can have arrays of measures (perhaps a series of sensor readings), arrays of records (hmm, that sounds like a table!), and, since an array is a composite type, we can have arrays of arrays if we find that useful.

Key Points

- Logical record types are composite types.

- We must be careful not to encapsulate every logical record type with methods. It may be better to encapsulate a higher-level logical record type that has exclusive access to logical records it references.

- By separately representing a logical record type, a collection of records of that type, and real-world entities represented by the collection of records, we can see how identification really works. We can see that it is the set of identifier values in a collection of records that identifies real-world entities, and not the type of the identifier itself.

- COMN supports stepwise refinement, which is the gradual addition of detail to a model.

- It is common to use one type to represent another type.

- Composite types are a wonderful means to standardize representations, ensure correct operations on values of the types, and enable reuse of the correct and standard representations.

- It is normal for types to nest, though E-R notations and SQL cannot express nesting.

- Documents are nested types.

Chapter Glossary

logical record type : a composite type that is intended to be used as the type of data records stored singly or in a collection of records

measure : a composite type consisting of a number and a type of thing being measured or counted

identifier : any value that represents exactly one member of a designated set

array : a collection of some integral number of variables or objects of the same type or class

References

[Parnas 1972] Parnas, D. L. "On the Criteria to be Used in Decomposing Systems into Modules." *Communications of the ACM,* 15, 12. New York: Association for Computing Machinery, 1972, pp. 1053-1058.

Chapter 13
Subtypes and Subclasses

Before the type/class split, we could consider the terms "subtype" and "subclass" to be synonyms. But now that a type designates a set while a class describes a computer object, these two terms take on distinct meanings. Both meanings are quite useful, separately and together.

SUBTYPES

The modern era of biological classification started in about the Sixteenth Century, as biologists began to recognize common characteristics across classes of animals, and began to create "super-classes" of animals. For instance, elephants, lions, and tigers were all classified as "mammals". Lions, tigers, jaguars, and other similar mammals were recognized as a subclass of mammals called "cats". A full taxonomy (system of classification) was developed by a number of scientists, and refined over time.

There are many taxonomies that classify many things besides animals. For example, there are systems for classifying currency (for example, hard and soft), crimes (for example, misdemeanors and felonies), and passenger cars (for example, 2-door, 4-door, and SUV). There can even be multiple classification systems for a single set of things. For example, here are just a few ways the cards in a standard deck of 52 playing cards can be classified:

- by suit: diamonds, hearts, spades, clubs
- by suit color: red, black
- by rank: face card, number card

Many of the most fascinating card games classify playing cards by complex criteria, and even by dynamically changing classification criteria. For example, some games allow a player to designate a suit of cards to be "trump", making all cards of that suit rank higher than any other card for the duration of one round (hand) of the card game. In the next round, the trump might be different.

A **subset** is a set of things drawn from a larger set of things. Just as a type designates a set, *a* ***subtype*** *designates a subset*. A subtype is always related to the type that designates the larger set; that is its **supertype**.

As an example, let's consider the nature of some forms of government. Figure 13-1 shows a brief taxonomy of forms of government. All of the shapes and connecting lines are both dashed and bold. They are dashed to show that they are about concepts, not material objects. They are bold because they are about real-world concepts, not data concepts.

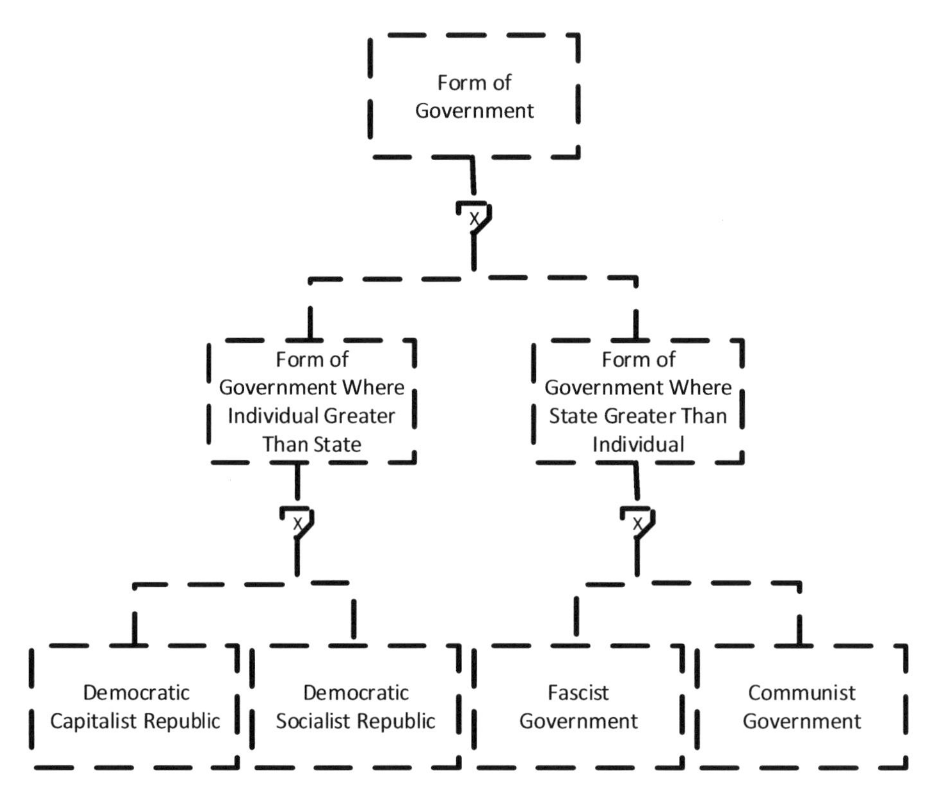

Figure 13-1. A Taxonomy of Forms of Government

You've seen the type rectangles before. The new shape in this figure is the pentagon, which depicts a **restriction relationship**. The wider side of each pentagon is towards the type that designates the set with more members; in other words, the supertype. The pointed side of each pentagon is towards the type that designates the set with fewer members; in other words, the subtype.

For each subtype, there is some restricting condition, not directly modeled, that determines whether a member of the supertype is included in the subtype. For instance, it's clear from the labeling of the type rectangles that, out of the set of all possible forms of government, only those governments where the individual is considered to be greater than the state are in the set designated by the type, "Form of Government Where Individual Greater Than State".

The X in each pentagon indicates that the subtypes connected through it to a common supertype are exclusive of each other. In other words, a given member of the set designated by one subtype is not designated by the other subtype.

It is very common to define subtypes as restrictions on supertypes. But we can go the other way around, too. For example, we can define the type called "alphanumeric character" as a supertype of the types "letter" and "number". Figure 13-2 is a model of the alphanumeric character type. The symbols are mostly the same as in Figure 13-1. Let's look at the differences.

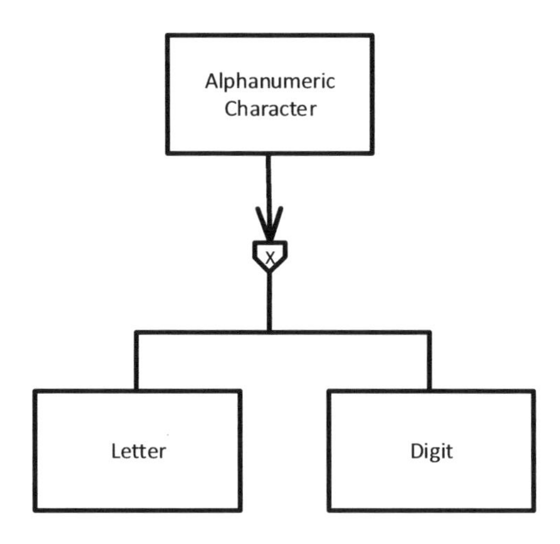

Figure 13-2. Alphanumeric Character as a Supertype of Letter and Digit.

First of all, the shapes and connecting lines in this figure are solid and bold. They are solid because characters are material objects. An individual character doesn't exist unless it can be seen. It has to exist as some relatively stable configuration of matter. It could be ink on paper, or liquid crystals on a computer display, or even objects on a flat surface juxtaposed to form characters. The COMN shapes are bold because the material objects being described exist outside a computer's memory. Something we refer to as a character that's inside a computer's memory exists only as a representation of a character, and not a character itself. Those kinds of characters don't get bold outlines.

The second difference is that there is an arrowhead on the line from Alphanumeric Character to the pentagon. Arrowheads on lines in COMN always indicate a direction of reference. This arrow says that the Alphanumeric Character type references the Letter and Digit types, and not the other way around. This is what tells us that Alphanumeric Character is defined in terms of its subtypes. Such a supertype is called a **union type**, because the set it designates is the union of the sets designated by its subtypes. When a type is defined like this, it is more accurate to call the relationship represented by the pentagon an **inclusion relationship**, especially since there is no restriction in effect. But the sub/super-type relationships that result are the same as those in a restriction relationship.

Figures 13-1 and 13-2 show simple strict type hierarchies, where each type has only one supertype, except for the type at the top, which has no supertype. But not everything is that simple, and it is a major mistake in analysis to force all things into a single type hierarchy with a single root. To illustrate, let's go back to our deck of playing cards. Realize that any standard deck of playing cards can be divided in half based on the color of the suits (excluding jokers): all cards in a red suit (hearts and diamonds) can be put in one pile, and all cards in a black suit (spades and clubs) can be put in the other pile. We could then further subdivide the two piles by the four suits. Figure 13-3 shows this type hierarchy. The shapes and lines are in bold outline because they describe real-world things. Since the things they describe are material objects, they are in solid outline. The rectangle at the top represents any playing card, regardless of suit, color, or rank. Each of the middle two rectangles represents the class of card whose suit is in one of the two colors. The rectangles at the bottom reflect the four suits.

This is not the only way to divide a deck of cards. Figure 13-4 shows an alternative way of classifying playing cards, by type of rank: face card (king, queen, and jack) and number card (ace through ten).

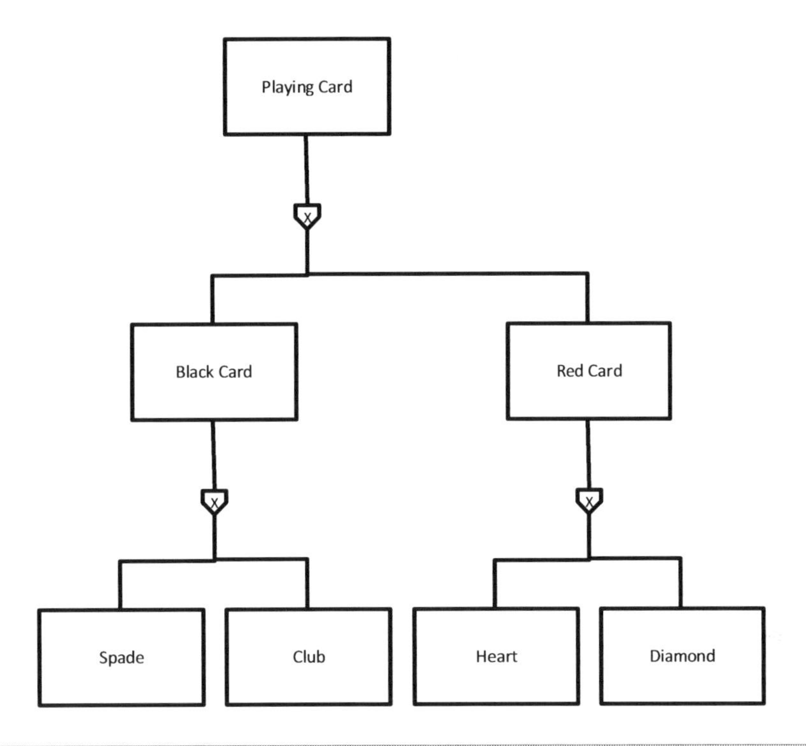

Figure 13-3. Playing Cards Divided into Suits

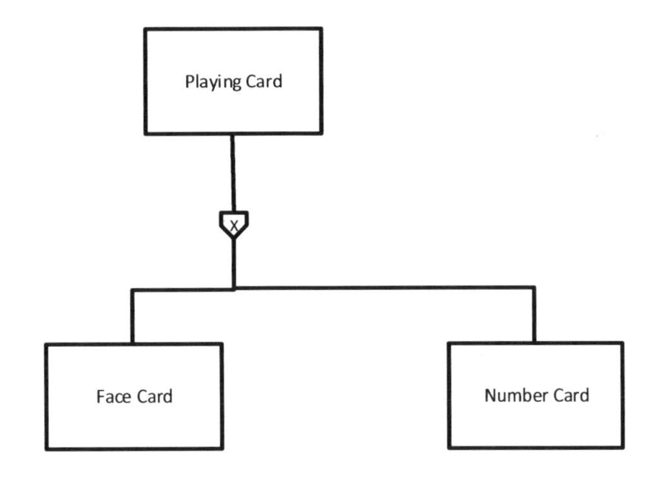

Figure 13-4. Playing Cards Divided by Rank

Figure 13-5 shows a deck of cards classified by all of the criteria above. Now we can see that, although a given classification system may be complete, there can be multiple classification systems side-by-side.

The symbols at the bottom of this figure deserve some attention. Two particular cards are shown: jack of hearts and nine of diamonds. But each is shown twice, once as a type and once as an object. That's to emphasize that "jack of hearts" and "nine of diamonds" are still *types* of cards, not individual cards. Yes, it's true that in a single deck of cards there will be only one card which is a jack of hearts and one card which is a nine of diamonds. But there is more than one deck of cards in the universe, and each deck contains one of those cards, so "jack of hearts" and "nine of diamonds" identify, not just one card, but a potentially unlimited set of cards. If we want to talk about hypothetical single cards, we show them using object symbols with the name beginning with the indefinite article, "a" (or "an"): "*a* jack of hearts" and "*a* nine of diamonds".

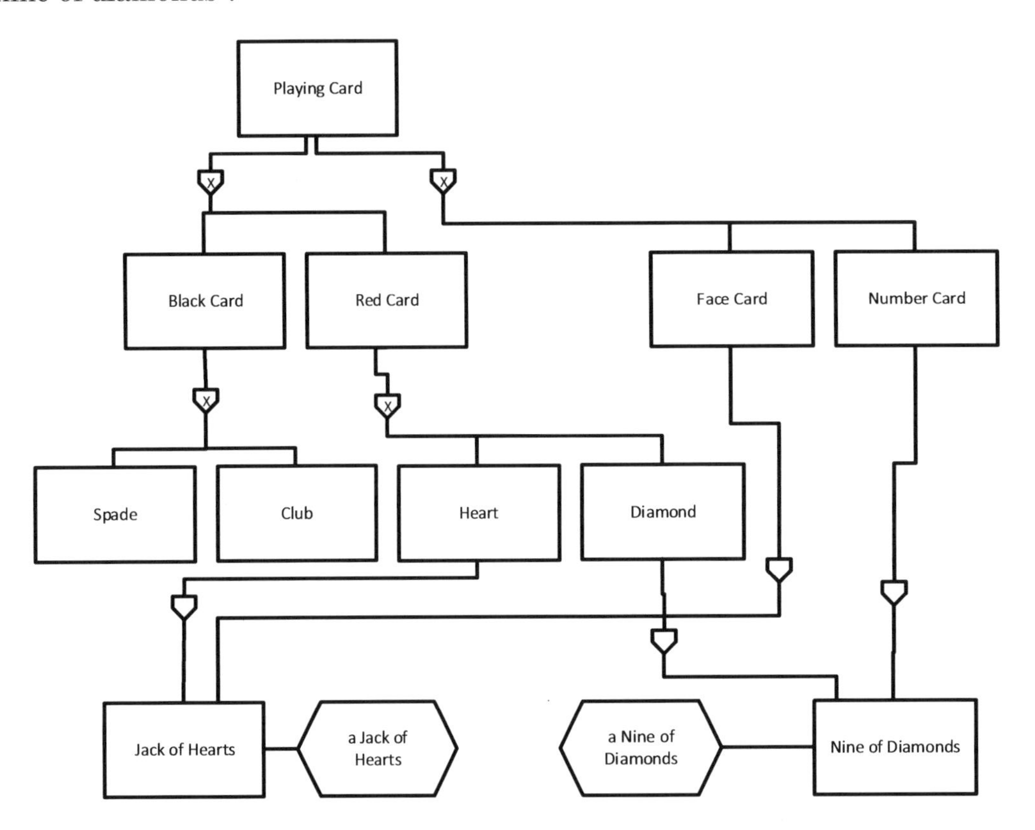

Figure 13-5. Playing Cards Divided by Multiple Criteria

Each of the types "jack of hearts" and "nine of diamonds" is connected to two type hierarchies, the hierarchy that classifies by suit and the hierarchy that classifies by rank. This shows that a type can have more than one supertype. This is sometimes referred to as **multiple inheritance**, but we'll avoid that term for now.

These illustrations of subtype/supertype relationships specified by restriction and inclusion have used real-world concepts and objects as examples, rather than data and computer objects. Subtype/supertype relationships work the same with data and computer objects. Since subtype/supertype relationships have to do with selecting members from supersets or combining members from subsets, no alterations to the structure of the types occur as a result of these operations. Because of this, no issues arise when an individual object (or concept) has multiple types. The problems of multiple inheritance only arise when one is dealing with subclassing, which we'll review in the next section.

RESTRICTION IS SUBTYPING

Recall that we said in chapter 4 that a type could be defined in a number of ways, including:

- by selection
- by enumeration
- by generation

By far the most common method of defining a subtype is by selection from a supertype using some criteria. The criteria restrict which members of the supertype may be members of the subtype.

It turns out that *every restriction defines a subtype*. If you scan through any data system design, you will find many data definitions that are defined as restrictions on more general data definitions. These are all subtypes. Here are some examples:

- An edit control on a user interface page normally accepts any character, but code on the page restricts the control to accepting only decimal digits. The restricted edit control only accepts values of type "numeric string", which is a subtype of "string".

- A field in a database is defined with the database's built-in type of "string", but a constraint is defined on the field such that only strings matching a certain regular expression can be stored in it. The regular expression defines a subtype of string.

Here is a powerful analysis technique: When analyzing any system or its requirements, look for expressions that restrict possible values, and label that expression a subtype. Identify the set of values being restricted, and label that expression the supertype.

SUBCLASSES

We know that types designate sets while classes describe objects. Let's see how the physicality of objects affects what it means to have a subclass.

Recall from chapter 10 that the world of object-oriented programming defined the term "class" as a description of something in the memory of a computer. In object-oriented programming, a subclass is *derived* from a *base* class. The subclass includes ("inherits") all of the components defined by the base class, and adds its own components to them. The methods of the base class continue to be valid for operating on objects of the subclass, but since they were written without knowledge of the subclass, they won't operate on any components of objects that are only defined in the subclass. It is common practice for a subclass to *override* many of the methods inherited from the base class, in order to *extend* them to operate on components added by the subclass in addition to those of the base class.

This description of the structure of subclasses is complete without making any reference to meaning. The world of object-oriented programming has put a strong and fixed set of ideas on the meaning of subclasses, but we are going to keep those ideas on the side for now, and come back to them in the next section of this chapter. For now, we will focus only on the physicality of objects and the *mechanism* of subclassing. This is consistent with COMN's view that, at their base, computer objects and their states have no intrinsic meaning.

A type designates a set. A class describes objects, but by so doing also designates a set, which is the potential and/or actual set of objects described by a class. The burning question, then, is, is a subclass equivalent to a subtype as described in the previous section?

To examine this question, let us consider the following base class and subclass:

- The base class is Circle. This class describes an object representing a circle drawn on a graphical display. It holds three values: the X and Y coordinates of the center of the circle, and the radius of the circle. This is all the data that is needed to draw the circle on the display. The Circle class does not support the concept of color. A circle is always drawn in white on a black background. The methods of the class are simply setPosition (X, Y) and setRadius(r).

- The derived class is Colored Circle. This class inherits the X, Y, and radius components of Circle, and adds a fourth component, which is color. The setPosition and setRadius methods still work, but now there's an additional setColor() method.

Figure 13-6 shows this design. The triangle between Circle and Colored Circle indicates **extension**, where the extending class adds components to those already in the base class, adds its own methods, and may override methods in the base class[2]. The way to remember the direction is that the wider side of the triangle is toward the class that adds components, while the narrower side of the triangle is toward the base class.

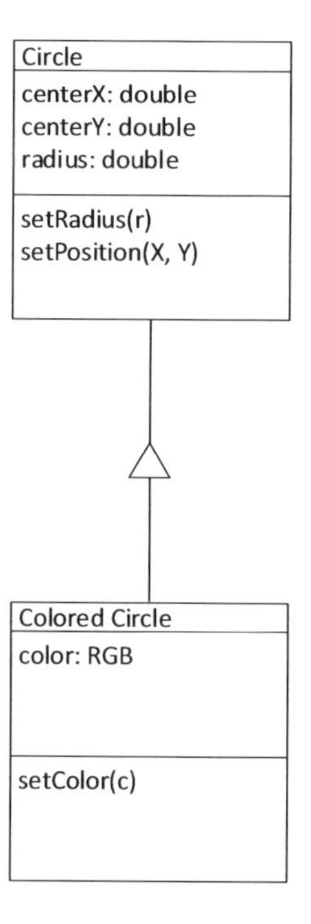

Figure 13-6. Circle and Colored Circle

[2] This idea of extension has nothing to do with RDF's extension.

Is Colored Circle a subtype of Circle? If it were, then it would describe fewer objects than Circle. In fact, it describes more objects than Circle. All Circle objects are white, while Colored Circles can have many more colors than white. In fact, every Circle object can be represented by a Colored Circle object whose color is set to white. A Circle is a subtype of a Colored Circle!

So we see, then, that—at least in this case—a subclass is not a subtype. In fact, the subtype relationship can be in the opposite direction of the subclass relationship.

COMN describes this kind of derivation relationship between two classes as **extension**. In order to avoid confusion with the term "subtype", COMN avoids the term "subclass" and calls the class that adds components to the base class the **extending** class.

Since objects of an extending class have more components than those of their base class, objects of an extending class have more potential states.

Extension only applies to composite types and classes, because one can only add components to something that can have components. In contrast, subtyping applies equally to simple and composite types and classes, since it depends on restricting the (simple or composite) values and states of, respectively, variables and objects.

As object-oriented programmers know, defining a class as extending more than one base class can get pretty gnarly pretty fast. It is mostly out of the scope of this book to discuss that kind of multiple inheritance, but two comments are relevant. First, recall that *restricting* multiple supertypes is not a kind of multiple inheritance that leads to any problems. Only *extending* multiple base classes or types can become difficult. Second, if one is careful to define the type a class represents, and possibly a type hierarchy, before designing a class extension hierarchy, one is likely going to be guided to use extension in valid ways that are quite workable in implementation.

SUBTYPES AND EXTENSIONS: PERFECT TOGETHER

Let's put these two ideas together, and see how they enable COMN to precisely model a common situation, which is a database of persons playing multiple roles. Let's imagine we are developing a database in support of a coffee shop. (It could be a bank, or a retailer, or any business that has individuals as customers.) We have the usual "rewards" program, where regular customers earn points with every purchase. We therefore need to represent customers in our data. We also need to represent employees in our data, so that we can track their working hours and pay them. We need to know when an employee is also a customer, because we give our employees discounts on their purchases.

Naïve early data models for such situations would use two separate tables: one for employees and one for customers. This approach sounds good enough until you consider common scenarios:

- Each table would need the person's name. The employee/customer would be obligated to enter his name twice, which is rather annoying.

- There would be the task of tracking which employee/customer pairs were in fact the same person. Personal names are notoriously difficult to use to achieve this, for many reasons, including:

    - People's names have many forms, and people can't be depended upon to enter their names the same way every time. For example, I might use "Theodore" in the employee database and "Ted" in the customer database.
    - People's names aren't unique.

For all these reasons and more, it would make much more sense to design a database with three tables:

- a table of persons, holding the data common to persons regardless of whether they are customers or employees

- a table of customers, holding data unique to customers, such as the dates of their last purchases

- a table of employees, holding data unique to employees, such as their dates of hire

The tables of customers and employees would refer back to the table of persons for data common to both.

See Figure 13-7 for a depiction of such a design. Let's take a close look at this model. In the top right-hand corner of the diagram we have Coffee Shop Person, which is the type that designates the set of real-world persons that matter to the coffee shop, namely employees and/or customers. Below the Coffee Shop Person type we have two subtypes, connected by the restriction pentagon. Some are customers, or, to be more technically accurate, persons playing the role of being a customer. Some are employees, similarly playing a role. The pentagon has no X in it, meaning that you might find the same person as a member of both subtypes—in other words, a person who is both a customer and an employee.

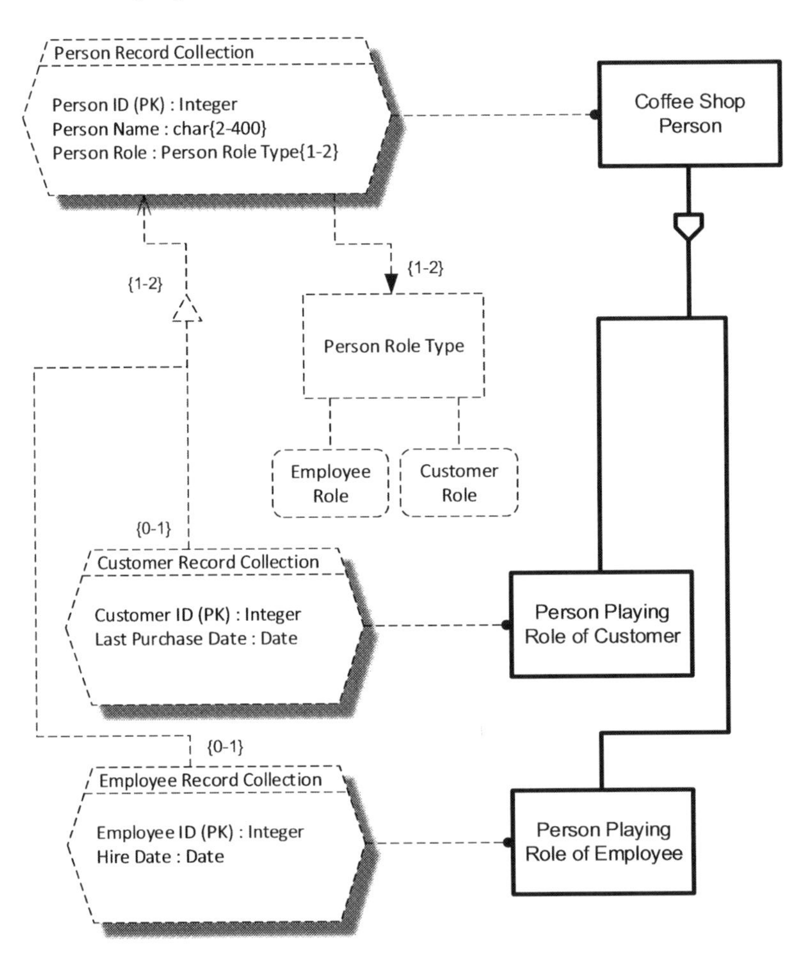

Figure 13-7. Coffee Shop Persons

To the left of the Coffee Shop Person rectangle we have a dashed hexagon representing the collection of logical records that will hold data about these persons. This is our first example of a hexagon divided into two parts. The top part contains the name of the collection of records, and the bottom part contains the names and types of the components of each record. This form of COMN enables one to model a set of composite variables or objects without an explicitly named type.

Each record in the Person Record Collection has three components: the internally generated meaningless number, called Person ID, which we use to distinctly identify each person; each person's name as Person Name; and the role(s) played by each person. The component name Person ID is followed by the letters PK in parentheses, indicating that it is a key to any set of Person data. The relationship line from Person to Coffee Shop Person is a representation relationship. *It is the values of the key* of Person Record Collection, namely Person ID values, which *represent*, or *identify*, Coffee Shop Persons.

The Person Role component of a person record is defined as an array of one to two variables of type Person Role Type. This tells us all we need to know about the Person Role component, but we'd like to know more about the Person Role Type, so that has been drawn, connected to the Person Record Collection with a line having a solid arrowhead, which indicates aggregation. When variables are defined in-line in a data structure, they are juxtaposed, and their types are effectively aggregated together in the structure's type.

There are two values depicted as values of the Person Role type, namely Customer Role and Employee Role. Each of the one or two elements of the Person Role component of a person record can be bound to either of these role values. We presume that there is a business rule that eliminates the possibility that a person could be recorded as playing the employee role twice or as playing the customer role twice. This rule is not expressed directly in this model, but it is expressed indirectly through the relationships to the customer and employee record collections, as we shall see.

Below the Person Record Collection we have two more record collections, one each for Customers and Employees. These are connected to the Person logical record type via a triangle, which is COMN's symbol for *extension*. The wider base of the triangle is on the side towards the types that extend the Person type, in an analogy to the fact that these types have more components than

Person. Don't read the triangle as indicating direction of reference. The direction of reference is given by the arrowhead pointing to Person.

The multiplicity of the extension relationship is given differently above and below the triangle symbol. Below the triangle, the text "{0-1}" indicates that a customer record might or might not extend a person record, and an employee record might or might not extend a person record. Above the triangle, the text "{1-2}" indicates that a person record will be extended at least once and possibly twice. The model therefore indicates that a person record must not be created without creating at least one extending record. This prevents the system from keeping records of data about persons who are neither customers nor employees—probably a good thing.

The Customer and Employee logical record types include their own IDs, which are in addition to Person ID. You can imagine customers with key-ring cards with bar codes on them holding their customer IDs, and employees with identification badges showing their employee numbers. Customers and employees will typically not know their Person IDs.

It is an implementation question whether Person ID values will be carried on Customer and Employee records, or whether two or three records of these types will be aggregated, such that Person ID is immediately accessible. This design decision is influenced by whether we implement in a SQL or NoSQL database. We can document the logical design, and defer that physical question. We will examine physical database design issues in chapter 18.

The Customer and Employee logical record types each hold data that is applicable only to customers and employees, respectively. Only customers have a Last Purchase Date, and only employees have a Hire Date. Extension is meant whenever a composite type or a class is extended with additional components, such that instances of the extending type or class may have more values or states, respectively, than the base type or class.

This picture is completed by the representation lines drawn from the Customer and Employee record collections to these Person Playing Role types. We see that the Customer Record Collection represents the type of Person Playing Role of Customer, and the Employee Record Collection represents the type Person Playing Role of Employee. A Customer ID identifies a customer, and an Employee ID identifies an employee.

Thus we see that extension and subtyping are very different but often exist side-by-side.

INHERITANCE

Both subtyping and extension are valuable because they enable us to define data and write software that **inherits** components and/or methods of a supertype, base type, or base class. The derived type or class can then be defined merely in terms of what's different from or in addition to the base. This makes the task of writing software more efficient. It also makes software more reliable, because it is easier to verify the correctness of a base type or class, and then separately verify the correctness of a derived type or class assuming that the base is correct, than it is to verify two separate but redundant implementations, especially when one implementation—the one that would have been derived—is more complex than the other.

Inheritance multiplies reuse when you realize that variables, values, and objects of derived types or classes can sometimes be used in places where only the base types or classes were contemplated in the original design. These are extremely powerful mechanisms for expanding software and data reuse. But this kind of reuse is subject to certain limitations—limitations that, it turns out, guarantee the correctness of the reuse. Let's look at these more closely.

USING SUBTYPE VARIABLES AND VALUES

Suppose we have a logical record type with a component defined as a number of up to 5 decimal digits. Suppose we have a user interface page with an edit box allowing the entry of up to 4 decimal digits. The type "4 digit decimal number" is a subtype of the type "5 digit decimal number". We can see that it will always be safe to store numbers entered in the user interface in the logical record type's 5-digit component. In fact, if the system knows of these type definitions, it doesn't even need to check values before allowing the storage, because it can depend on the subtype relationship to guarantee that the values coming from the user interface are within the range provided by the storage system.

Clearly, going in the reverse direction is not so safe. If our system retrieves a 5-digit number from a record, and attempts to display it in a 4-digit field in a user-interface, it had better first check whether the value from the record is no greater than 9,999. If the value were too large, it would be truncated on display and mislead the user as to the actual value. It would be better for the system to report an error (an "exception"), so that someone could either correct the data or the software. This simple example illustrates truths about rules regarding subtype variables and values.

- A value of a subtype can always be safely assigned to a variable of its supertype.
- Because of the above fact, any variable of a subtype can be safely assigned to a variable of its supertype.
- A value of a supertype might be able to be assigned to a variable of a subtype, but its value needs to be checked first to see if it meets the subtype's constraints.
- Because of the above fact, any variable of a supertype might be able to be assigned to a variable of a subtype, but its value needs to be checked first to see if it meets the subtype's constraints.

USING EXTENDING TYPES AND CLASSES

Recall our Circle and Colored Circle classes. If we pass a Colored Circle object to software written before circles had color, that software should be able to use the setPosition and setRadius methods of the Colored Circle object and get the right behavior out of the circle. It won't be able to affect the color of the object, but that's OK: through extension we have made it possible for software written to be able to operate on objects of the base class to be able to operate on objects of the extending class, too.

Things don't work so nicely in the reverse direction. If we try to pass an object of a non-colored Circle to software expecting Colored Circles, that software could fail when it tried to invoke the non-existent setColor method of the plain (white) Circle object. This simple example illustrates truths about rules regarding extending class objects.

- An object of an extending class may be passed to software expecting an object of its base class.
- An object of a base class may not be passed to software expecting an object of an extending class (of the base class).

PROJECTION: THE INVERSE OF EXTENSION

Just as inclusion is the inverse of restriction, projection is the inverse of extension. Projection is the process of eliminating components from a base class or type.

Projection is a common operation in SQL databases. The process of selecting a subset of a table's columns in a query or view is projection. Projection is just as meaningful for types or classes in memory, except that projection can invalidate any methods that reference components that have been projected away.

The extension triangle represents projection when it is read in the reverse direction. A direction of reference arrow indicates when the projecting model element references the base model element. We'll see some uses of projection in chapter 17 on physical design.

Key Points

- Subtyping and extension work in different ways and are often used together.
- Just as a type designates a set, a subtype designates a subset.
- Anything that creates a restriction on values, by format, size, or other means, defines a subtype.
- A major mistake in analysis is to force things into a single hierarchy with a single root. There are no problems with multiple type hierarchies and multiple supertypes of a single type when subtyping is only of the restriction variety.
- Extension adds components and/or methods to a base class or type. It only applies to composite classes and types.
- We avoid the terms "subclass" and "superclass" to avoid confusion with "subtype" and "supertype". Instead, we say "extending class" and "base class". Similarly, when speaking of the extension of composite types, we say "extending type" and "base type".

Chapter Glossary

subtype : something that designates a subset of the set designated by another type, called the **supertype**

restriction relationship : a relationship between two types, where one type, called the subtype, is defined in terms of a restriction on members of the set designated by the other type, called the supertype; inverse of inclusion relationship

inclusion relationship : a relationship between types, where the supertype is defined as a union of its subtypes; inverse of restriction relationship

extending class (or type) : a class (or type) that is defined in terms of another class (or type), called a **base class (or type)**, by defining components and/or methods to what are already available in the base class (or type)

extension : the addition of components to a base class or type; its inverse is **projection**

Chapter 14

Data and Information

We have been using the terms "data" and "information" throughout this book, but do we know what they really are? This chapter lays the foundation for understanding how data combines with predicates to form information, which is the topic of the next chapter. Predicates generalize information. Meaning is given by information, and meaning is the focus of semantics.

INFORMATION

When we attempt to define the words "information" and "data" in ways that are more precise and yet compatible with natural language, we encounter problems right away. Consider these definitions from Merriam-Webster.

information : FACTS, DATA

fact : a piece of information presented as having objective reality

Here we have a circularity: Information consists of facts, and a fact is a piece of information! Let's see if the word "data" can help us escape the circle.

data : information in numerical form that can be digitally transmitted or processed

So data is a kind of information: it's numerical information. That's fine, but we still don't know what information is!

Of course, I have deliberately selected these definitions from several possibilities Merriam-Webster gives for each of these words, in order to show that, to some extent at least, a good definition of "information" is hard to find. A study of the alternative definitions of these words begins to widen the circle to include the word "knowledge", among others, but there is no strong definition of "information" in this dictionary. Our task, then, is to develop a definition of "information" that is precise, consistent, and useful as a building block.

It is at least indisputable that the word "information" refers to a mass quantity. It is much like when we refer to "water": we aren't referring to any particular quantity of water, and we certainly aren't counting water molecules: we just mean water *en masse*.

The human race did not need to know about water molecules before we could benefit from or harness the power of water, but our understanding of the physical world took a great leap forward when we learned of the existence of water molecules, and in fact this understanding helped to usher in the modern era where we have much greater control over the physical world. If we are to understand information in a deep way, and truly gain control over it, it is essential that we understand information at the molecular level, so to speak. We already get value out of information, but by understanding information at the molecular level, we will enable even greater insights and accomplishments. We need to answer the question, What is the fundamental piece of information?

For the answer, I will look to the field of mathematical logic, specifically propositional logic and first-order predicate logic, for the terms proposition and predicate. We gain a tremendous advantage by linking the definition of information to the field of logic, because we can harness all of the proven techniques of formal logic systems to assist in information analysis and processing. Propositional logic and predicate logic are what link the fields of data and semantics.

Merriam-Webster's defines the word **proposition** as follows:

> **proposition 2 a :** an expression in language or signs of something that can be believed, doubted, or denied or is either true or false

For example, the statement, "It is raining outside right now," is a proposition, because at this very moment the statement is either true or false—or at least one may argue about whether it is true or false. (Perhaps it is only drizzling.)

A proposition is the most fundamental piece of information. A collection of propositions constitutes **information**.

Let's see what this means in practice. Here is a series of propositions, which I believe most of us intuitively consider to be, collectively, information.

- The Dow Jones Industrial Average is down 100 points today, finishing the week 1% lower, at 10,194.
- The Secretary of State will be representing the United States at this year's G8 Summit in Paris.
- Average SAT scores were up this year, reversing a five-year trend.
- According to a recent Gallup poll, over 45% of Americans are in church every Sunday.

(In fact, each of these propositions is a *compound proposition*, because each asserts more than one claimed truth. We will save consideration of decomposing propositions—moving from the molecular level to the atomic level—until a later time.)

IS INFORMATION ALWAYS TRUE?

In natural language we sometimes speak of "false information". The above definition of information, as a collection of propositions, allows for the possibility that information is false, since a proposition may be true or false. Thus, our definition of information enables us to use the word in this natural-language way. In contrast, the word "fact" carries with it the notion of truth. When a supposed statement of fact turns out to be false, we don't call it a "false fact"; instead, we say that it is *not a fact*.

Given this definition of the word:

> **fact 5 :** a piece of information presented as having objective reality— **in fact :** in truth (Merriam-Webster)

, we can say that a **fact** is a proposition (a piece of information) that is true.

Those familiar with fact-based modeling, which was reviewed in chapter 7, will recognize that the facts of fact-based modeling are propositions.

FROM INFORMATION TO DATA

Here is a proposition in the context of employment:

Employee #952 works in Department 4567 and earns a salary of $5000 per month.

We would expect the Human Resources department of a corporation to make many similar propositions. Here are a few more examples of such propositions:

Employee #956 works in Department 4567 and earns a salary of $4000 per month.

Employee #891 works in Department 4566 and earns a salary of $5000 per month.

Clearly these propositions, being of the same form, repeat a lot of text. By separating the unique parts of each proposition from the common parts, we can simplify the expression of this information. We will take the common parts of these propositions and place variables where the unique parts fit, as follows.

Employee #EmpId works in Department DeptNr and earns a salary of $SalaryMnthUsdAm per month.

We call a statement of this form a **logical predicate**, or **predicate** for short. (This definition of "predicate" is the one used by logicians, and is different from its use in the field of semantics and in ordinary English. We will look at both of those other meanings later on in this chapter.) We will take the unique parts of these propositions and arrange them in a table such that it is obvious how they are to be substituted into the predicate, in place of the variables, to "re-constitute" the original propositions.

The values in Table 14-1 are called data, which is a plural word. Each value individually is a datum.

EmpId	SalaryMnthUsdAm	DeptNr
952	5000	4567
956	4000	4567
891	5000	4566

Table 14-1. Employment Data

Let's examine Webster's definition:

> **datum 1 a :** something given or admitted especially as a basis for reasoning or inference

In this context, a datum is *given* to a predicate as a value for one of its variables. Observe that a datum may have some intrinsic meaning, but its full meaning in context is known only after it is substituted into its related predicate. For example, the number 5000 could indicate many different things, including a monthly salary, the number of people attending a concert, or the cost of a computer. We wouldn't know which unless we knew the predicate with which it is associated.

It is also important to understand that a value is not a datum *unless it is intended to be bound to a predicate's variable.* For instance, the value 39 is just a number. If, however, the value 39 is associated with some predicate variable (for example, 39 is the x in "I just bought x apples"; or 39 is the y in "I am y years old"), then in that context 39 is a datum. This is important, because it reveals that the terms datum and data connote *roles that values play*. There's a lot of over-use of the word "data" to describe values and/or symbols regardless of whether or not those values play the role of being bound to some predicate's variable. We'll talk a lot more about roles that data play in chapter 15.

DATA *EN MASSE*

We tend to deal with data *en masse*. That's because the value of data processing lies in the capability of computers to process large quantities of data. This is the reason we see the singular form of the word, datum, so seldom. It is also the reason that the word "data" has come to be treated as a mass noun, like "water" and "information": we treat it not as a plural noun ("the data are . . ."), but as a singular noun ("the data is . . ."). In this perfectly legitimate usage, we ignore that any quantity of data is composed of many elemental particles, in the same way that we ignore that any quantity of water is composed of many molecules. We need to accept both the singular and plural usages of the word "data", reserving the plural usage for more technical contexts where we are paying attention to the fact that data is composed of multiple atoms, each of which is a datum.

In order to deal with data *en masse*, we separate data from information. That is, we reduce a number of propositions of the same form to a single predicate and a set of data per proposition. We then store the data in a **database management system**, which is a computer system specifically designed to manage large quantities of data. In order to recover the original information, we must retrieve the data from the database system and marry it to its associated predicate. This latter operation is rarely done in an automated fashion. That is, it is usually done by humans, outside any computer system. For instance, a worker in a human resources department might bring up an employee's record, and see, on a screen, values labeled Employee ID, Salary, and Department. Because the values are appropriately labeled on the screen, the human computer user understands the implicit predicate and re-constitutes the original proposition in his mind ("Employee #956 works in Department 4567 and earns a salary of $4000 per month."). Rarely does any so-called information system represent this whole proposition. (Rarely does any so-called information system even represent the predicate, but that is a topic for a later section.)

VARIABLE NAMES

To make things easy for ourselves, we humans typically try to choose variable names that remind us of what the variables stand for—in the example above, we are reminded by the variable names EmpId, DeptNr, and SalaryMnthUsdAm that these variables stand for employee ID number, department number, and monthly salary, respectively. But the computer attaches no such meaning to variable names; in fact, it attaches no meaning to them at all. As far as the computer is concerned, the predicate could be

> Employee #<u>X</u> works in Department <u>Y</u> and earns a salary of <u>Z</u> per month.

, and everything would be just fine.

SUMMARY

Keep in mind that

> A **proposition** is the fundamental piece of **information**; to put it another way, one or more **propositions = information**.

A **predicate** + **data** (as values for the predicate's variables) = a **proposition**.

I like to say that data is dehydrated information; just add predicates.

Information and Data as Colloquialisms

What have been presented above are very precise and technical definitions for the words "information" and "data" that are quite different from many common uses of the words. These other uses remain legitimate. I believe you will see that most of these other uses relate in an approximate way to the tight definitions given above, usually by sharing some core concept. Let's look at some of those other meanings.

INFORMATION *EN MASSE*

The word "information" is sometimes used to refer to insights gained by analyzing some quantity of data. For example, retailers often analyze how well a certain product is selling and correlate this to, for instance, the price of the item and the geographical region in which it is sold.

Given "information" as defined above, the results of analyses are certainly a kind of information. However, if we use the term "information" solely to mean the results of analyses, we lose the more fundamental capability to reason about information as a collection of propositions. Therefore we will keep the definition of "information" a tight one. We will use the term "analytics" or "insight" for the data or information obtained by analyzing data.

IT'S JUST DATA

The term "data" is sometimes used as a pejorative term, to imply that there is insufficient meaning or value in some data or information, and that a context must be supplied for the data, or further analysis of the so-called data is required. It is sometimes said, "This is just data; we need information."

That which is referred to as "just data" might really be data in the strict sense, in which case a context is definitely needed (more precisely, a predicate) in order to understand what the data indicates. By the definition above, data is separate from the context (a predicate) which gives it meaning.

If that which is referred to as "just data" is in fact information in the strict sense—a set of propositions—then the complaint is saying either that not enough supporting information has been supplied in order for the information to be useful, or that analysis of the information (usually a large quantity of information) is required in order to extract valuable insights from it.

PUTTING IT ALL TOGETHER

Consider this progression from data to information to analytics.

> just a number: 39
>
> probably data: 39 degrees
>
> probably data: 39 degrees Celsius
>
> information: The patient's temperature is 39 degrees Celsius.
>
> information: The outdoor temperature is 39 degrees Celsius.
>
> analytics (a kind of information): The average high temperature in Tucson, Arizona in the month of July for the last twenty years has been <data: list of monthly average temperatures>
>
> insight (a kind of information): It sure is hot in Tucson in July!

The pure number "39", without any other context, cannot be assumed to be data: it's just a number. When the pure number "39" is combined with units of measure—degrees (of something unspecified) or degrees Celsius—we can begin to suspect that the values are data, because it would be unlikely that temperatures would be presented apart from some context. But without further information, such as a predicate for which the values were suited, even these measurement values are just values.

When a proposition is made—that is, when an assertion is made that can be agreed or disagreed with, or believed, doubted, or denied—then we have information. Before that line is crossed, the values presented do not form any kind of proposition, and therefore there is no information, nor can we confidently assert that the values are data.

Analytics are information derived from other information or data, and insights are information derived from analytics.

"UNSTRUCTURED DATA" AND "SEMI-STRUCTURED DATA"

Although corporations store vast quantities of data in databases, a great deal of storage is occupied by artifacts designed primarily for human consumption, such as text documents, graphical presentations, audio and video recordings, etc. These kinds of artifacts have come to be known by the unusual term **unstructured data**. This term is relative to the term **structured data**, so before we can understand why some things are called *un*structured data, we must understand what structured data is.

Table 14-1 above provides a structure for data. It is clear from the context surrounding the table that the EmpId column should only contain employee IDs, the DeptNr column should only contain department numbers, and the SalaryMnthUsdAm column should only contain monthly salaries. To a limited extent, database systems can enforce these requirements by preventing the insertion of data that violates certain rules. For example, given a second table of department numbers, a database system can ensure that the DeptNr column of Table 14-1 only contains values found in the table of department numbers.

One of the chief advantages of database systems is that they can be used to impose structure on data. A structure organizes data so that it is easier to understand, easier to process efficiently, and easier to verify that it is correct. A typical database has hundreds of tables, each of which imposes structure on the data it contains. That's a lot of structure!

In contrast, the software that is used to create and maintain text documents, audio recordings, etc., does not impose any structure on those artifacts other than the structure necessary to ensure that they are in fact text documents, audio recordings, etc. This is why they are called unstructured. So-called unstructured data, then, needs to be considered at two levels. At the lower level, there is a structure. Text is represented by data that is interpreted as text; audio is represented by data that is interpreted as sound; video is represented by data that is interpreted as a sequence of pictures plus audio, etc. There is structure expected of and imposed on the data at this lower level. At the higher level, no additional structure is imposed (in general). Whether the text forms sentences, the audio is meaningful, or the images are interesting, is not something that software guarantees. At this higher level, the "data" is unstructured; or, to state it more precisely, the lower-level data, which is structured, expresses things which may or may not have structure.

Despite the lack of guarantees, generally text documents contain complete sentences, audio files contain meaningful sounds, etc.; in other words, unstructured data contains information. It is also common for unstructured data to express what is, strictly speaking, data. For instance, page numbers on a multi-page text document are, in fact, data, because the numbers generally appear in a structured manner so that they can be recognized as page numbers and not part of the text. There is an implicit predicate around a page number that says, The page on which this page number appears is the *n*th page in this document.

Additionally, unstructured data can contain what is potentially data. For example, consider residential mortgage agreements. Such agreements are often 40 pages long, and contain many statements (which are propositions) that give information about the responsibilities of mortgagor and mortgagee, the term of the loan, the schedule of payments, etc. If one had a pile of, say, 100 such mortgage agreements, all issued by the same lender in a month's time, one would discover that the bulk of the 40 pages were identical. If one separated out the customer-specific variable parts of the agreements from the non-varying parts, and put placeholder variables where the customer-specific variable parts should be inserted, one would have customer-specific *data* plus (mostly) non-customer-specific *predicates*: we would have given structure to the otherwise unstructured data.

There are, of course, artifacts that would not easily lend themselves to a separation of data from other content; for example, video and audio recordings containing little repetition. Referring to these as "unstructured data" makes the term a bit of a misnomer. "Unstructured information" would be a better moniker.

"Semi-structured data" refers to information stored in a way that separates data from other content, but not in a system such as a database system that enforces a stricter pre-defined structure on the data. A spreadsheet is an example of semi-structured data. So is an XML document, where the XML markup has added some structure to an otherwise unstructured string of text.

Data Object

Whether or not something is a datum depends on the use to which the entity is put. As the example above showed, the number 39 is just a number unless it is known that it is intended to be substituted for a variable in a predicate. Strictly speaking, then, there is no special "data object". An object is a data object only if its states represent values intended for use in a variable that is part of a predicate.

One may construct objects for dealing with data in general, but then such objects will likely deal, not with individual objects representing individual values, but rather with more complex objects representing logical records, tables, and other data structures. Such objects are then indeed "data objects", but modeling them generically and distinctly from non-data objects probably has no value unless one is designing a database management system. A value is data only if it plays the role of data. In our next chapter we will focus on roles played by data.

Key Points

- Data is dehydrated information—values separated from the variables of the predicates that give the data meaning.
- Propositional logic and predicate logic link data to semantics.
- Calling some values "data" indicates that the values play a certain role. They are intended to be bound to the variables of a predicate.
- "Data" and "information" are mass nouns, like "water". Mass nouns indicate some unknown plural quantity but are treated as if they were singular.

CHAPTER GLOSSARY

proposition : an expression in language or signs of something that can be believed, doubted, or denied or is either true or false (Merriam-Webster)

information : a collection of propositions

fact : a proposition that is true or believed to be true

predicate : short for logical predicate

logical predicate : a statement containing variables which, when the variables are bound, yields a proposition

predicate : a statement containing variables which, when the variables are bound, yields a proposition

datum : that which is intended to be given to a predicate as a value for one of its variables

data : plural of datum

analytics : information derived from other information or data

insight : information derived from analytics

structured data : collections of data items stored in a database that imposes a strict structure on that data

unstructured data : data representing text, audio, video or other data which have no structure imposed on what they represent

semi-structured data : collections of data items stored in a way that supports but does not enforce a structure

Chapter 15

Relationships and Roles

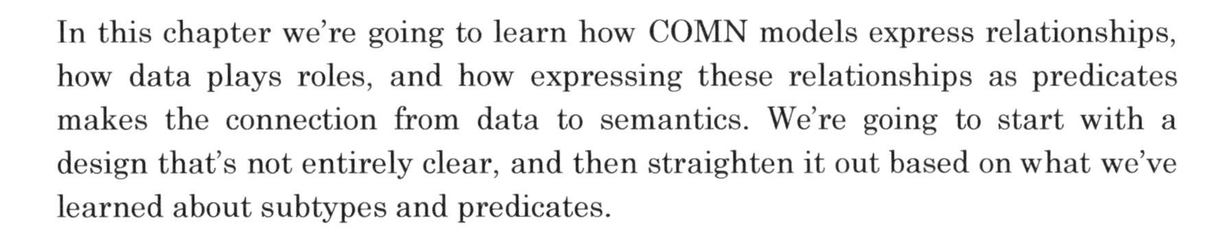

In this chapter we're going to learn how COMN models express relationships, how data plays roles, and how expressing these relationships as predicates makes the connection from data to semantics. We're going to start with a design that's not entirely clear, and then straighten it out based on what we've learned about subtypes and predicates.

ARRIVALS AND DEPARTURES

Suppose you were in an airport and glanced up to see a display screen with the following information on it:

Flight Number	City	Time
351	Charlotte	11:05 AM
295	Chicago	11:00 AM
445	Gary	9:17 AM
1023	Topeka	10:47 AM

Table 15-1. A Flight Schedule

Aha, you say, a flight schedule! There's just one very important piece of information missing: are these departures or arrivals? You typically have to search for a title over the display screen for that information. This shows that two or more sets of data can have the same structure even though they are meant for substitution into different predicates (that is, the logical predicates of chapter 14). Even though the structure of departure and arrival data is the same, there is a great difference in meaning between the proposition that flight 351 is departing for Charlotte at 11:05 AM and the proposition that flight 351 is arriving from Charlotte at 11:05 AM. If you're a passenger, confusing those two meanings can result in a missed flight, and if you're an air traffic controller, confusing those two meanings can result in pandemonium!

Figure 15-1 shows the common Flight Schedule Record Type as the type of both the Departures and Arrivals record collections.

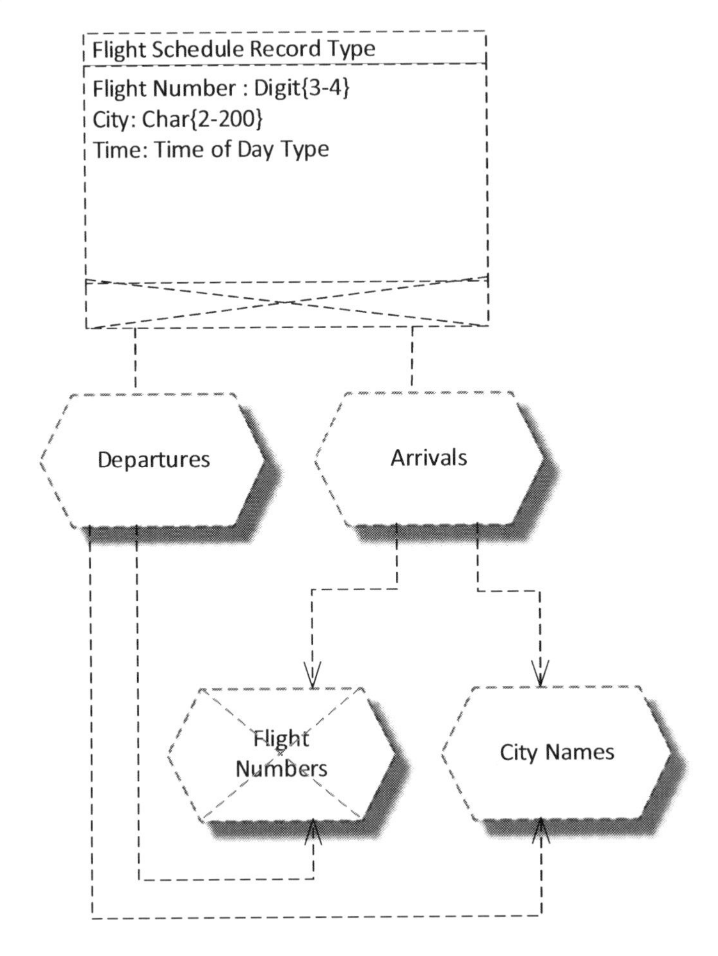

Figure 15-1. Departures and Arrivals

Since we know that not every 3- or 4-digit number is an actual flight number, nor that every string of up to 200 characters is an actual city name, we want to keep collections of the legitimate values. Before a record of data is stored in the Departures or Arrivals collection, we can check these collections to ensure that the flight number and city name are known. The Flight Number and City Name collections are shown at the bottom of Figure 15-1. Flight Numbers are just integers, and integers are simple types; hence the crossed lines through the hexagon. City Names are character strings, which are arrays of characters and therefore composite types, and so there are no crossed lines. (A single character is a simple type.)

The Departures and Arrivals collections reference the Flight Numbers and City Names collections, as shown by the relationship lines with open arrowheads indicating the direction of reference. This kind of relationship expresses reference without any kind of composition.

Logically—ignoring implementation details—the references to Flight Numbers are made by the Flight Number components of Departures and Arrivals, and the references to City Names are made by the City components of Departures and Arrivals. In a SQL database, the Flight Number and City components are called **foreign keys**. A foreign key is a component that can only take on values that are found as key values in the referenced table. In this way, a flight schedule's flight number is *restricted* to be only known flight numbers and not just any 3- or 4-digit number, and a flight schedule's city name is *restricted* to be only known city names and not just any string of characters. No relationship is shown to a table of times. We'd rather not keep a table of all 1440 minutes in a day! Instead, we depend on the Time of Day Type to enforce that the time reference hours and minutes in a day in a customary format.

By this point in the book your COMN antennae may have gone up when you read the words "restricted", and you might suspect that there are subtypes somewhere here—and in fact there are. Let's examine the Flight Number component. Its format is defined to be a 3- or 4-digit number. But only some 3- or 4-digit numbers are listed in the Flight Numbers collection, and only those are legitimate flight numbers. Thus, we have two sets:

- the set of all 3- and 4-digit numbers
- the subset of 3- and 4-digit numbers found in the Flight Numbers table.

The **foreign key constraint** that restricts a Flight Schedule's Flight Number component is in fact a type, because it designates a set, that set being the flight numbers listed in the Flight Number table.

This shows that it is always true that *a foreign key constraint is a subtype*. The supertype is the underlying type of the key. The subtype designates the set of key values actually in the referenced table.

This is a really radical observation, because up until now we have always said that the lines in a data model represent *relationships*, and now we're learning that some of the lines in fact represent *types*! To be specific, a reference to a collection without aggregation or assembly, shown in COMN with an open arrowhead, amounts to the definition of a subtype, if the collection has a key.

Many document DBMSs, and other NoSQL DBMSs, don't have the concept of a foreign key, and will allow flight number and city name fields to accept any digit strings or character strings. But the fact that these DBMSs don't enforce the type constraints doesn't mean that the types don't logically exist. For your NoSQL database design, you should still document that these types exist at the logical level. When you move to physical database design, and have no way to represent or enforce these logical types physically, it will be important to document that these fields are wide open, and the database is dependent on the application code to store only data that is of the correct logical type.

LABELING RELATIONSHIP LINES

It is customary in E-R notations and in the UML to label a relationship line with any or all of the following:

- the name of the relationship type (for example, employment)
- verb phrases for reading the relationship in one or both directions (for example, employs / is employed by)
- the role played by the data at each end of the relationship (for example, employer, employee)

These labels are given in fact-based models by labeling the role boxes that are connected by lines to so-called object types (which we would simply call types in COMN).

These labels correspond directly to the predicates that give the data meaning, so they're pretty important. The roles are the predicate variables, and either one of the verb phrases or the name of the relationship type can be used as the name of the predicate.

Looking at Table 15-1, we can deduce the predicates implicit in the data, as follows:

```
Flight #Flight Number departs to city City.
```

```
Flight #Flight Number departs at time Time.
```

or

```
Flight #Flight Number arrives from city City.

Flight #Flight Number arrives at time Time.
```

These predicates have been broken down into simple predicates (no AND conjunction) so that each one expresses a binary relationship—just two variables. I've done that so we could put these predicates on relationship lines, which connect just two entities. We haven't yet covered how to show relationships between three or more entities.

We would like to label the relationship lines in our Departures and Arrivals model—specifically, the reference relationships with open arrowheads—but we have several problems. We can easily label the line from Departures to City Names with "departs to city", and the line from Arrivals to City Names with "arrives at city". But where do we put the labels "departs at time" and "arrives at time"? And is there any meaningful way to label the lines from Departures and Arrivals to Flight Numbers?

We have a model, then, that can't support the annotation of all of the meaning that it expresses.

We're going to address this situation by doing two things:

1. We are going to clean up the model of Figure 15-1, so that it contains more type information and less redundancy.
2. We are going to borrow the role box notation of fact-based modeling to enable us to document relationships even when we don't have relationship lines to label.

CLEANING UP THE MODEL

We learned in the previous section that foreign-key reference relationships actually represent subtypes. Our Flight Schedule Record Type does not benefit from this reality, because its types for Flight Number and City are very weak: those components will accept any 3-4 digit numbers and any 2-200 character strings, respectively, whether or not they are known flight numbers and known city names. To fix this, we should have the Flight Schedule Record Type reference the Flight Numbers and City Names collections. This will also remove the parallel references to those collections from the Departures and Arrivals collections, making the model less cluttered. Of course, this removes some of the relationship lines we'd like to label, but we'll address that problem with role boxes.

We'll use role boxes to give us places to record the predicates relevant to this model.

The result is shown in Figure 15-2.

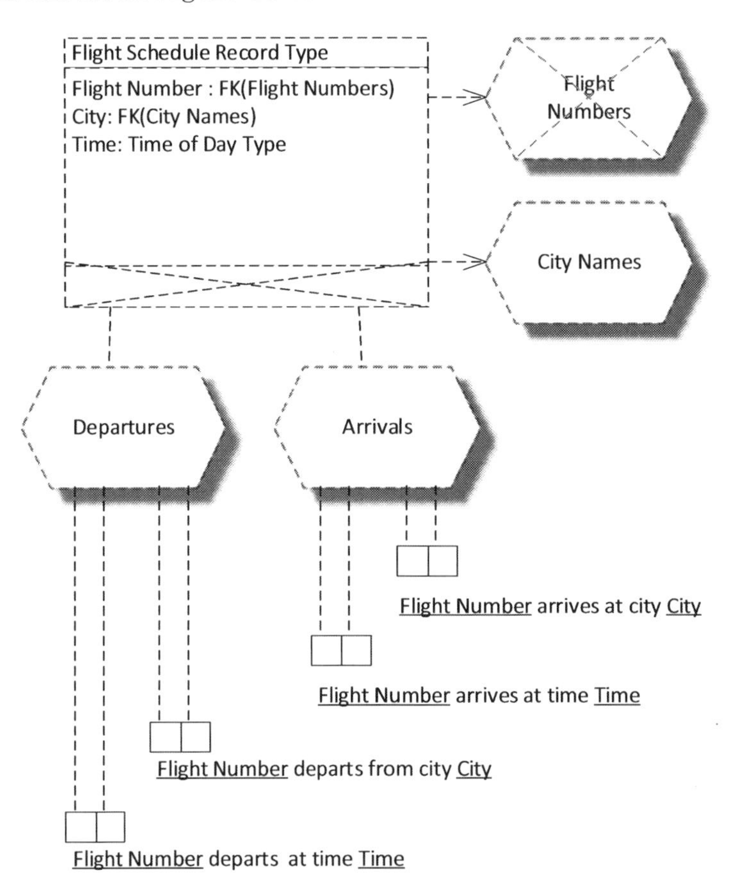

Figure 15-2. Flight Schedules with Role Boxes

Within the Flight Schedule Record Type rectangle, we've changed the types of the components Flight Number and City. The type of Flight Number is now given as FK(Flight Numbers), meaning that a Flight Number's type designates the set of all key values found in the Flight Numbers collection. "FK" stands for foreign key. Likewise, the type of City has been changed to FK(City Names). If we wanted to know the underlying types of Flight Numbers and City Names—that is, the types of the keys, which are the supertypes involved here—we'd have to look at the logical record types for Flight Numbers and City Names. They aren't shown in this model just to keep the clutter down. This change further reduces redundancy in the model, because now those underlying types are defined only once, rather than both at their origin and at their point of reference.

At the bottom of Figure 15-2 you'll see the role boxes used in fact-based modeling. Each group of small role box rectangles represents a predicate, and the number of boxes in the group gives the number of variables in the predicate. The phrase near a group spells out the predicate, and uses logical record type component names (underlined) as variable names.

The role boxes illustrate that, in a record-oriented design, relationships exist between components of a single logical record. Foreign-key relationships are really subtype specifications.

If you're lucky enough to have a design where all the important relationships correspond to the subtype/foreign key relationships, you can skip the role boxes and label those relationship lines. But you can see from this example that you might not always be so lucky.

Which notation should one use? That is almost entirely an issue of preference. There is a large community of data modelers and business people who are comfortable with E-R notations, and the very similar UML notation. The community of data modelers and business people familiar with fact-based modeling is much smaller. This would tilt the preference for notation in favor of foreign-key/subtype relationship lines over small-box relationship notation. However, if one wished to show the relationships that exist between components of a single logical record type when no foreign key is involved, or when the diagram doesn't show the referenced logical record type as a rectangle, role-box notation can be used.

Furthermore, role-box notation can show relationships involving three or more data items—predicates with three or more variables—without forcing the inclusion of a so-called "associative entity" in the diagram.

Roles, Predicates, and Relationships

Recall our discussion in chapter 13 about how a person related to a coffee shop can play either the role of a customer or the role of an employee, or both. This shows that a person can play multiple roles in life. (Certainly, actors play multiple roles!) We saw in chapter 13 how to illustrate data about these multiple roles in COMN.

Now we see that even data plays roles. In fact, as we saw in the previous chapter, a value isn't even data *unless* it plays a role as a value for a variable in a predicate.

We've also seen that relationships exist between the components of a single logical record type, and that predicates express those relationships.

It turns out that the great struggle to find good names for logical record type components (data attributes) is a struggle to name the variables of logical predicates. This struggle is not made any easier by the fact that we rarely write down the predicates. Understanding that data attributes play roles should focus us on naming logical record type components based on the roles played by them in relationships.

We have used the term "relationship" heavily throughout this book. It is time to give it a robust definition. A **relationship** is *a proposition concerning two or more entities*. Thus, the statement that "Flight #351 is departing for the city of Charlotte" is a relationship. So is the statement that "Flight #351 departs at 11:05 AM."

A collection of logical records expresses a set of relationships, which are propositions that we would intuitively recognize are *all of the same type*. Using our COMN terminology, we would search for something that designates that set of relationships, and whatever designates that set is the type.

It turns out that, just as we have two types involved in every foreign key relationship—the type of the key, which is the supertype, and the collection of key values, which are the set designated by the foreign key—we have two types involved in every table of records.

The logical record type, apart from any particular collection of values, creates the potential to have a set of values which contains every possible combination of flight number, city name, and time. (It's highly unlikely that we'd ever create a table with all those values.) So the logical record type is a type because it designates that set.

The Departures and Arrivals collections both draw from that same supertype. Their particular values are those values for which their related predicates are true. Thus, the predicates in effect designate sets of values, and that means—you guessed it!—a predicate is a type. We can say specifically that *a logical predicate is a relationship type*, because it designates a potential set of relationship propositions.

Key Points

- Relational database foreign key constraints are actually subtypes, because they designate the set of key values in the referenced table, which are a subset of the values designated by the key's type.
- Foreign-key relationship lines in E-R diagrams depict subtype relationships.
- Relationships exist between the attributes of a single logical record.
- Role boxes can be used to express relationships between components of a single logical record type.
- Data are values that play roles in predicates, as values for predicate variables.
- A logical predicate is a relationship type, because it designates a potential set of relationship propositions.

Chapter Glossary

relationship : a proposition concerning two or more entities

relationship type : a logical predicate

Chapter 16

The Relational Theory of Data

We've gotten quite far in our investigation of data models, including discussions of what data and information are, and what relationships are. It's finally time to take a look at the fundamental theory behind all of this.

We've already established, and the world has already proven, that you can do a lot with data without understanding relational theory. It's also true that you can do a lot with water power without understanding the water molecule, H_2O. So why are we bothering at this juncture to look at relational theory? Because so much thinking will be clarified, and so many new vistas will open before us, when we understand what relational theory is all about.

For the NoSQL aficionados among my readers, you should realize that relational theory matters as much to NoSQL databases as it does to SQL databases—even more so, in one sense. Relational theory is a theory of data that matters whether you're storing your data in a document, a graph, or a table. SQL is strongly associated with relational theory, but that doesn't mean that the theory only works with SQL. It works whenever there's data. You don't know it yet, but if you've read the book this far, you've already encountered many of the important concepts in relational theory.

In my experience, I've often seen folks struggle to understand relational theory. If you've read this far in this book and understood most of it, you've already grasped concepts that are more difficult than those in relational theory. The reason that relational theory escapes many people is because of one of the greatest terminological tragedies in our field, which is that, in relational theory, *a "relation" is not the same as a "relationship"*! Once you get past that, the rest is relatively easy.

WHAT IS A RELATION?

In overly simplistic terms, a relation is a table. So why do we use this fancy word "relation", instead of the more easily understood term "table"? Because there are some important differences, namely:

1. The order of rows in a relation has no significance whatsoever, while the order of rows in a table may carry information.

2. The repetition of rows in a relation has no significance whatsoever, while the repetition of rows in a table may carry information.

Below I will explain these differences, and why they matter.

THE ORDER OF ROWS

As soon as a list of data is written down on a piece of paper, it has an order; that is, the order in which the data is written down. But does that order mean anything? To understand this issue, we will consider two examples from everyday life.

Imagine a cash register receipt from a grocery store. See Figure 16-1 for an example of part of a cash register receipt.

```
TOMATO CAN 16 OZ              1.69
MILK 128 OZ                   3.39
CARROTS 2.30 LB @ 0.69        1.59
TOMATO CAN 16 OZ              1.69
FACIAL TISSUE                 4.59
```

Figure 16-1. Part of a Grocery Store Cash Register Receipt

When cash registers were mechanical devices that printed item prices on paper, cash register receipts showed the prices of grocery items in the order in which the cashier rang them up. This custom has been preserved even in the age of computerized registers and bar code scanners. Thus, not only does the printing on the paper register tape show each item purchased together with its price, but it also shows the order in which the items passed by the scanner. If, for some reason, we wished to re-order the items in the list, say by sorting them so that the least expensive item appeared first, we would lose track of the order in which they were rung up or scanned. We observe that there is information carried in the order of the items in the list. In contrast, consider a printed telephone directory. See Figure 16-2 for an example of part of a telephone directory.

Doe Jack	**123 Main St.**	**555-1234**
Doe Jane	**222 Axle Ave.**	**555-9999**
Doe John	**27 Red House Ln**	**555-8877**
Doe Joseph	**1 Pennsylvania Rd**	**555-3333**

Figure 16-2. Part of a Telephone Directory

This list also has an order. It is apparent that the order of this list is determined by sorting the names of telephone subscribers in alphabetical order. The telephone directory publisher established this order so that it is easy to find listings by name: one simply searches alphabetically through the directory for the name of the desired listing.

If you took a telephone directory, cut off the binding while leaving the contents of the pages intact, and shuffled the pages like a deck of cards, you would not lose any information. Every listing would still be in those pages, though it would take much longer to find any one listing because of the loss of order. With enough time and patience, one could re-sort the pages to alphabetical order, by consulting the listing at the top of each page. Because the order can be restored using the information still on each page, one can see that the directory's physical property of alphabetical order carries no information. However, that order is valuable for efficiency when searching the directory.

Consider again the cash register receipt. To record all of the information from the receipt explicitly, including the significance of the order of the rows, and preserve the information when the rows are re-ordered, we would have to add a column to the table that lists the sequence in which items were rung up, as shown in Figure 16-3 below.

12	TOMATO CAN 16 OZ	1.69
13	MILK 128 OZ	3.39
14	CARROTS 2.30 LB @ 0.69	1.59
15	TOMATO CAN 16 OZ	1.69
16	FACIAL TISSUE	4.59

Figure 16-3. Part of a Grocery Store Cash Register Receipt with Explicit Order

Now if we re-order rows by price, or alphabetically by product name, or by any other criteria, we can still know the order in which each item was rung up.

It is not always possible to predict how we wish to search some data for a desired relationship. For instance, although most of us want to find entries in a telephone directory by name, the caller ID feature of a telephone system must look up an entry by telephone number in order to find the name to display. A direct-mail advertising company might wish to take listings from a telephone directory and sort them by address for more efficient postal delivery. As soon as we take any data and write it down, we have a table, which has order to its rows. However, we want the freedom to establish that order differently for different uses. That is why it is so important to ensure that we represent data as relations—without order to their rows—while storing data as tables, which have order to their rows. Database systems that store information in the order of rows have a significant disadvantage, in that they cannot re-order rows for faster access without losing information. One of the main advantages of relational database systems over other kinds of database systems is this so-called **data independence**, where the physical order of data storage can be changed to speed up various styles of access without changing the information stored.

THE UNIQUENESS OF ROWS

Consider a telephone directory with a printer's error, as shown in Figure 16-4 below.

Doe Jack	**123 Main St.**	**555-1234**
Doe Jane	**222 Axle Ave.**	**555-9999**
Doe John	**27 Red House Ln**	**555-8877**
Doe John	**27 Red House Ln**	**555-8877**
Doe John	**27 Red House Ln**	**555-8877**
Doe Joseph	**1 Pennsylvania Rd**	**555-3333**

Figure 16-4. A Printer's Error

The printer's error is to print one listing three times, which is entirely unnecessary and a waste of paper and ink. No matter how many times John Doe's listing is printed, it is still only true once, so to speak, that his telephone number is 555-8877. This repetition does not indicate that, for instance, he has three telephones in his house. He might have four, or only one: the directory does not carry such information.

In contrast, the cash register receipt of Figure 16-1 has two rows that are identical, and this repetition carries information, specifically that two 16-ounce cans of tomatoes were purchased. Thus, a telephone directory is much more like a relation than a cash register receipt is, because neither the order of its rows nor any repetition of rows carries any information.

We say that a table depicts a relation because it is like a picture of a relation. A table is a *physical representation* of a relation. It is not the relation itself. You can't see the relation itself, because the relation is a concept. Just as no one has ever seen the number one, even though we've all seen thousands of *representations* of the number one in words and symbols, no one has ever seen or will ever see a relation.

THE SIGNIFICANCE OF COLUMNS

We all know intuitively that a table has rows and columns. In the examples above, it is easy to see what the columns are. Table 16-1 below shows the cash register receipt with columns explicitly labeled.

Item Description	Price
TOMATO CAN 16 OZ	1.69
MILK 128 OZ	3.39
CARROTS 2.30 LB @ 0.69	1.59
TOMATO CAN 16 OZ	1.69
FACIAL TISSUE	4.59

Table 16-1. A Grocery Store Cash Register Receipt as a Table with Column Headings

The column headings create an expectation as to what data we will find in the corresponding fields of each row. For example, we would be very surprised to find the words "FACIAL TISSUE" in the Price column. In fact, if that occurred on a cash register receipt or in a corresponding table in a computer's memory, we would consider it to be an error.

By definition, each column in a relation can only carry one type of data; that is, data drawn from only one set of values. For instance, values in the Price column of a cash register receipt can only be drawn from a set of numbers that represent prices, with two digits to the right of the decimal point. Further, the values in each column carry a significance which is usually indicated by the column heading. For instance, we expect that values in the Item Description column describe the items purchased.

We can describe the form of the cash register receipt and the telephone directory using a logical record type. We know from the previous chapter that relationships exist between the components of a logical record type, so this means that relationships must exist between the columns of these tables.

SUMMARY

A relation is a conceptual record of data, where there is no significance to the order of rows, nor to repetition of data. We represent relations as tables, which do have order to their rows, and which can repeat row values. However, by avoiding the use of the physical order of data in a database to record information, data can be re-ordered in order to make retrieval faster, without losing information. In any relation, relationships between data exist between (not necessarily adjacent) columns.

TECHNICAL RELATIONAL TERMINOLOGY

In thinking of relations, mathematicians start with three things:

1. a name for the role a value plays
2. a type for that value (that is, the designation of the set from which the value is drawn)
3. a value

Together, these three entities are called a **data attribute value**[3].

Let's take our Departures and Arrivals example from chapter 15 and expand it to show a full schedule for each flight. See Table 16-2 below.

---

[3] A data attribute value is often called simply an attribute value, but we're going to explore the difference in a later section.

Flight Number	Departure City	Departure Time	Arrival City	Arrival Time
351	Charlotte	11:05 AM	Philadelphia	12:40 PM
295	Chicago	11:00 AM	Los Angeles	4:30 PM
445	Gary	9:17 AM	Topeka	11:47 AM
1023	Topeka	10:47 AM	Gary	12:05 PM

Table 16-2. A Full Flight Schedule

This table shows many data attribute values. Here are a few examples:

<Departure City, FK(City Names), Charlotte>
<Departure City, FK(City Names), Chicago>
<Arrival Time, Time of Day Type, 4:30 PM>
<Flight Number, FK(Flight Numbers), 445>

The angle brackets (< >) indicate that the order of terms inside them is significant. This is important: we don't want to confuse the name of a role that data plays with the name of the set from which it is drawn. For instance, it is important not to confuse a particular Flight Number with the set of possible Flight Numbers.

A set of data attribute values, taken together, is called a **tuple value**, or, more simply, a **tuple**. This strange name comes from the names we use for sets of particular numbers of things: single, double, triple, quadruple, quin*tuple*, sex*tuple*, sep*tuple*, ... (You can pronounce "tuple" to rhyme with "couple" or to rhyme with "scruple"; both are acceptable.)

Table 16-2 shows four tuples, each one as a row of the table. Here is the tuple represented by the first row of the table.

{
<Flight Number, FK(Flight Numbers), 351>,
<Departure City, FK(City Names), Charlotte>,
<Departure Time, Time of Day Type, 11:05 AM>,
<Arrival City, FK(City Names), Philadelphia>,
<Arrival Time, Time of Day Type, 12:40 PM>
}

The outer braces around this list of data attributes indicate that they are members of a set, and therefore the order of items in the list is insignificant. I listed the data attribute values in the same order in which they were depicted in Table 16-2—in column order—but since each data attribute value carries its role name (which equals the column name), the order of data attribute values in the set is irrelevant. One could rearrange the data attribute values within the tuple without losing any information.

Technically, a **relation** is a set of tuples that all have the same set of role names and types in their data attribute values. Table 16-2 depicts a relation with four tuples as four rows. Each field in a row, at the intersection of a row and a column, depicts a data attribute value. Each column name is the role name of the data attribute value.

One can see that writing out each set of data attribute values—each tuple—is a very inefficient way of displaying the data in a relation. If one were to show a relation as a set of tuples, it would take a great deal of space, indeed. (This, by the way, is unfortunately the manner in which XML depicts tuple values, and it is so inefficient that it disallows XML from use in many demanding applications that involve structured data.) We prefer the compact depiction in a table such Table 16-2. The only disadvantage to the table notation is that it provides only two of the three parts of a data attribute value, namely, the role name and the value: nowhere is the data attribute type specified. That is a problem easily addressed by adding an additional header row to the table; see Table 16-3, where the types are given as non-bold headers directly below the column names.

Flight Number	**Departure City**	**Departure Time**	**Arrival City**	**Arrival Time**
FK(Flight Numbers)	FK(City Names)	Time of Day Type	FK(City Names)	Time of Day Type
351	Charlotte	11:05 AM	Philadelphia	12:40 PM
295	Chicago	11:00 AM	Los Angeles	4:30 PM
445	Gary	9:17 AM	Topeka	11:47 AM
1023	Topeka	10:47 AM	Gary	12:05 PM

Table 16-3. A Full Flight Schedule with Column Types

If we store many, usually related, relations in one place, we have what is called a **relational database**. In relational theory, a database is a collection of **relation variables**, where each relation variable can take on the value of some relation. The logical record type collections, represented in COMN as shadowed and dashed hexagons, are relation variables. In practice, a relational database is implemented using a physical table for each relation variable.

TUPLE AND RELATION SCHEMES

We have already talked about how a tuple has data attribute values, each of which has a name and a type, in addition to a value, and how a relation is a set of tuples that have the same data attribute names and types. If one takes just the name and type pairs from a tuple value, then one has a **tuple scheme**.

For example, the scheme of each tuple in Table 16-2 can be expressed as follows.

{
<Flight Number, FK(Flight Numbers)>,
<Departure City, FK(City Names)>,
<Departure Time, Time of Day Type>,
<Arrival City, FK(City Names)>,
<Arrival Time, Time of Day Type>
}

Each of these <name, type> pairs is called a **data attribute** of a tuple scheme. (Contrast this with a data attribute *value* of a tuple [value].)

We can then describe a relation as a set of tuples all of which have the same scheme.

Given this, we can see that a **relation scheme** has the same set of <name, type> pairs as the tuple scheme of any of its tuples.

GIVING DATA TO THE SYSTEM

Given a tuple scheme, one can imagine all of the possible tuple values conforming to that scheme. For example, we could imagine an airline flights table showing every possible combination of flight numbers, departure and arrival cities, and departure and arrival times. There would be thousands of rows in such a table, with each row depicting one possible tuple conforming to the tuple scheme. This set of tuple values is called **the universal type of the tuple scheme**.

Such a set of values isn't very useful. We are only interested in tuple values representing actual scheduled flights, and we can't deduce which those are just by examining the thousands of tuples in the universal type. Someone must *give the system* the tuples conforming to the tuple scheme that represent actual scheduled flights. The relevance of the term *datum* (plural: *data*) appears here: **datum** is a Latin word meaning "that which is given". From any database's table definition, which specifies a tuple scheme, a computer could deduce all possible row (tuple) values, but that isn't useful. One must *give* the relevant rows (tuple values or data) to the table.

DATA ATTRIBUTE VERSUS ATTRIBUTE

Most relational theorists refer to the components of a relation or tuple simply as an attribute rather than as a data attribute. This shortened form isn't incorrect, but it can lead to confusion when we're trying to model the real world along with our model of data about the real world. Here's why.

The ordinary English definition of **attribute** is "an inherent characteristic" (Merriam-Webster). An inherent characteristic is something you can't remove from an entity—it's not a component of the entity, but is a property that's intrinsic to the entity. For example, matter has mass. There is no "mass component" to matter. So we say that mass is an *attribute* of matter—but not a data attribute. If you weigh a hunk of matter—a material object—you can measure its mass and write that measure down. If that measure is intended to be used as the value for some predicate's variable—say, X in the predicate, "The rock weighs X", then the value is a *data attribute value*, and X is a *data attribute.*

As another example, every person has an age, which is the measure of time that has elapsed since the person was born. There is no age component to a person. Age is an inherent characteristic or *attribute* of a person. We often record a person's date of birth as a *data attribute* about that person, and that enables us to calculate a person's current age at any moment.

When modeling things in the real world, whether objects (solid bold outline) or concepts (dashed bold outline), we want to be able to represent some of their inherent characteristics—their attributes. We can use the middle section of the composite type or class rectangle to record these attributes, as long as we remember that, in that context, they are not data attributes—optional and removable components. Rather, they are attributes, which are non-removable inherent characteristics.

By making this distinction, we can use COMN to model the real world and to model data about the real world, and we can show the mapping between the two parts of the models, thus representing our data designs fully.

RELATIONAL TERMINOLOGY REPRISE

In this section and the remainder of the chapter, relational terminology will be used, but you can probably already detect how COMN has used more familiar terms for the same things. A full terminology map is at the end of the chapter, to help you connect our terminology of modeling practice to the technical terminology of relational theory.

COMPOSITE DATA ATTRIBUTES

Let's consider a new table, the Employee Data Table, shown in Table 16-4.

Employee Number	Employee Last Name	Employee First Name	Employee Middle Name	Employee Home Phone Number
FK(Employee Numbers)	FK(Personal Names)	FK(Personal Names)	FK(Personal Names)	Phone Number Type
1012	Smith	John		609-555-1234
1096	Jones	John	Paul	212-555-9876
0967	Tally	Sally	A.	310-555-5678

Table 16-4. The Employee Data Table

With a quick glance at the table heading we observe that there are three name columns that, taken together, give an employee's full name. Each of the three name columns reference a Personal Names table, so that, as employees' names are added to the table, a system can check whether a certain name has ever been seen before. If a name is not found, the system can ask the data entry person, "Are you sure this is a personal name?", allowing entry, and adding the name to the Personal Names table, only after the data entry person has confirmed the spelling. This helps ensure high data quality on personal names, which are so varied as to be difficult to check in any other way.

However, with the table as defined, we have no means to deal with an employee's full name as a whole. Rather, we are forced to deal with an employee's name as three separate components.

We can improve on this situation. See Table 16-5 below.

	Employee Name			
Employee Number	**Last Name**	**First Name**	**Middle Name**	**Employee Home Phone Number**
FK(Employee Numbers)	FK(Personal Names)	FK(Personal Names)	FK(Personal Names)	Phone Number Type
1012	Smith	John		609-555-1234
1096	Jones	John	Paul	212-555-9876
0967	Tally	Sally	A.	310-555-5678

Table 16-5. The Employee Data Table with a Sub-Scheme

In this version of the Employee Data table, we have collected three data attributes under a new heading, Employee Name. Note the change in the role names under Employee Name. The word "Employee" has been removed from the role names of the sub-attributes. It is the "big attribute" that tells us that this is a name of an employee. We intuitively recognize that the sub-attributes—Last Name, First Name, Middle Name—are applicable not just to the names of employees, but also to the names of customers, parents, taxpayers, etc.

How do we understand this in relational terms? Table 16-5 introduces a new tuple scheme, with three data attributes: Last Name, First Name, and Middle Name. All three data attributes have the same type, FK(Personal Names), but this is purely coincidental and not significant. The important aspect is that we are now using a tuple scheme as the type for the data attribute Employee Name. We call data attributes like Employee Name, whose types are tuple schemes, **composite data attributes**. We recognize that a composite data attribute is merely an attribute whose type is a composite type; that is, a type defined using a scheme.

Now, we haven't given this new tuple scheme a name: it is anonymous. But it would make perfect sense to call this tuple scheme Person Name, and then we could re-use this tuple scheme to represent the names of persons in many different contexts. Table 16-6 depicts this same table with the additional tuple scheme type shown as Personal Name Type, and Figure 16-5 shows the COMN logical data model corresponding to this table.

	Employee Name (Personal Name Type)			
Employee Number	**Last Name**	**First Name**	**Middle Name**	**Employee Home Phone Number**
FK(Employee Numbers)	FK(Personal Names)	FK(Personal Names)	FK(Personal Names)	Phone Number Type
1012	Smith	John		609-555-1234
1096	Jones	John	Paul	212-555-9876
0967	Tally	Sally	A.	310-555-5678

Table 16-6. The Employee Data Table with a Sub-Scheme with Explicit Type

This is classic type nesting. We do this all the time in the context of programming languages, where the components of a class may be other classes, to any level. We do this in XML, where an XML element can contain other XML elements, nested to any level. We do this in JSON, where an object or an array can contain other objects or arrays, nested to any level. We now understand type nesting as it relates to tables and relations. This is made possible by two aspects of COMN:

- separation of the idea of a composite type from a record collection that conforms to that type
- recognition that a foreign key constraint is a subtype

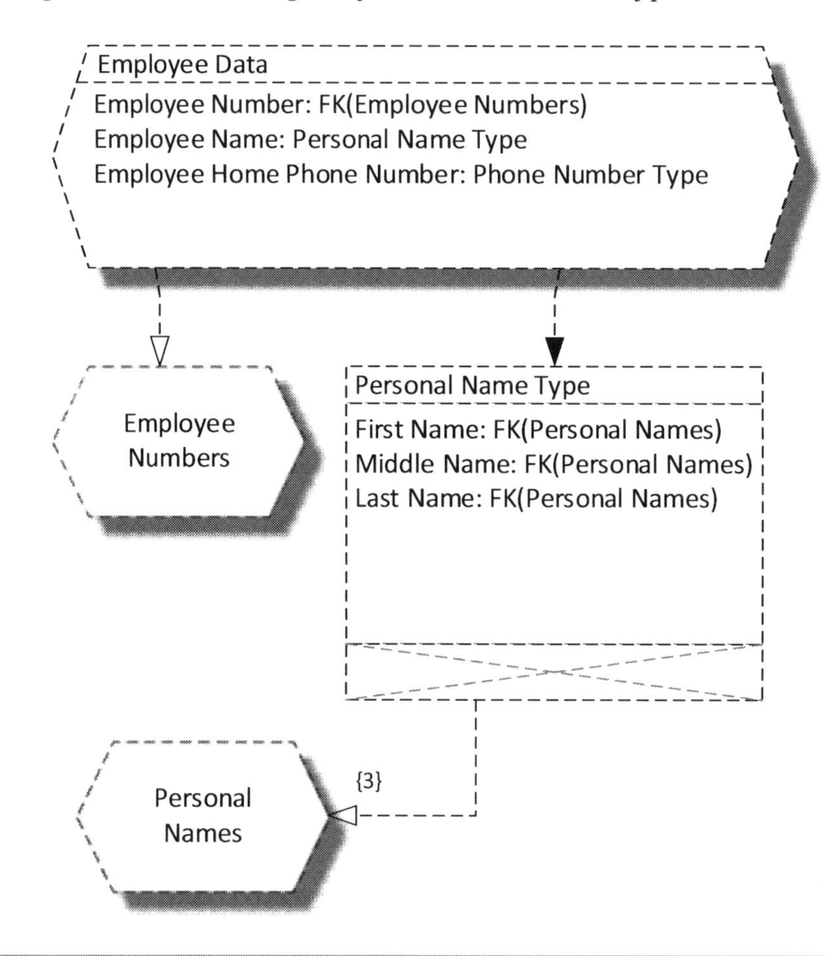

Figure 16-5. A COMN Model for the Employee Data Table

Relational Operations

There are nine relational operators that return relations as results: select (or restrict), join, project, union, intersection, difference, extend, rename, and divide. These relational operators show up directly or indirectly in SQL, and are often present in NoSQL DBMSs as well, of necessity. For instance, an operation that selects documents from a document database based on the value of a particular document element is performing the relational operation of restriction.

Encapsulating data in classes—a common practice in object-oriented programming—disables the relational operators. Relational operators need free access to the data attributes of relations in order to recombine them in useful ways. SQL DBMSs, and other DBMSs that implement the relational operations, provide powerful means to manipulate large quantities of data very efficiently and with minimal programming.

The NoSQL community is in danger of leaving that efficiency and expressiveness behind, and manually replicating the same operations repeatedly at the application level. This is costly and inefficient, and requires that what is (or should be) essentially the same logic be tested over and over. It's important to be aware that relational theory and relational operations are not tied to SQL or any particular physical implementations, and are best implemented once in a DBMS for all to use.

NoSQL Versus the Relational Model

Relational theory is not about tables; rather, it is about relations, tuples, and types. When we associate relations and tuples with predicates, we add semantics to relational theory.

Most of the time, relations are discussed, just as I have done above, in terms of tables. This leads us to thinking about highly structured and highly repetitive data. But there's nothing in relational theory that says that a relation has to have many tuple values in it, nor that we can't have a highly varied set of relations of different schemes, each with one tuple value. So, no matter the context, if you have a data structure of any sort—document, graph, key/value, whatever—where each data attribute has a name that corresponds to its role and a type that limits its possible values, you have a tuple scheme, and relational theory applies. This is true of XML and JSON, even when the typing is so weak as to allow any string of characters to be a value for the data attribute.

What makes NoSQL stand apart from SQL is not that it leaves the relational model behind. It is impossible to leave the relational model behind. It will tag along behind all your data structures. NoSQL is distinctive because its various physical realizations are usually optimized for data exhibiting a great variety of tuple and relation schemes, rather than large sets of data conforming to a small number of schemes. NoSQL is also distinctive because of its more varied approaches to things such as consistency and availability. We'll explore those in greater depth in the next chapter.

SQL Versus the Relational Model

SQL (Structured Query Language) databases are the best-known representatives of the relational model of data, and relational theory is usually judged by the characteristics of SQL databases, most of which are physical and not related to relational theory directly. We will dig into many of those differences in the next chapter on NoSQL and SQL physical database design. For now, we will focus only on the extent to which SQL is an implementation of the relational model.

A database definition in SQL always starts with a CREATE TABLE statement. There is no CREATE RELATION statement in SQL. It follows from this that the SQL language describes physical tables, which have the characteristics of order and repetition explained above. Now, any physical table, including a SQL table, has order to its rows, and there is no possibility of preventing this. SQL DBMSs do state up front that the order of rows in a table is not necessarily preserved across operations on a table, nor across changes to the DBMS software, so it is impossible to store information in the order of a table's rows. (Well, almost impossible: I knew of one system that failed because a programmer expected a certain SQL query to return rows from a table in a certain order; when the DBMS software was upgraded, the order changed and the code depending on that order failed. Fortunately, the bug was easily fixed by adding an explicit ORDER BY clause to the SQL query.)

SQL tables allow two or more rows to represent the same values; they therefore allow repetition. With the addition of a PRIMARY KEY or UNIQUE INDEX to a table, a SQL DBMS will prevent this from happening, making a SQL table a true representative of a relation from relational theory.

In other words, unless additional steps are taken, a SQL table can contain two or more rows representing identical values.

Now, there's nothing *wrong* with tables as tables, but given that SQL DBMSs do not promise to preserve the order of rows in tables, the only aspect of tables as opposed to relations that remains available for use is the ability to store the same row value more than once. If this can be useful in some application, great, but it's more likely to be a source of error, where a table allows duplicate data to be stored inadvertently.

But a data design properly executed in COMN will indicate the key data attributes for each logical record type, and this translates directly into SQL as a table with one or more unique indexes, thereby preventing duplicate data and making a table an accurate representation of a relation.

TERMINOLOGY

Relational Term	COMN Term
attribute	**data attribute**
(no relational equivalent)	**attribute**: an inherent characteristic
attribute value	**data attribute value**
tuple scheme	**composite type** **logical record type** if intended to be used as such
tuple variable	a variable having a composite type a **logical record** if intended to be used as such
tuple, tuple value	value of a composite type
relation scheme	composite type for a collection of logical records
relation variable	a variable having a relation scheme as its type
relation, relation value	value of a relation variable

Key Points

- The relation of relational theory is not a relationship. This is a great terminological tragedy that has impeded comprehension of relational theory.
- A relation is like a table where the order of the rows is irrelevant, and any repeated row values are irrelevant.
- Making order irrelevant enables data independence, so that data can be reordered for faster access.
- Type nesting is compatible with relational theory, but the lack of support for type nesting in SQL and E-R notations have led to the belief that one must abandon relational theory in order to gain type nesting.
- Relational operators are powerful means for recombining data in useful ways. Encapsulating data disables these operators, and leaving them out of NoSQL DBMSs forces them to be implemented repeatedly in applications, with resulting higher costs, lower quality, and lower reliability.

Chapter Glossary

attribute : an inherent characteristic (Merriam-Webster)

data attribute : a <name, type> pair. The name gives the role of a value of the given type in the context of a tuple scheme or relation scheme.

data attribute value : a <name, type, value> triple

tuple : a tuple value

tuple value : a set of data attribute values

tuple scheme : the specification of the data attributes of a tuple, together with any constraints referencing a tuple value as a whole

relation : a relation value

relation value : a set of tuple values all having the same tuple scheme; informally, a table without significance to the order of or repetition of the values of its rows

relation scheme : the specification of the data attributes of a relation, together with other information such as keys and other constraints on a relation value as a whole

tuple variable : a symbol which can be bound to a tuple value

relation variable : a symbol which can be bound to a relation value

data independence : the ability to re-order data without losing any information

Chapter 17

NoSQL and SQL Physical Design

As you can see, the bulk of this book is spent explaining concepts of analysis and design, and teaching you how to represent things in the real world, and data about those things, in COMN models. Now we get to the final step that follows from analysis and design: expressing a physical database design in a COMN model. There are several goals for such a model:

1. We want the model to be as *complete and precise* as an actual database implementation, so that there's no question how to implement a database that follows from the model. This is especially important if we want to support model-driven development.

2. We want assurance that *the physical design exactly represents the logical design*, without loss of information and without errors creeping in.

3. We want the database implementation to *perform well*, as measured by all the criteria that are relevant to the application. We want queries by critical data to be fast. We want updates to complete in the time allowed and with the right level of assurance that the data will not be lost. The physical design process is the place where performance considerations enter in, after all the requirements have been captured and the logical data design complete.

WHAT'S DIFFERENT ABOUT NOSQL?

The most obvious difference between NoSQL and SQL databases is the support, or lack of it, for the Structured Query Language (SQL). However, times have changed, and it's no longer so easy to divide DBMSs into two strictly separate camps of SQL and NoSQL. Some NoSQL DBMSs have added SQL interfaces, to make it easier to integrate them into traditional database environments. The former distinction of ACID and BASE is melting away, as NoSQL DBMSs add ACID capabilities, and SQL databases provide tunable consistency to enable greater scaling. Finally, both SQL and NoSQL DBMSs are adding more ways to organize data. Some NoSQL DBMSs support tabular data organizations, and some SQL DBMSs support columnar and document data organizations.

As a result, the rejection of SQL has been softened, so that now "NoSQL" has been reinterpreted to mean "not only SQL". This reflects the realization that it's generally better to have a selection of physical data organization techniques at one's disposal. Being able to arrange one's data only as, say, a graph, can be just as limiting as being able to arrange one's data only as a set of tables. It's just as mistaken to have only a screwdriver in one's toolbox as it is to have only a hammer. One wants a toolbox with a hammer, a screwdriver, a hex wrench, and many other tools as well.

So, rather than present all of these DBMS characteristics divided into two overly simplistic categories of NoSQL and SQL, I will present the full list of DBMS capabilities regardless of whether SQL is the main data language.

DATABASE PERFORMANCE

Our task as physical database designers is to choose the physical data organization that best matches our application's needs, and then to leverage the chosen DBMS's features for the best performance and data quality assurance. This might lead us to choose a DBMS based on the data organization we need. However, sometimes the DBMS is chosen based on other factors such as scalability and availability, and then we need to develop a physical data design that adapts our logical data design to the data organizations available in the target DBMS.

The task of selecting the best DBMS for an application based on all the factors below and the bewildering combinations of features available in the marketplace, at different price points and levels of support, is far beyond the scope of this book to address. This chapter will equip you to understand the significance of the features of most of the DBMSs available today, and then—more importantly for the topic of this book—show you how to build physical models in COMN that express concrete representations of your logical data designs.

Physical design is all about performance, and there are several critical factors to keep in mind when striving for top performance:

- scalability: Make the right tradeoffs between ACID and BASE, consulting the CAP theorem as a guide. Know how large things could get—that is, how much data and how many users. You will need to know how much of each type of data you will accumulate, so that you can choose the right data organization for each type.

- indexing: Indexing overcomes what amounts to the limitations of the laws of physics on data. If a field is not indexed, you will have to scan for it sequentially, which can take a very long time. Add indexes to most fields which you want to be able to search rapidly, and consider the various kinds of indexes the DBMS offers you. But be aware of the tradeoffs that come with indexes.

- correctness: Make sure the logical design is robust before you embark on the physical design. There's nothing worse than an implementation that is fast but does the wrong thing. In this context, "robust" means complete enough that we don't expect that evolving requirements will require much more than extension of the logical design.

ACID versus BASE and Scalability

ACID

Almost all SQL DBMSs, plus a few NoSQL DBMSs, implement the four characteristics that are indicated by the acronym ACID: atomicity, consistency, isolation, durability. These four characteristics taken together enable SQL databases to be used in applications where the correctness of each database transaction is absolutely essential, such as financial transactions (think purchases, payments, and bank account deposits and withdrawals). In those kind of applications, getting just one transaction wrong is not acceptable.

Here is a guide to the four components of ACID.

Atomicity

A DBMS transaction that is **atomic** will act as though it is indivisible. An update operation that might update a dozen tables will either succeed completely or fail completely. Either all affected tables will be updated, or, if for some reason the update cannot completely succeed, tables that were updated will be rolled back to their pre-update state. A transaction might not complete because of errors in the update, or because a system crashed. It does not matter: An atomic transaction will appear to a DBMS user as if it either completely succeeded or completely failed.

Consistency

A DBMS can enforce many constraints on data given to it to store. The most fundamental constraints are built-in type constraints: string fields can only contain strings, date fields can only contain dates, numeric fields can only contain numbers, etc. Additional constraints can be specified by a database designer. We've talked a lot about foreign-key constraints, where a column of one table may only contain values found in a key column of another table. There can be what are called check constraints, which are predicates that must be true before data to be stored in a table is accepted.

Consistency is the characteristic that a DBMS exhibits where it will not allow a transaction to succeed unless all of the applicable constraints are satisfied. If, at any point in a transaction, a constraint is found which is not met by data in the transaction, the transaction will fail, and atomicity will ensure that all partial updates that may have already been written by the transaction are rolled back.

Isolation

Isolation is the guarantee given by a DBMS that one transaction will not see the partial results of another transaction. It's strongly related to atomicity. Isolation ensures that the final state of the data in a database only reflects the results of successful transactions; isolation ensures that, if a DBMS is processing multiple transactions simultaneously, each transaction will only see the results of previous successfully completed transactions. The transactions won't interfere with each other.

Durability

Durability is the guarantee that, once a transaction has successfully completed, its results will be permanently visible in the database, even across system restarts and crashes.

BASE AND CAP

ACID sounds great, and it really is great if one has an application where preserving the result of every transaction is critical. But ACID comes at a cost. It is difficult to build DBMSs that can leverage large farms of parallel servers to increase processing capacity, while achieving ACID. Large farms of parallel servers are needed to support millions of users and billions of transactions. Such databases are seen in companies like Facebook and Amazon. These large databases are designed to **scale horizontally**, meaning that greater performance is achieved by putting many computers side-by-side to process transactions in parallel, and the data is replicated many times over so that multiple copies may be accessed simultaneously for retrieving requested data. This is in contrast to the traditional approach of **scaling vertically**, meaning that a faster computer and larger storage are used for the DBMS. There are limits on how fast and large a single system can be made, but the limits are much higher on how many computers and how much storage can be set side-by-side.

Horizontal scaling is great, but the CAP theorem, put forward by Eric Brewer in 2000 [Brewer 2012], proves that, in a distributed DBMS, one may only have two of the following three attributes:

- **consistency**: This is a specialized form of the consistency of ACID. It does not refer to the enforcement of consistency constraints. Rather, it is the requirement that, in a DBMS that has many copies of the same data, all of the copies match each other. In a horizontally scaled database, one can guarantee that all the copies match each other, but only if either availability or partition tolerance is sacrificed.

- **availability**: With lots of computers accessing lots of storage over many network connections, there are bound to be failures at various points. That much hardware just has to have some pinpoint failures from time to time. But the motivation for having so many computers and so many copies of the same data is that, for any data request, there's a good likelihood that some working computer can access some copy of the data and satisfy the request, even if some of the computers are down or some of the storage is unavailable. 100% availability can be achieved, even in a network with some failures, but only if either consistency or partition tolerance is sacrificed.

- **partition tolerance**: A partitioning of a distributed system is a case where a network failure causes one subset of the computers in the distributed system to be unable to communicate to the rest of the computers. The result of a partitioning is that copies of the database maintained by different computers can get out of sync with each other. An update completed in one set of computers will be missed by the other set. A DBMS can be programmed to tolerate partitioning, but only at the sacrifice of either consistency or availability.

The CAP theorem forces you to see that you can't have your cake and eat it too. If your plan is to scale a DBMS horizontally by linking lots of computers side by side to maintain lots of copies of the same data, then you have to choose just two features out of consistency, availability, and partition tolerance.

Most NoSQL databases are designed to scale horizontally, and so because of CAP they can't offer ACID. They are described as achieving BASE (cute acronym):

- **Basic Availability**: Most of the data is available most of the time.
- **Soft state**: Unlike ACID, a "commit" of an update to a database might not always succeed. Some updates will be lost.
- **Eventual consistency:** After some internal failure, out-of-sync copies of data will eventually "catch up" with the correct copies.

BASE sounds a little scary, but sometimes it's all that's needed. For example, Facebook serves hundreds of millions of users, and probably couldn't do so effectively with ACID-strength guarantees. So they allow users to post with only a soft-state guarantee. Every now and then, a user's post gets lost. (It has happened to me.) The downside is minimal: a few users are occasionally slightly annoyed by having to re-type a short update. As long as this doesn't happen too often, Facebook is able to fulfill its mission of enabling hundreds of millions of users to share their personal lives and thoughts. This would not be possible with a traditional ACID approach.

A particular application might use both an ACID DBMS and a BASE DBMS, in combination, to achieve a certain mission. For example, a retail Web site might deliver product information and user reviews using a BASE DBMS, but run purchases and financial transactions on an ACID DBMS. A user would probably tolerate a review being lost, but not a purchase being lost or an account double-charged for one purchase.

NoSQL and SQL Data Organization

Under the covers, NoSQL and SQL DBMSs all use the same set of data structures that were worked out decades ago for organizing data for fast access. These structures include things called trees, linked lists, queues, arrays, hashes—and those venerable data structures, tables. What distinguishes DBMS types from each other is how they present these varied data storage structures to the DBMS user. NoSQL databases can be categorized into four types of data organization:

- key/value: an extremely simple data organization, where each record has a single key data attribute which is indexed for high-speed searching, and a "value", which is really just an object for storing arbitrary data whose structure is not known to the DBMS
- graph: storage of data defining graph nodes and edges
- document: storage of data in a form similar to ordinary text documents; usually using lots of nesting
- columnar: storage of data as columns of a table rather than in the traditional organization of rows of a table

When we add tables to this list—the traditional data organization of SQL databases—we see that we have five ways to organize our data physically.

KEY/VALUE DBMS

A system that organizes data as key/value pairs is arguably the simplest means of managing data that can justify calling the system a database management system. The main focus of a key/value DBMS is on providing sophisticated operations on key values, such as searching for exact key values and ranges of key values, searching based on hashes of the key values, searching based on scores associated with keys, etc. Once the application has a single key value, it can speedily retrieve or update the "value" portion of the key/value pair.

Key/value terminology is somewhat problematic, since the keys themselves have values. In reality, the "value" portion of key/value is just an object of some class that is unknown to the DBMS.

Because of the simplicity of key/value DBMSs, it is relatively easy to achieve high performance. The tradeoff is that the work of managing the "value" is left to the application. Some DBMSs are beginning to provide facilities for managing the "value" portion as JSON text or other data structures.

Mapping a logical record type to a model like this involves the following considerations:

- Each physical record class can have only one key, which could consist of one component or of a set of components treated as a unit (in other words, a composite key). This will be the only component that can be searched rapidly. If records need to be found by the value of more than one component, the data might have to be split into several physical record classes.

- To the DBMS, the "value" component is a blob, but to the application it's quite important. Therefore, it will behoove the designer and implementer to fully define the "value" components of the logical record.

Because key/value DBMSs don't support foreign key constraints, a greater burden is put on the application to ensure that only correct data is stored in a key/value database.

GRAPH DBMS

A graph DBMS supports the organization of data into a graph. There are only two kinds of model entities in a graph: **nodes** and **edges**. Graph data is usually drawn using ellipses or rectangles to represent nodes and lines or arcs to represent edges. In contrast to common practice in most applications of data modeling, graph data models usually depict entity instances rather than entity types. Figure 17-1 shows some graph data expressed using the COMN symbols for real-world objects (Sam), simple real-world concepts (Employee Role), and data values (2016-01-01).

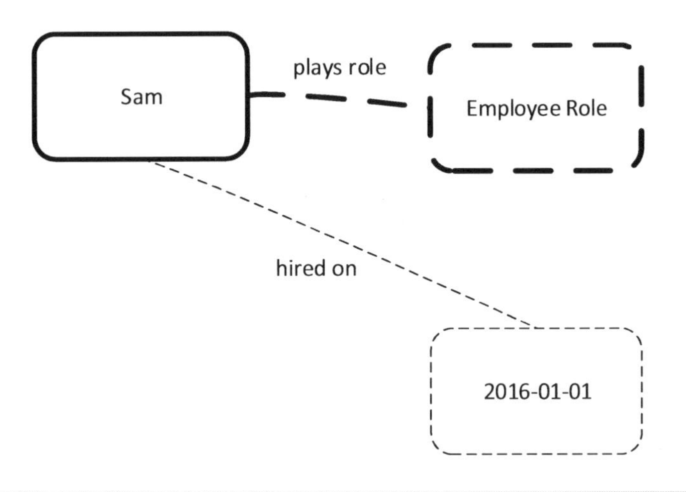

Figure 17-1. A Data Graph

Data expressed in the Resource Definition Framework (RDF), described in chapter 8, is especially suited to representation as a graph. An RDF triple maps directly to a graph. The subject and object of a triple are graph nodes, and the predicate is an edge. In RDF terms, the graph of Figure 17-1 illustrates two triples.

A data graph is valuable for expressing and exploring the relationships between various entities, and between entities and data attributes about them. Representing data in a graph makes it possible to use dozens of graph algorithms to analyze the data. Graph algorithms can be used to find the shortest way to visit many points, to search for similarities in large quantities of data, or to find graph nodes that are strongly related to each other. A data graph makes no distinctions between entities and their attributes, or, for that matter, data attributes. If the data in question is to be represented in a graph database, then such distinctions do not matter. However, one must be aware that such distinctions are lost in a graph database. Whether or not that matters depends on the nature of the application.

If one wishes to illustrate the permissible values of nodes in a graph database—in other words, add type and class information—one can do this by using the COMN symbols for types and classes. Figure 17-2 below expresses the expected types of the actual graph data in Figure 17-1.

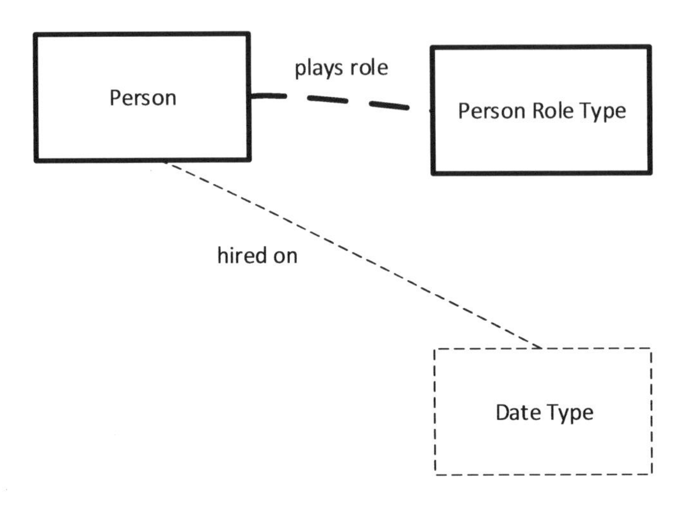

Figure 17-2. A Model of a Graph Type

Figure 17-2 is a mini-ontology, in that it expresses relationships which exist between a class of real-world objects (Person), a type of behavior of persons in the real world (Person Role Type), and a type of data (Date Type). As mentioned in chapter 8, COMN can be used as a graphical notation for ontologies.

DOCUMENT DBMS

At its interface, a document DBMS stores and retrieves textual documents. A document DBMS usually supports some partial structuring of documents using a markup language such as XML. Some so-called document DBMSs support JSON texts, often mistakenly called documents. A document is a primarily textual composite record type with possibly deep nesting. Usually, many of a document's components are optional. It is straightforward to model any document's structure in COMN as nested composite types; however, a non-trivial document might involve many types and might need to be split across a number of diagrams.

As with any database, speedy access to data will depend on important components being indexed. A database index is built and maintained by a DBMS by taking a copy of the values (or states) of all instances of a specified component or components, and recording in which documents those values are found. This is represented in COMN as a projection of data from the record or document collection to the index, and then a pointer back to the collection. DBMSs usually offer indexes in many styles. The particular index style can be indicated in the title bar of the index collection, in guillemets, as in «range index». This notation gives the class (or type) from which the current symbol inherits or is instantiated. See Figure 17-3 for an example. The Employee ID Index is defined as a physical record collection that is a projection from the full Employee Resume Collection of just the Employee ID component. The index is also an instance of a unique index, a class supported by the DBMS. The pointer back to the collection is implicitly indicating a one-to-one relationship from each index record to a document in the collection, which is true of a unique index. A non-unique index would require a "+" at the collection end of the arrow, indicating that one index record could indicate multiple documents or records in the collection.

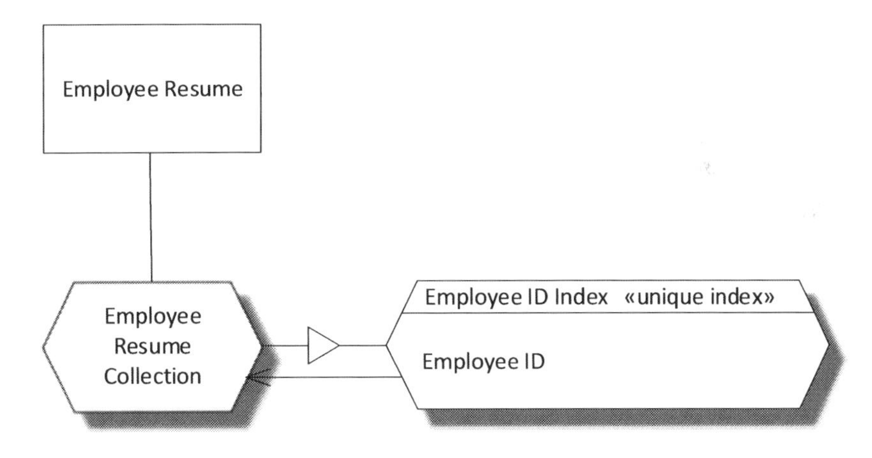

Figure 17-3. A Document Database Design with a Unique Index

COLUMNAR DBMS

A columnar DBMS presents data at its query interface in the form of tables, just as a SQL DBMS does. The difference is in how the data is stored.

Traditional table storage assumes that most of the fields in each row will have data in them. Rows of data are stored sequentially in storage, and indexes are provided for fast access to individual rows.

Sometimes it would be better if the data were sliced vertically, so to speak, and each column of data were stored in its own storage area. A traditional query for a "row" would be satisfied by rapidly querying the separate column stores for data relevant to the row, and assembling the row from those column queries that returned a result. However, columnar databases optimize for queries that retrieve just a few columns from most of the rows in a table. Such queries are common in analytical settings where, for example, all of the values in a column are to be summed, averaged, or counted. Columnar databases optimize read access at the cost of write access (it can take longer to write a "row" than in a row-oriented database), but this is often exactly what is needed for analytical applications.

Consider, for example, a database of historical stock prices. These prices, once written, do not change, but will be read many times for analysis. In a row-oriented database, each row would repeat a stock's symbol and exchange, as well as the date and open, high, low, and close prices on each trading day. A columnar database can store the date, open, high, low, and close each in their own columns and make time-series analysis of the data much more rapid.

Representing a columnar design in COMN involves modeling the columns, which are physical entities. This is quite straightforward to do, as a column is a projection of a table. Figure 17-4 below shows our example design, where the physical table class that represents the logical record type is shown projected onto a row class and five columnar classes.

TABULAR DBMS

Let's not forget about traditional tables as a data organization. Traditional tables can, of course, be used in SQL DBMSs, but increasingly NoSQL DBMSs support them, too.

The physical design of tabular data emphasizes several aspects for performance and data quality:

- indexing: Probably the most important thing to pay attention to in a tabular database design is to ensure that all critical fields are indexed for fast access. Add indexes carefully, because each index speeds access by the indexed data, but also increases the database size and slows updates.

- foreign keys: Foreign key constraints are valuable mechanisms for ensuring high data quality. They were covered in chapter 15.

- partitioning: Many DBMSs enable the specification of table partitions (and even index partitions). The idea is that each partition, being smaller than the whole table, can be searched and updated more quickly. Any query is first analyzed to determine which table partition(s) it applies to, and then the query is run just against the relevant partition.

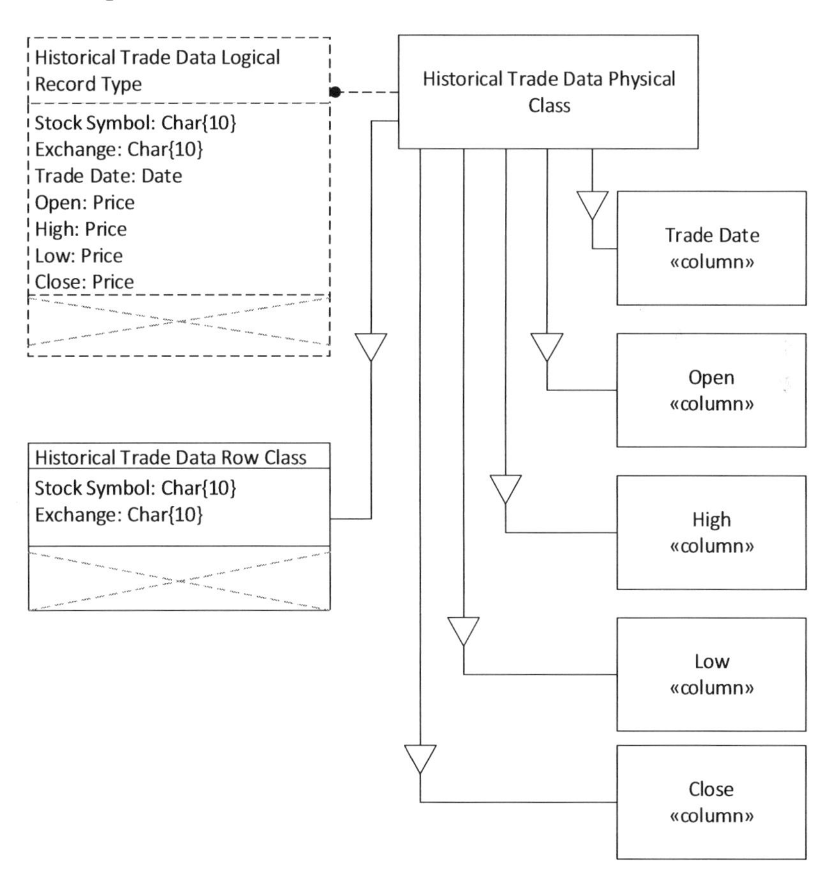

Figure 17-4. A Columnar Data Design

As explained under document DBMSs, an index is a projection of the table data into another table. The index type is given in the shape's title section, surrounded by guillemets.

Foreign key constraints were covered in depth in chapter 15. A physical design illustrating foreign key constraints would use the same symbols but solid outlines to connote physical classes implemented by the DBMS, rather than the dashed outlines used in logical data design. The only new thing to consider is how to model partitioning a table by rows—so-called horizontal partitioning. Each partition can be thought of as a table in its own right, containing a subset of the data. The subset is usually defined by some restriction on the data based on a value found in the data, such as a date. Figure 17-5 illustrates a horizontally partitioned row-oriented table.

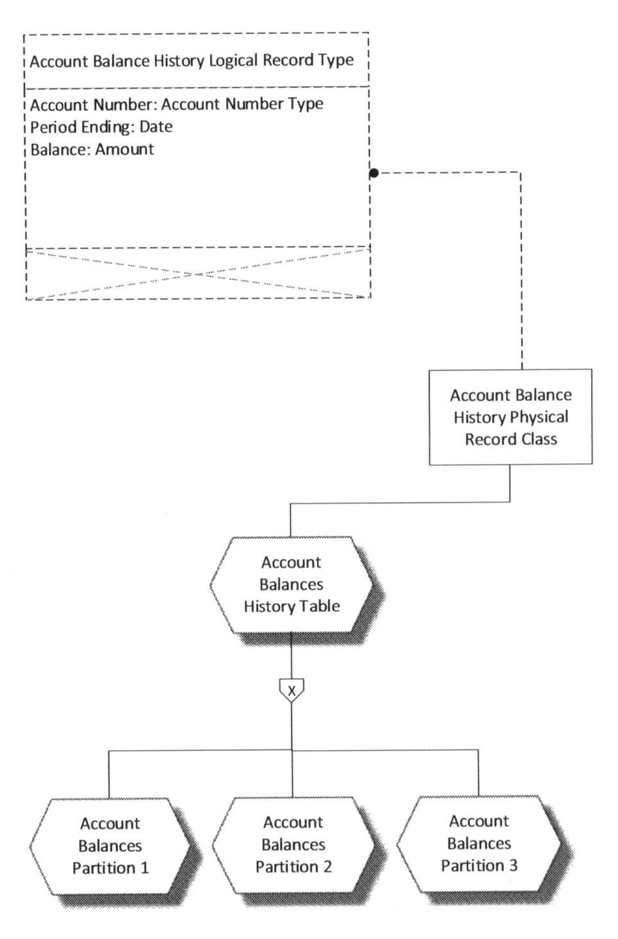

Figure 17-5. A Partitioned Row-Oriented Table

SUMMARY

COMN's ability to express all the details of physical design for a variety of data organizations means that the physical implementation of any logical data design can be fully expressed in the notation. COMN enables a direct connection to be modeled between a logical design and a physical design in the same model, enabling verification that the implementation is complete and correct. The completeness of COMN means that data modeling tools could use the notation as a basis for generating instructions to various DBMSs to create and update physical implementations. This makes model-driven development possible for every variety of DBMS.

REFERENCES

[Brewer 2012] Brewer, Eric. "CAP Twelve Years Later: How the Rules Have Changed." New York: Institute of Electrical and Electronic Engineers: *IEEE Computer,* February 2012, pp. 23-29.

Key Points

- Physical database design is the place where performance becomes paramount.
- Physical design should not begin until a robust logical data design has been completed.
- There are many physical data organizations available for implementation, including key/value, document, graph, columnar, and row-oriented tabular. Some DBMSs are specialized for exactly one form of data organization, and some are hybrid, supporting multiple organizations.
- DBMSs vary to the extent to which they can be scaled in size, and to the extent they support ACID and BASE transactional characteristics.
- DBMS selection must sort through the various intersections of data organization, ACID/BASE, scaling, performance, price, and support that appear in the marketplace. Matching a DBMS's data organization style to an application's needs is just one important aspect of DBMS selection.
- Many DBMSs achieve speed and scale by omitting features that applications have often used to achieve high data quality, such as type safety and foreign key constraints. Be sure to consider these aspects when selecting a DBMS.
- Data to be stored in a key/value DBMS should be modeled in its entirety, even though the DBMS sees the "value" only as a blob, because the application will need to know the structure of the "value".
- Graph data can be modeled in COMN using value and object symbols. A graph schema can be modeled with a graph of COMN type and class symbols.
- Database indexes, whether for documents or tables, are modeled in COMN as projections of the main record collection. A DBMS-specific index class can be noted in a shape's title, surrounded by guillemets (« »).
- A columnar data organization is modeled as projections of the record class onto multiple column classes.
- A horizontally partitioned row-oriented table is shown as a set of exclusive subsets of the main table.

Part IV

Case Study

In this section we will walk through a case study to document a sample business as it would exist in the real world, design the data needed to operate the business, and design a hybrid physical implementation that uses a document database and a tabular database. The result will be a single COMN model documenting data requirements, logical data design, and physical database implementation.

Chapter 18

The Common Coffee Shop

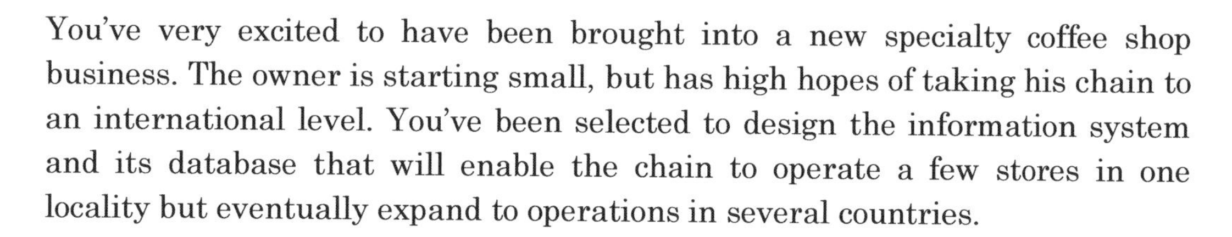

You've very excited to have been brought into a new specialty coffee shop business. The owner is starting small, but has high hopes of taking his chain to an international level. You've been selected to design the information system and its database that will enable the chain to operate a few stores in one locality but eventually expand to operations in several countries.

You've learned the value and discipline of model-driven development. You understand that your first task is to understand the business owner's requirements, and the business itself. You plan to document relevant aspects of the business, in COMN, so that you can then figure out what data will be needed to support operations and what analytics will be needed to support marketing. Only then will you begin the work of selecting appropriate DBMSs and designing the implementation classes for a high-quality, high-performance information system that will help this business go from inception to success.

Analysis: Documenting Real-World Entities

Every business involves certain real-world object classes and certain types of concepts which we can very quickly identify as relevant to our data modeling task. Real-world object classes include customers, employees, physical facilities, vendors, and products. Concept types include orders, purchases, and accounts payable and receivable.

Let's look first at where commerce begins in a coffee shop. A customer walks in, walks up to the counter, and places an order by speaking. The order could be as simple as, "Black coffee to go." It could be as complicated as, "I'd like two lattes: one small and one medium; a large hot chocolate with no whipped cream; and a bag of French-roast coffee. Could you grind the coffee for me, please?" This indicates the need for a data design exploding with possibilities.

Let's analyze. Figure 18-1 is a COMN model of some of the important things in the business that we must understand before we can begin to design data to represent these things. Some of these are objects and some are concepts.

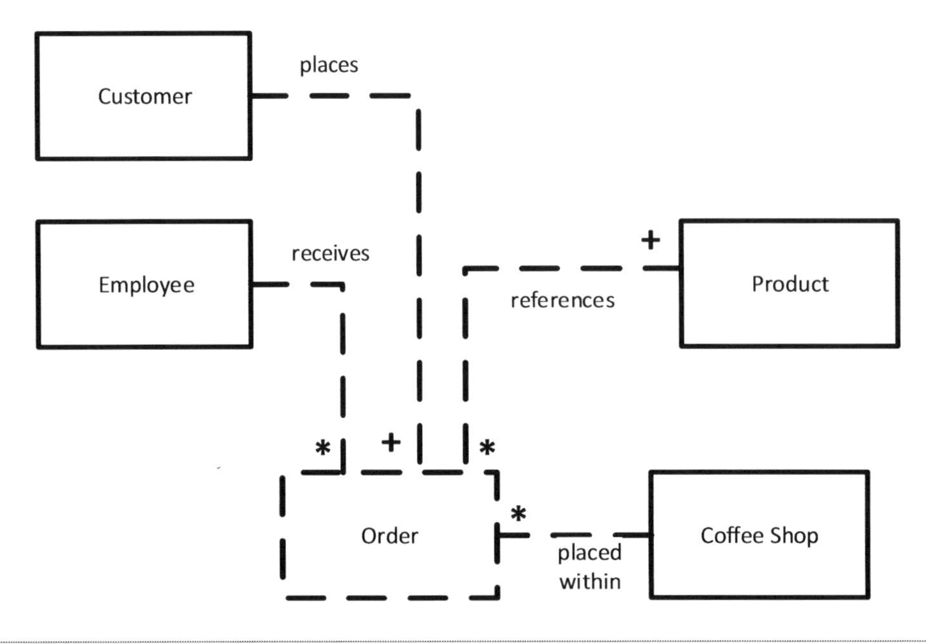

Figure 18-1. Real-World Entity Types in the COMN Coffee Shop

We saw back in chapter 13 that a customer is more specifically described as a person playing the role of customer. It was important to spell that out in chapter 13 so that we could understand how roles work, but now we'll abbreviate the name of that same real-world class, a subtype of the Person class, to merely Customer. The rectangle representing the set of customers gets a bold solid outline, because persons are real-world physical objects. The class of employee—persons playing the role of employee—is similarly represented as a rectangle with a bold solid outline.

A customer speaks, and an order is expressed. The order did not exist as a stable set of physical objects that we could observe. It existed first in the mind of the customer, then briefly as sound waves vibrating in the air, and finally the order existed in the mind of the employee working at the counter. The order is a real-world concept that is shared ever so briefly between customer and employee. To reflect this, we draw the type of orders as a bold, dashed outline.

A customer places an order. We annotate the relationship line from Customer to Order with the verb "places". Since this can be read correctly in a left-to-right direction, we don't include an arrow to indicate reading direction, although it would be not wrong to do so. Since Order is conceptual, its relationship to Customer is also conceptual, so the relationship line is drawn dashed. A particular customer may, at different times, place many orders. However, we don't consider a person a customer until she places at least one order. So we show a plus sign on the Customer to Order relationship line, next to the Order type, to indicate that the multiplicity of the relationship from Customer to Order is 1 or more. A particular order cannot be given by more than one customer, so we don't indicate multiplicity at the other end of the line. This indicates by default that an Order is placed by exactly one Customer.

A particular employee may, at different times, receive many orders. We have placed an asterisk on the Employee-to-Order relationship line, next to the Order type, to indicate this. Since an order is received by only one employee at a time, we don't indicate multiplicity at the other end of the line. This is in keeping with a business rule that any particular order is the responsibility of exactly one employee.

The order mentioned products. All of our coffee shop's products are physical objects, so we represent the class of products as a rectangle with a bold, solid outline. An order must mention at least one product, so the Order-to-Product relationship line has a plus sign at the Product end to indicate a multiplicity of one or more. Since any product can be referenced by any number of orders, including none (either because the product is being offered for the first time or is a total failure), there is an asterisk at the Order end of the line.

Each order must be placed within a coffee shop, so there is a Coffee Shop real-world class shown, and the multiplicity of the relationship from Order to Coffee Shop is exactly one, which is indicated by default in the absence of any explicit notation at the Coffee Shop end of the relationship line. In the reverse direction, there can be any number of orders placed within a given coffee shop, including none if the coffee shop just opened. Therefore there is an asterisk at the Order end of the same relationship line.

As the example orders above indicated, each product mentioned in an order can get pretty complicated, with sizes, flavors, and optional ingredients. There can be requests for processing products before delivery, such as a request to grind whole-bean coffee. Figure 18-2 shows a fraction of the product offerings. This diagram illustrates how straightforward it is for COMN to show the composition of real-world objects. Each object class that is a subtype of the Product class—indicated by an unadorned line connecting the class to the exclusive subtype pentagon—is the class of a product that is sold directly to a customer. Some of these products are also blended (double arrowhead) into other products. For example, espresso is sold as a product, but is also blended into cappuccino and latte. Hot chocolate is a blend of cocoa mix and one of four different types of a milk-type ingredient; whipped cream can be optionally added on top (aggregated).

It's important to note that, although Figure 18-2 clearly shows that there are three exclusive subtypes of bagged whole-bean coffee, we don't show that the supertype is a product. Instead, each of the three subtypes is a product. It would not be wrong to show the supertype as a product, and then provide a means to indicate which type of bagged coffee the customer wanted. However, we're thinking of the idea that each type of bagged coffee will have its own Universal Product Code (UPC) encoded in a bar code directly on the bag. We want to sell each type of bagged coffee as its own product, not as a subtype of some abstract supertype of product. Categorization is a process we humans do almost without thought, but it can get in the way of proper analysis and data design. We keep the supertype off to the side as a way to document that three of our products are bagged whole-bean coffee products, but we don't force that vocabulary on our customers and coffee shop workers. Later on we might want to classify sales of bagged whole-bean coffee products together in a marketing analysis report, so the supertype might be useful later on—but not when we're trying to understand how customers order products.

We are limited in this book to rather small diagrams. In a facilitated requirements-gathering session with business stakeholders, full-size models can be drawn on large whiteboards or large sheets of paper. Afterwards, these drawings can be entered into an electronic drawing tool that doesn't have strict size limitations.

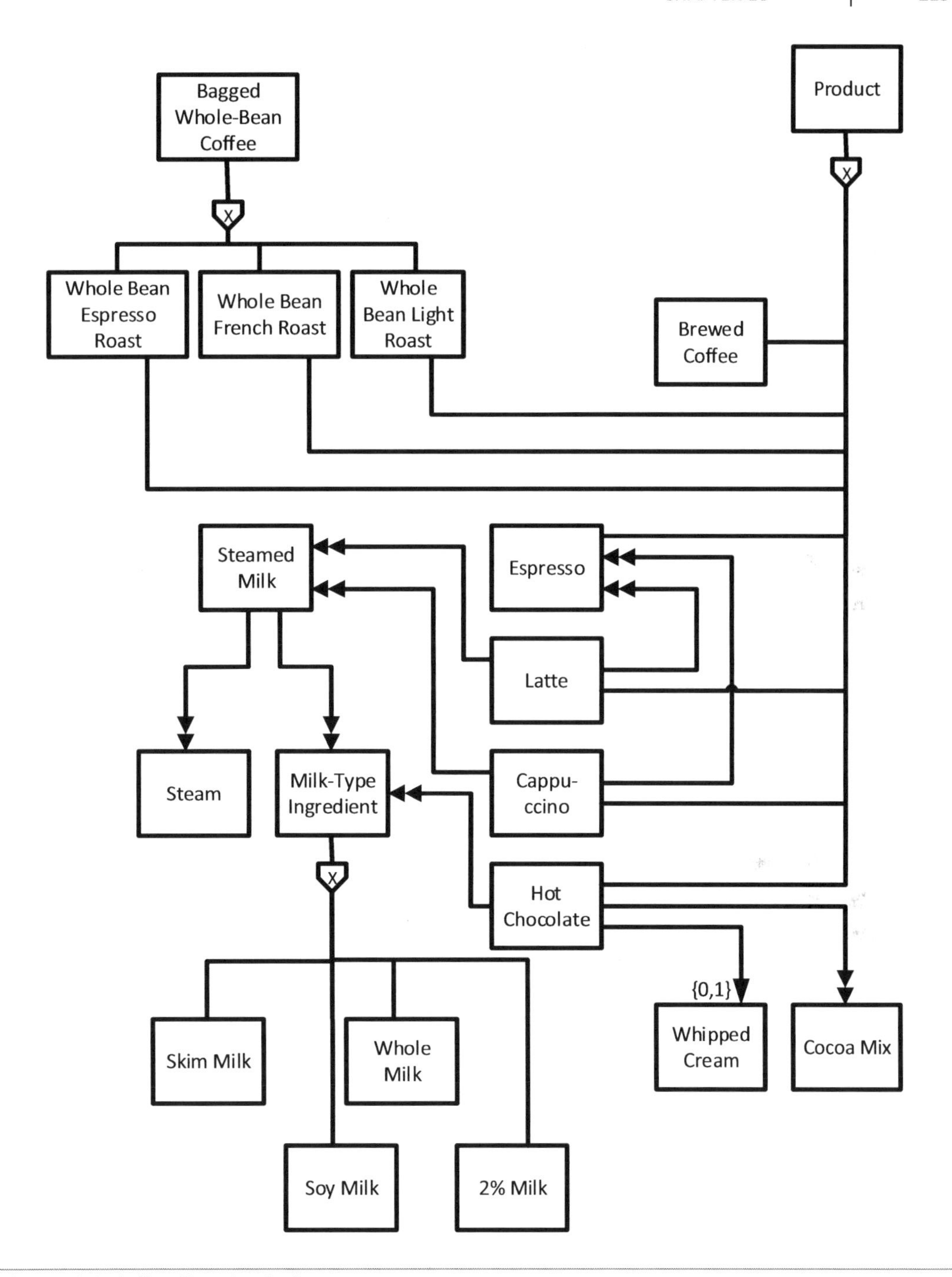

Figure 18-2. Coffee Shop Products

LOGICAL DATA MODELING: DESIGNING THE DATA

In chapter 13 we documented our logical data design for tracking data about customers and employees, and connected it to the real-world classes of Coffee-Shop Person, Employee, and Customer. Let's turn our attention to the order, which is a central part of our coffee shop business (and indeed, of any business).

Figure 18-3 shows a logical data design for orders that references the real-world entity types and classes of Figure 18-1. We can carefully examine this model to ensure that every real-world entity type in Figure 18-1 is represented by some data in Figure 18-3, and that the relationship multiplicities given in Figure 18-1 are able to be represented by the corresponding data types. Let's see how this works.

Each relationship line—each line with a solid circle at one end—shows a one-to-one relationship from some logical record collection to the real-world type or class it represents. For the most part, the relationships between the record collections and the real-world types that they represent are parallel. But it's a little more complicated with the order record collection. In the real world, an order references one or more products. However, in our data design an order does not represent products directly. Instead, we see that an order record collection is composed of one or more order items, and each order item references exactly one product in the product record collection. So the multiplicities of the relationship from order to product are preserved in the data: one order has one or more order items, and each order item references a product, so one order (indirectly) references one or more products. Thus, the multiplicities in the real-world model of the entity types in the business are preserved in our logical data model.

The relationship line from the Order data record collection to the Order Item data type indicates that an Order is composed of one or more Order Items. The multiplicity in the reverse direction says that an Order Item cannot stand alone; it must always be related to an order.

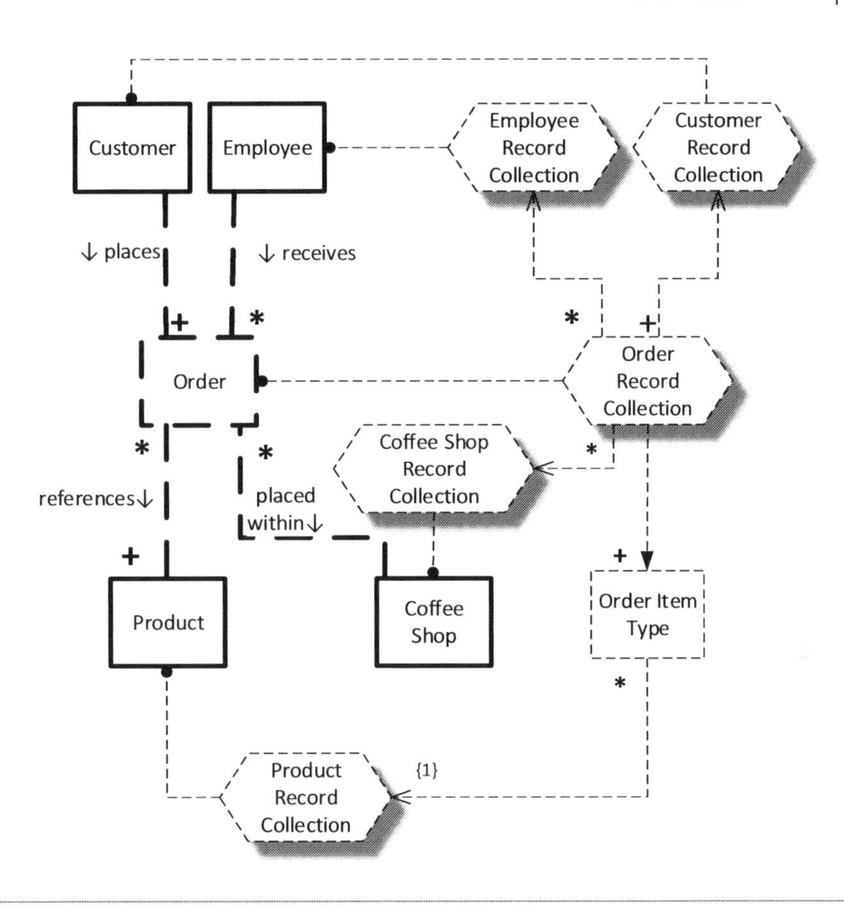

Figure 18-3. Coffee Shop Order

So far, so good. However, we have a few gaps. We have not yet decided how our order will identify our products, our employees, and our customers. We don't have a means for identifying the coffee shop within which each order is placed. Identification is an issue centered mostly in data. We're going to need more space in our diagram to develop our identification schemes. Since we've confirmed that our data model accurately represents the real world, in Figure 18-4 we've dropped the real entity types, and redrawn just the logical record collection hexagons and logical types of Figure 18-3 in the three-section form. This gives us the room we need to show the components of the records in the collections.

This diagram will illustrate the significant difference in a logical data design between composition and reference. An order *is composed of* order items, but merely *references* a customer, an employee, and a coffee shop. What's the difference here?

Data we can't identify separately can only exist as a component of some other data. In our data model we've decided that we must be able to reference data about employees, customers, products, orders, and coffee shops, because, in the real world, they all stand apart from each other. For one instance of data to reference another instance of data, it must have some value by which to *identify* the referenced data. From relational theory we know that the data attribute or attributes of some data record that distinguish it from all other data records in a set are its **key**, and that the value of a key is an *identifier* of a particular record in that set. This is a true statement whether the data in questions is stored in tables, in graph nodes, in documents, or in some other form. Relational theory is not limited to describing the storage of data in tables. In fact, we need to understand when we need keys in our data before we get to the question of how we'll store the data.

So, in order for us to enable an Order to reference a customer, an employee, and a coffee shop, we must have keys for the three corresponding record collections. They are indicated in each record collection rectangle as components with a (PK) suffix. "PK" stands for primary key. A composite data type may have more than one key. Each additional key is identified by "AK" for alternate key, and can be numbered, as in AK1, AK2, etc. No alternate keys are used in this design.

We also want to be able to reference orders by some kind of identifier. In a busy coffee shop, employees might need to communicate to each other about which order they are working on. And since we plan for the business to grow, we know we're going to want to analyze order data that's been collected across many coffee shops and many days. So orders need keys, too. The key for the Order data type is particularly interesting. It is composed of two components (two data attributes). We call such a key a **composite** (or **compound**) **key**. A key with a single data attribute is a **simple key**. Since an order is always placed within a single coffee shop, we have designed orders to be identified by a simple integer sequence, Order ID, but qualified by the Coffee Shop ID—the data attribute playing the role of describing In (which) Coffee Shop the order was placed. This design allows a database in each coffee shop to assign key values—identifiers—to orders that don't overlap with other coffee shops' key values, simply because each coffee shop has its own unique Coffee Shop ID.

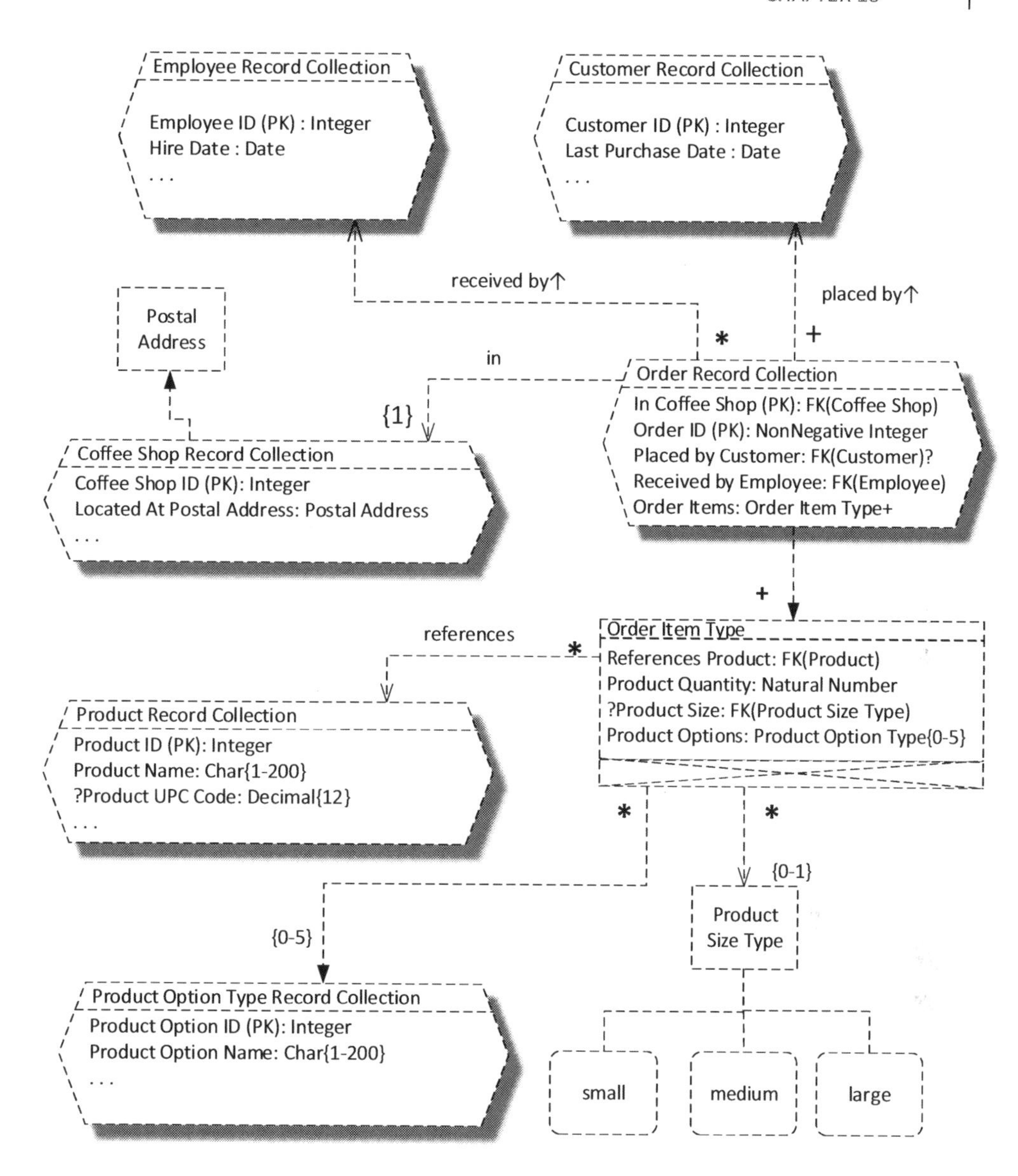

Figure 18-4. Coffee Shop Order Data Types with Components

An order's In Coffee Shop data attribute has an interesting type, FK(Coffee Shop). "FK" stands for foreign key. We learned in chapter 16 that a foreign key constraint defines a subtype. The type of the In Coffee Shop data attribute is the set of all values which are key values of the Coffee Shop record set. We can see that the primary key of the Coffee Shop data type is the data attribute Coffee Shop ID, which has a type Integer. Therefore, we know that Order's In Coffee Shop supertype is Integer. The FK(Coffee Shop) notation is much more informative than a mere "Integer". Order's key is therefore dependent on Coffee Shop's key.

Each order also references the Employee Record Collection and the Customer Record Collection using foreign keys. But the type of the data attribute Placed by Customer—the foreign key—is followed by a question mark. When a data attribute's type is followed by a question mark, this means that it is possible that, at the time a record is written, the value for this data attribute might not be known. There is no question that every order is placed by a customer—there is no question mark before the data attribute's name—but we are well aware that we don't always know the identity of each customer, and that's OK. We'll record the identities of those customers who have signed up for our frequent buyer program, but for the rest we'll just leave the customer ID value as "unknown".

"Unknown" is completely different from "optional", which we'll see is used in the order item record collection and elsewhere.

Product Quantity is simply a natural number. A natural number is a counting number (1, 2, 3, . . .) and so is always greater than zero. It doesn't make sense to have an order item for zero products. By choosing a natural number type rather than a rational number type, we disallow fractional quantities of products. A customer can't order half a cup of coffee.

It would be so tempting to aggregate Product Size Type directly into Order Item Type, as it appears on the surface that nothing could be simpler than indicating whether a product size ordered is small, medium, or large. However, we're thinking about our business expanding globally. As soon as we expand into a multi-lingual market such as Canada, we will need to support expressing the same product sizes in multiple languages; for example, *petit*, *médium*, and *grand*. Therefore we've chosen for Order Item Type to reference Product Size Type, so that we can look up the appropriate language in which to express size to the customer. The Product Size component is preceded by a question mark, meaning that it's optional. Size does not apply to every type of product. As explained above, an optional data attribute, indicated by a question mark preceding its name, is not the same as a potentially unknown, indicated by a question mark following its type. If size does apply to a product, we must know which size the customer selects.

Our design allows for up to five options to be specified as values of the Product Option Type. For the sake of brevity, we've omitted the design for data about product options. As with product size data, we want to reference product option data so that we can support multiple languages.

The designs for Employee Record Collection and Customer Record Collection were described in chapter 13. We have two remaining record collection designs to look at, namely Coffee Shop Record Collection and Product Record Collection.

Each coffee shop will be identified by a simple natural number, which carries no particular meaning, other than indirectly through the fact that the first coffee shop we open will be coffee shop #1. The most distinct fact about a coffee shop that we'll record is its postal address. We will aggregate the Postal Address type directly into each coffee shop record, since we don't need to make sure that coffee shop postal addresses can stand alone. Therefore, no key is needed for coffee shop postal addresses. We might make a different choice for customer postal addresses. For example, we might want to know when two customers share an address, as that might indicate that they are part of the same household, and we might want to combine marketing efforts to all customers in the same household. We will not explore such a design here. The ellipsis indicates that there are other coffee shop record components that are not shown. These could include such things as the date on which the coffee shop was opened, the date on which it was closed if it is no longer in operation, etc.

Products will also be identified by simple, meaningless natural numbers. A product record optionally carries a Universal Product Code (UPC), which is that number associated with a scannable bar code. Some products, such as bagged coffee, will be marked with UPCs, but it doesn't make sense to have a UPC on a product that can't be scanned, such as a cup of coffee. As with Product Size Type, we want to be able to refer to our products with language-specific names, so we've separated product names into their own record collection. The primary key for Product Name Record Collection is a composite key. One data attribute of the key is a foreign key to the Product Record Collection. The other data attribute has the ISO 639-1 Code as its type. That code is the international standard for referencing human languages. The two data attributes together identify a language-specific name for a product.

In summary, we can see that one of the most important issues driving logical data design is whether a given type of data needs to be able to be referenced separately from other data or can be incorporated into other data without its own key.

PHYSICAL DATA MODELING: DESIGNING THE IMPLEMENTATION

We've reviewed the logical data model with our business stakeholders, and we're reasonably certain that our data as designed will adequately represent all of the entities involved in daily coffee shop operations. Now it's time to choose a physical representation for the data.

It is at the point of physical data design that performance considerations come in. We want to make sure that access to the data is efficient in the contexts where it's used. We are going to think about two usage contexts. The first usage is in coffee shop operations, where orders must be able to be captured quickly. Fast update is a concern. The second usage is in marketing analytics, where we collect orders from coffee shops throughout our empire, and want to look across all of the data to be able to compare such things as which kinds of products sell best in which regions and which are the busiest times of day.

For coffee shop operations, the most straightforward design is to represent an order, together with its items, as a single document. We'll choose a NoSQL document database for our in-coffee-shop operational database management system. That means that each of the independent logical record collections of Figure 18-4 will be represented as a document collection. Figure 18-5 shows the physical design.

The physical record collections depicted here have type names given in guillemets (« »). A type name in guillemets in a record collection indicates the type of the instance. For example, the Customer «document collection» is an instance of a DBMS document collection named Customer. In a physical data model targeting a specific DBMS, the DBMS's type name would be used within the guillemets.

The modeling of indexes deserves special attention. The Customer «unique index» is an instance of a DBMS unique index named customer. The extension symbol with its narrow side towards the index expresses the fact that the index contains a *projection* of the document collection—a vertical slice, so to speak—where only certain data attributes of each document are included in the index.

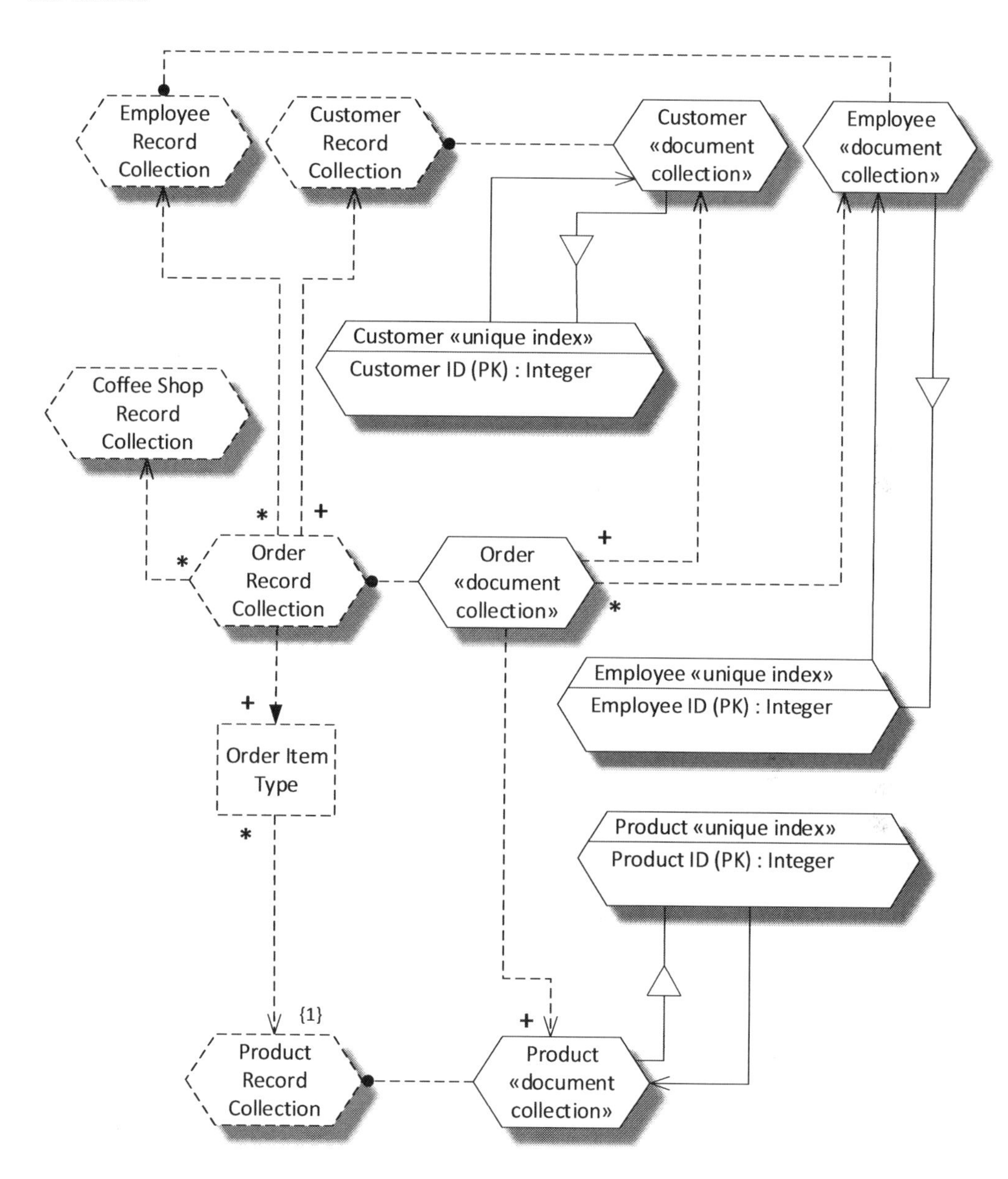

Figure 18-5. Coffee Shop Document Database

The Customer «unique index» symbol shows that only the Customer ID is included. This use of projection of a record collection expresses physical data copying. Fortunately, the DBMS takes care for us that the copied data in the index always stays in sync with the original data in the document collection. The non-dashed arrow pointing to the Customer «document collection» indicates that each record in the index has a one-to-one *physical* relationship to a record in the document collection. If an index were non-unique, then it would have a plus sign at the document collection end of the arrow, showing that a single index entry might reference multiple records, but would always reference at least one.

Most, but not all, of the logical record collections and types are represented by document collections. We intend each coffee shop to have its own copy of the database, and we don't see the need to store data about all the other coffee shops in each coffee shop's database, so there's no document collection representing the coffee shop record collection. The Order Item Type is aggregated into the Order record collection, so it doesn't need a separate representation by its own document collection. All the rest of our logical record collections are represented by document collections.

The unique indexes on the primary keys of the document collections enable fast lookup of customers, employees, and products, which is all we need for fast order entry in the shop. But when we want to analyze this data later, we will need much more flexible navigation through the data. Figure 18-6 shows a data warehouse designed to represent the same logical data with an entirely different physical structure. This is a dimensional warehouse design to be implemented in a SQL database. In this design, the Order Item «SQL Table» is the central fact table, and there are separate tables for the Customer, Employee, Product, Order, and Coffee Shop dimensions. Unlike our operational database, Coffee Shop data is now represented, as we're collecting data in our warehouse from all of our coffee shops.

Following the physical data modeling pattern presented for the coffee shop operational database design, we can use this diagram to confirm that we've represented multiplicities correctly, then create another diagram that drops the logical data and expands the tables to show their components. We can show unique and non-unique indexes on the tables. Following traditional techniques for dimensional data warehouse modeling, we can add additional fact tables and additional dimensions.

Using the expressive Concept and Object Modeling Notation, we can model the types of entities—types of concepts and types of objects—that are present in a problem domain, model at a logical level the data we will use to identify and describe those types of entities, and model at a physical level how we will arrange our representations of that data.

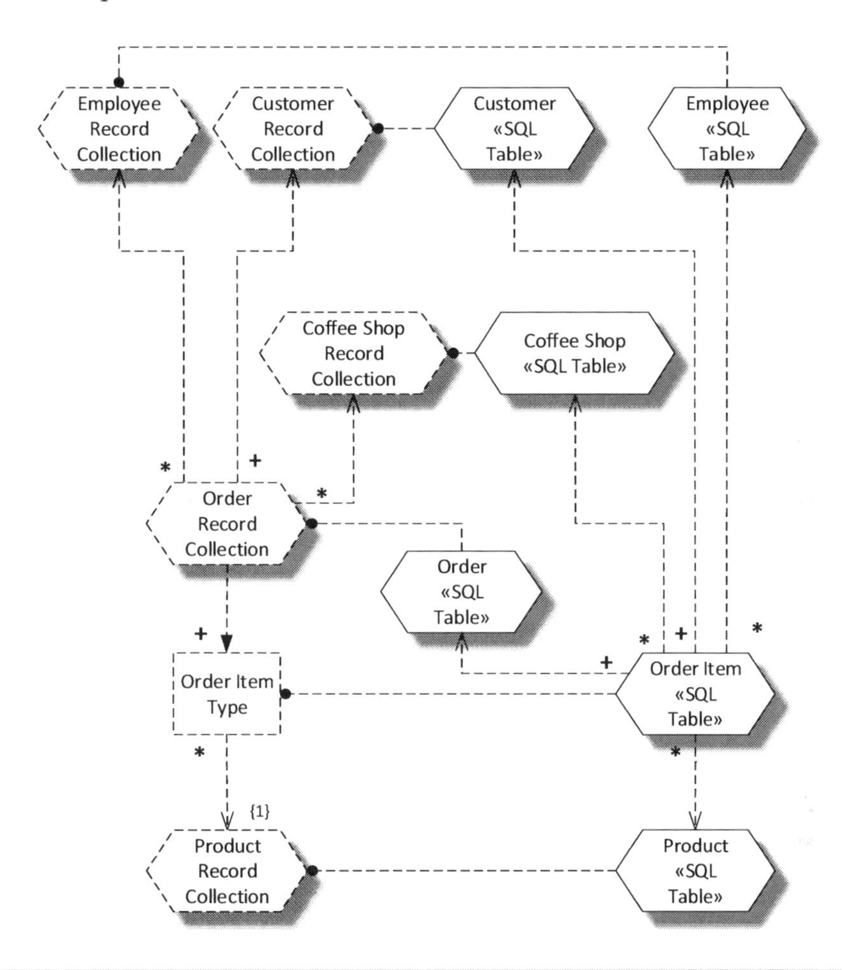

Figure 18-6. The Order Item Fact Table in the Coffee Shop Data Warehouse

We can model how the data will represent the real-world entities in the problem domain, and confirm at every stage of modeling that we have preserved the same relationships in the data as exist in the real-world entities. We can take the physical model to a level of detail where implementation in a NOSQL database and/or a SQL database can be mechanically derived from the physical model, and therefore something that could be fully automated. COMN enables model-driven development from the identification of problem-space entity types all the way through to multiple physical implementations of the same data.

APPENDIX
COMN Quick Reference

A complete reference for the Concept and Object Model Notation can be found at the author's Web site at http://www.tewdur.com/. This appendix provides a quick reference for use with this book.

Figure A-1 shows the hexagons, rectangles, and rounded rectangles used by COMN to represent entities, types of entities, and the states or values of entities. It also illustrates the meaning of the four different types of outline. A shadow on a shape represents a collection of that which is represented by the shape. The symbols as shown represent composite entities. Add crossed lines through a shape to indicate that it is simple, representing entities that have no components.

Figure A-2 shows the kinds of relationship lines that do not express composition, and Figure A-3 shows the kinds of relationship lines that express composition. Arrowheads on the lines indicate the direction of reference (and not data flow). Arrows that are part of the label text indicate reading direction. Labels on the lines having arrowheads are unnecessary, as such lines only ever have a single meaning. However, labels are strongly recommended to provide the names and readings of relationships, and to identify the roles played by participants in the relationships. Labels on unadorned lines are always necessary unless the lines are between dissimilar polygons, in which case they have only one meaning. Line weights (normal, bold) and style (solid, dashed) indicate whether the relationship is in the computer (normal weight) or the real world (bold weight) and whether the relationship is physical (solid line) or conceptual (dashed line).

Figure A-4 shows the pentagon symbol for restriction (that is, subtyping) and the triangle for extension. Extension can only apply to composite base types or classes. The relationships may be read in either direction. The labels on the lines are unnecessary, as the meaning of the lines is fixed when connecting these kinds of symbols. An arrowhead may be placed on a line to indicate direction of reference. An X in the center of the pentagon or triangle indicates exclusivity. Restriction and extension also applies to variables and objects.

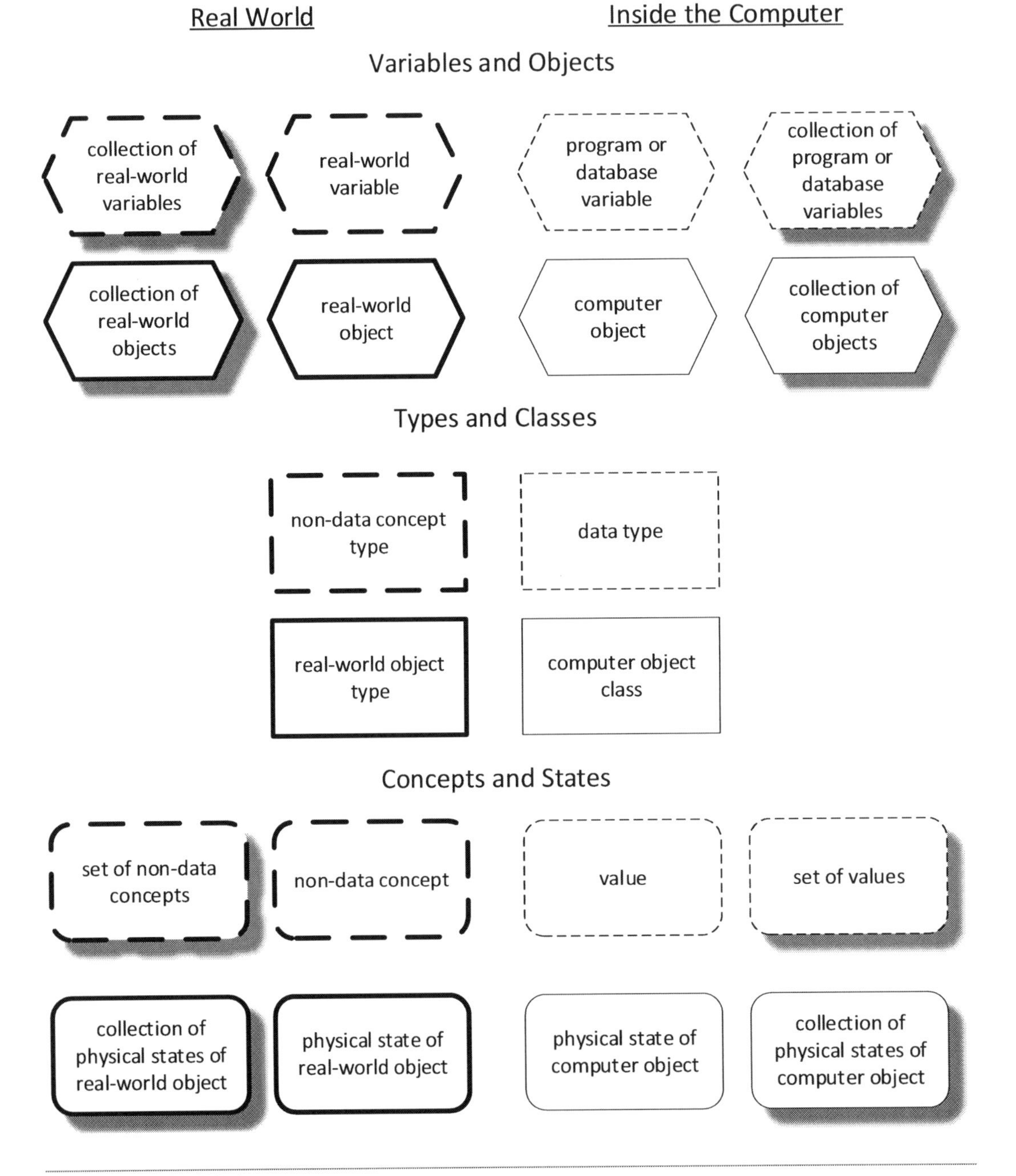

Figure A-1. COMN Polygons

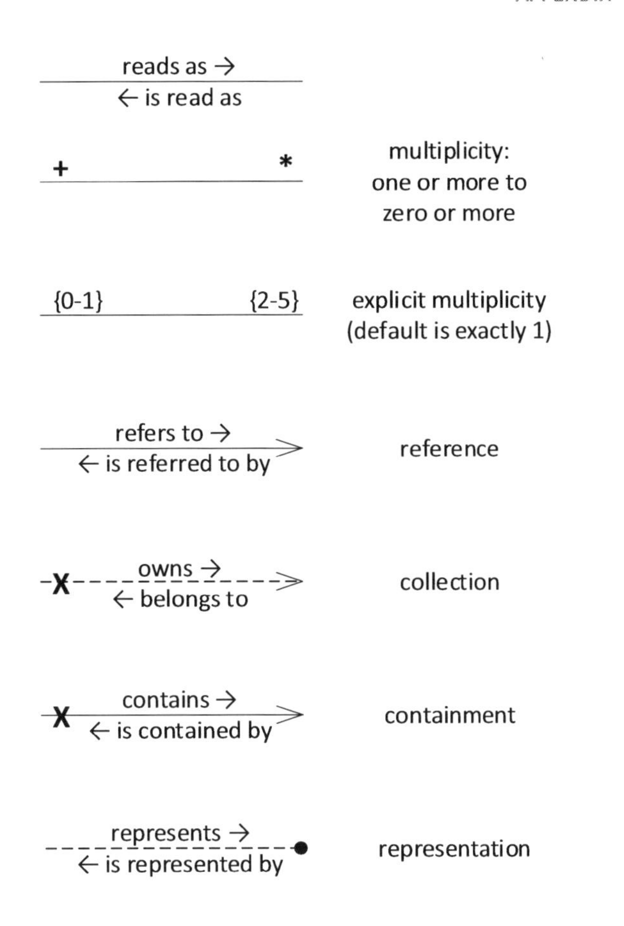

Figure A-2. Non-Composition Relationship Lines

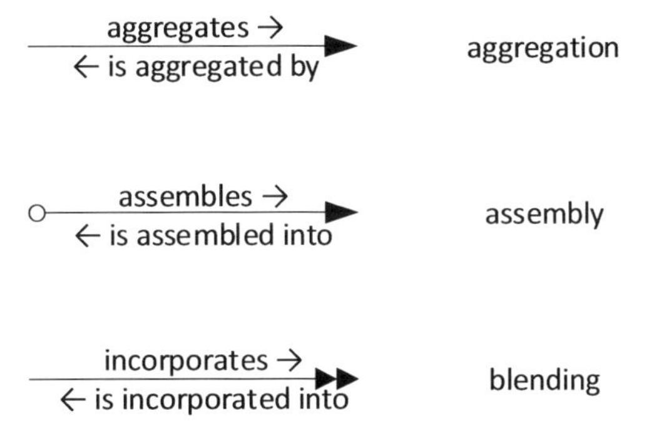

Figure A-3. Composition Relationship Lines

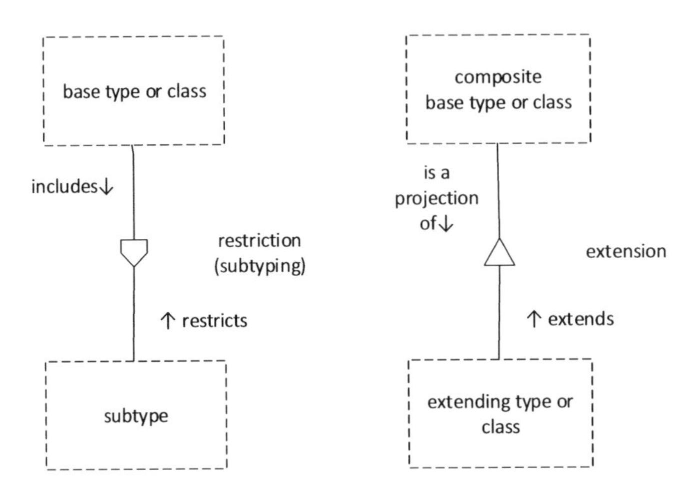

Figure A-4. Restriction (Subtyping) and Extension.

Figure A-5 shows the symbols for composite types, variables, and concepts, when it is desired to list their components. The outlines of these symbols may be varied to depict real-world (bold) and/or physical (solid) entity types, entities, and concepts or states. If a type or class does not encapsulate its components, then the bottom section for methods is crossed out.

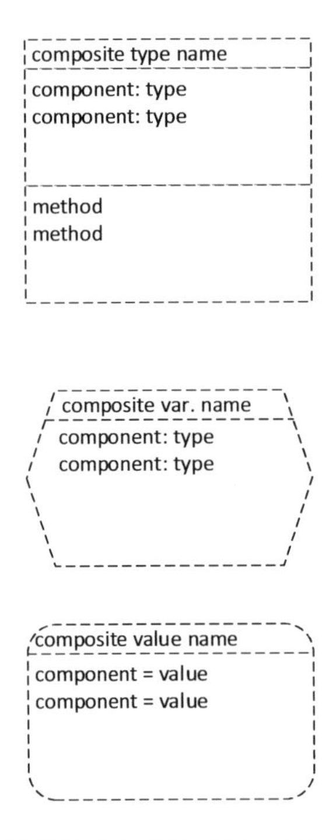

Figure A-5. Symbols for Composite Entities Showing Components

Glossary

Definitions marked (Merriam-Webster) are taken from Merriam-Webster's Online Dictionary at http://www.merriam-webster.com/dictionary/.

aggregation : combining two or more objects in such a way that they retain their integrity, but it is difficult or impossible to separate them again (like a layer cake)

analytics : information derived from other information or data

array : a collection of some integral number of variables or objects of the same type or class

assembly : combining two or more objects in such a way that they retain their integrity, and it is relatively easy to separate them again (like an engine)

attribute : an inherent characteristic (Merriam-Webster); see also data attribute

blending : combining two or more objects in such a way that they lose their integrity (like eggs, flour, milk, and sugar in a cake)

class : a description of the structural and/or behavioral characteristics of potential or actual objects

collection : a set of objects having a single owner

component : a constituent part (Merriam-Webster)

composite : made up of distinct parts (Merriam-Webster)

composite type : a type that designates a set whose members have components

computer object : a stateful material object whose state can be read and/or modified by the execution of computer instructions

concept : something conceived in the mind : thought, notion (Merriam-Webster)

conceptual : relating to a concept or concepts

container : an object that can contain other objects (like an egg carton)

contents : the objects inside a container (like the eggs in an egg carton)

data : plural of datum

data attribute : a <name, type> pair. The name gives the role of a value of the given type in the context of a tuple scheme, relation scheme, or composite type; see also attribute

data attribute value : a <name, type, value> triple

data independence : the ability to re-order data without losing any information

datum : that which is intended to be given to a predicate as a value for one of its variables

encapsulate : to authorize only a certain set of routines (called **methods** of the class) to operate on the components of objects of a class

entity : something that has separate and distinct existence and objective or conceptual reality (Merriam-Webster)

extending class (or type) : a class (or type) that is defined in terms of another class (or type), called a **base class (or type)**, by defining components and/or methods to what are already available in the base class (or type)

extension : the addition of components to a base class or type; its inverse is projection

fact : a proposition that is true or believed to be true

fact type : see relationship type

hardware object : a computer object which is part of the physical composition of a computer

identifier : any value that represents exactly one member of a designated set

inclusion relationship : a relationship between types, where the supertype is defined as a union of its subtypes; inverse of restriction relationship

information : a collection of propositions

insight : information derived from analytics

juxtaposition : arranging objects in a fixed spatial relationship without connecting them (like a place setting)

logical predicate : a statement containing variables which, when the variables are bound, yields a proposition

logical record type : a composite type that is intended to be used as the type of data records stored singly or in a collection of records

measure : a composite type consisting of a number and a type of thing being measured or counted

method : a routine authorized to operate on the components of software objects of the class of which it is a part

object : something material that may be perceived by the senses (Merriam-Webster)

predicate : short for **logical predicate**

projection : the removal of components from a base class or type; its inverse is **extension**

proposition : an expression in language or signs of something that can be believed, doubted, or denied or is either true or false (Merriam-Webster)

relation : a relation value

relationship type : a logical predicate

relation scheme : the specification of the data attributes of a relation, together with other information such as keys and other constraints on a relation value as a whole

relation value : a set of tuple values all having the same tuple scheme; informally, a table without significance to the order of or repetition of the values of its rows

relation variable : a symbol which can be bound to a relation value

relationship : a proposition concerning two or more entities

relationship type : a logical predicate

restriction relationship : a relationship between two types, where one type, called the subtype, is defined in terms of a restriction on members of the set designated by the other type, called the supertype; inverse of inclusion relationship

semi-structured data : collections of data items stored in a way that supports but does not enforce a structure

simple type : a type that designates a set whose members have no components

software object : an object composed of hardware objects and/or other software objects by exclusively authorizing only certain routines to access the component objects

state : the physical condition of an object

stateful : having more than one state

stateless : having only one state

structured data : collections of data items stored in a database that imposes a strict structure on that data

subtype : something that designates a subset of the set designated by another type, called the **supertype**

tuple : a tuple value

tuple scheme : the specification of the data attributes of a tuple, together with any constraints referencing a tuple value as a whole

tuple value : a set of data attribute values

tuple variable : a symbol which can be bound to a tuple value

type : something that designates a set

unstructured data : data representing text, audio, video or other data which have no structure imposed on what they represent

value : a concept that is fully specified by a symbol for the concept; also, a symbol for such a concept

variable : a symbol that may be bound to a value

Photo and Illustration Credits

p. 2, oil refinery: Philadelphia Energy Solutions
http://pes-companies.com/wp-content/themes/responsive/_images/home_page_hero.jpg

p. 7, Figure 1, Defects per Object: courtesy of Ron Huizenga

p. 17, Figure 2-1, elementary particles:
https://commons.wikimedia.org/wiki/File:Standard_Model_of_Elementary_Particles.svg

p. 30, Russian matryoshka dolls:
https://commons.wikimedia.org/wiki/File:Russian-Matroshka2.jpg

p. 31, layer cake
https://commons.wikimedia.org/wiki/File:Meyer_lemon_chiffon_cake,_chocolate.jpg

p. 31, engine
https://commons.wikimedia.org/wiki/File:Mercedes_V6_DTM_Rennmotor_1996.jpg

"Mercedes V6 DTM Rennmotor 1996". Licensed under CC BY-SA 3.0 via Commons

p. 32, place setting
https://en.wikipedia.org/wiki/Table_setting#/media/File:Formal_01.jpg

"Formal 01" by No machine-readable author provided. KillerChihuahua assumed (based on copyright claims). - No machine-readable source provided. Own work assumed (based on copyright claims).. Licensed under CC BY-SA 3.0 via Commons -
https://commons.wikimedia.org/wiki/File:Formal_01.jpg#/media/File:Formal_01.jpg

p. 35, art museum: Barnes Foundation

p. 39, elephant herd
http://www.fond-ecran-hd.net/pc-driver/1314.jpg

p. 98, Figure 10-1, rock:
https://commons.wikimedia.org/wiki/File:SandstoneUSGOV.jpg

p. 98, Figure 10-2, flashlight:
https://commons.wikimedia.org/wiki/File:Led-flashlight.jpg

Index

abstraction, 6, 61, 73, 89, 98, 123
  multiple levels of, 48–50
ACID, 198, 199
aggregation, 31, 32, 33, 63, 100, 114, 129, 235
agile software development, 6
American Standard Code for Information Interchange. See ASCII
analytics, 161, 166, 235
array, 50, 51, 86, 132–34, 135, 149, 189, 235
ASCII, 123, 124
assembly, 32, 34, 100, 118, 235
association, 60, 63
associative entity, 48, 174
atom, 24
atomic, 200
attribute, 59, 186, 194, 235
Barker-Ellis, 45
BASE, 202
base class, 144, 152, 154, 236
base type, 146, 154, 236
bit, 96
Blaha, Michael, 61
blending, 30, 31, 33, 218, 235
byte, 96
C++, 83, 101
cake, 30, 31
CAP theorem, 199, 201, 202
cardinality, 133
carton, 29, 30, 33, 236
change request, 4
Chen, Peter, 45
class, 39–41, 41, 59, 60, 64, 84, 101, 102, 107, 116, 235
class diagram, 59–60
classification, 39, 107, 116, 137
collection, 35–36, 35, 36, 41, 42, 235
columnar, 198, 203, 207, 208, 212
COMN, 46, 63, 79, 211
  goals of, 11–12, 84
completeness principle, 122
component, 26, 28, 32, 100, 235
composite, 26, 28, 235
composite data attribute, 187, 189
composite key, 222
composite type, 52, 116, 117–18, 235
composition, 31–32, 100
computer object, 97–102, 104, 235
concept, 23, 26, 27, 28, 36, 42, 62, 89, 235
Concept and Object Modeling Notation. See COMN
conceptual, 57, 236
conceptual data model, 48, 49, 57
conceptual entity, 27
conceptual thing, 24
consistency, 200
container, 29, 33, 236
containment, 29–30, 30
contents, 29, 33, 236
CRM, 10
crow's feet, 47
customer relationship management. See CRM
data, 155, 157–61, 165, 166, 236
data architect, 7
data attribute, 45, 57, 64, 117, 174, 185, 194, 236
data attribute value, 182, 194, 236

data independence, 180, 194, 195, 236
data model, 8–11
data modeler, 7, 8, 11, 14, 51, 54, 85, 115
data modeling tool, 6, 8, 115
data object, 165
database, 6
database administrator, 7
database developer, 7
Database Management System. See DBMS
datum, 159, 166, 186, 236
DBMS, 9, 49, 106, 108, 114, 160, 201
document database, 120, 191, 203, 213, 226
Document Type Definition. See DTD
domain, 51
DTD, 131
durability, 201
edge, 205
egg, 29, 30
electron, 24
element, 130, 132
element number, 132
elementary particle, 24, 25, 27
elephant, 38, 41, 137
encapsulate, 102, 104, 236
encapsulation, 59, 118
entity, 23, 27, 28, 45, 46, 72, 89, 236
entity-relationship model, 45
enumeration, 40, 41, 42, 113, 143
extending class, 146, 152, 154, 236
extending type, 150, 152
eXtensible Markup Language. See XML
extension, 145, 146, 154, 236, 237
fact, 155, 157, 166, 236
fact type, 67
fact-based model, 70
fact-based modeling, 67
limitations of, 70–71
terminology of, 71–72
FCO-IM, 67
FK, 46, 169
flight schedule, 167, 169
flip-flop, 94
foreign key. See FK
foreign key constraint, 169
forward engineering, 6
Fully Communication-Oriented Information Modeling. See FCO-IM
generalization, 45, 63
graph, 203
graph DBMS, 205
hardware object, 98, 104, 236
Humpty-Dumpty problem, 19
IDEF1X, 45
identification, 119
identifier, 119, 135, 236
IE, 45, 61
implementation class, 64
inclusion relationship, 140, 154, 236
index, 132
induction, 24
information, 155–57, 160, 165, 166, 236
Information Engineering. See IE
Information Technology. See IT
inheritance, 144, 151–52
insight, 166, 237
Integration DEFinition for Information Modeling. See IDEF1X
isolation, 200
IT, 50
JavaScript Object Notation. See JSON
JSON, 10, 129, 131, 189
juxtaposition, 32, 33, 100, 149, 237
key/value, 191, 203, 204, 212
kind, 39, 42

location, 40, 42
logical data model, 48, 49, 53, 54, 55, 57, 189, 220, 226
logical E-R data model, 45–48
  limitations of, 50–56
  terminology of, 56–57
logical predicate, 77, 81, 158, 166, 167, 174, 237
logical record type, 45, 135, 237
main memory, 95
markup language, 132
material object, 90–97, 103
matryoshka doll, 30
matter, 24, 25
measure, 72, 125, 135, 237
member, 37
method, 59, 84, 90, 94, 101, 104, 237
Microsoft Visio, 9, 45
Microsoft Visual Studio, 67
model-driven development, 6
molecule, 24
Monet, 35, 36, 37
multiple inheritance, 142
multiplicity, 133
naming, 40
National Insurance Number. See NINO
natural language, 20, 21, 67, 69, 75, 76, 90, 92, 155, 157
Natural-language Information Analysis Methodology. See NIAM
nested type, 128–30
neutron, 24
Newman, Robert, 93
NIAM, 67
Nijssen, Sjir, 67
NINO, 117
node, 205
NORMA, 67, 69, 71, 74
normalization, 68
NoSQL, 50, 51, 120, 170, 192, 197
NoSQL Database Developer, 13
object, 23, 25, 27, 28, 29, 42, 59, 60, 71, 89, 131, 237
Object Role Modeling. See ORM
object type, 68, 70, 71, 72
objective thing, 24
object-oriented language, 107
object-oriented modeling, 83
  terminology for, 85–86
object-oriented software, 8, 10, 20, 59, 101
Old North Church, 92, 93, 94, 103
ontologist, 15
operations, 59
ORM, 67
OWL, 15, 75, 79, 81
OWL class, 77
PK, 46, 51
predicate, 75, 77, 158, 161, 166, 237
primary key. See PK
projection, 153, 237
proposition, 156, 160, 166, 237
proton, 24
quark, 24
RDF, 75, 76, 81
RDF statement, 76
real world, 49
record collection, 120
redundancy, 52
relation, 178–82, 194, 237
relation scheme, 185, 195, 237
relation value, 195, 237
relation variable, 185, 195, 237
relational database, 185
relational operation, 178–82
relationship, 63, 170, 174, 175, 176, 237
relationship line labels, 170–74
relationship type, 176, 237
RELAX NG. See RNG
Renoir, 35
Resource Description Framework. See RDF

restriction relationship, 138, 154, 238
reverse engineering, 6, 8
RNG, 131
round-trip engineering, 6
scale horizontally, 201
scale vertically, 201
schema-less, 9, 10
selection, 40
semantic modeling, 75
semi-structured data, 166, 238
set, 37–38, 107
set notation, 37
simple hardware object, 99
simple key, 222
simple type, 52, 112–15, 116, 238
Simula, 83, 116
slot, 60, 61, 64
SmallTalk, 83
Social Security Number, 119
software developer, 7, 14
software object, 98, 104, 238
specialization, 45
SQL, 6, 49, 192
SQL Database Developer, 14
state, 29, 90, 91, 104, 238
stateful, 91–94, 103, 104, 235, 238
stateful mechanism, 97
stateless, 91, 96, 104, 238
stepwise refinement, 6, 123, 134
stereotype, 60, 64
structured data, 163, 166, 238
Structured Query Language. See SQL
subclass, 63, 144–46
subroutine, 52
subset, 138
subtype, 63, 137–44, 138, 152, 154, 238
superclass, 62
supertype, 62, 138, 152, 154, 238
Supreme Court, 55, 70
tag, 130
taxonomy, 137, 138
thing, 23
tuple, 183, 194, 238
tuple scheme, 185, 194, 238
tuple value, 183, 194, 238
tuple variable, 195, 238
type, 39–41, 41, 64, 77, 83, 84, 105, 116, 238
type checking, 106
UML, 31, 59, 62, 129
  limitations of, 61–63
  terminology of, 63–65
Unified Modeling Language. See UML
union type, 140
Universal Product Code. See UPC
universal type of the tuple scheme, 186
unstructured data, 163, 166, 238
UPC, 225
value, 104, 238
value type, 68, 71, 86
Vehicle Identification Number. See VIN
VIN, 119
Web Ontology Language. See OWL
XML, 10, 76, 129, 130, 184, 189

Made in the USA
San Bernardino, CA
27 January 2018